The Last Days of the Confederacy

The Last Days of the Confederacy

★★★★★

A. A. and Mary Hoehling

The Fairfax Press
New York

Dedicated to the people of Richmond, 1861–65

Library of Congress Cataloging in Publication Data

Hoehling, A. A. (Adolph A.)
  Last days of the confederacy.

  Originally published under title: The day Richmond died.
  Bibliography: p.
  Includes index.
  1. Richmond (Va.)—History—Siege, 1864-1865.
I. Hoehling, Mary Duprey, 1914-   II. Title.
E477.61.H7   1986   973.7'38   86-1997
ISBN 0-517-60358-6
h g f e d c b

Contents

Acknowledgments

Snug little sum of $381—though small is much
better than nothing. Only think of the poor
Johnnies when their term of service expired.
Whatever was due them was entirely
worthless . . .

This mundane philosophy relating to the subject of back pay was scribbled by Sergeant Isaac Richardson, Company B, Tenth New Hampshire Volunteers, to his wife, "Dear Esther." It was dated May 26, 1865, from occupied Richmond.

It represents but one of a vast legacy of letters, diaries (published and unpublished), memoirs, little essays, magazine articles, all sorts of testimony bearing on those rich, unforgettable moments in the lives of our forebears when fate propelled them on collision courses—those who would preserve the Union; those who sought to carve out a little island labelled the Confederate States of America, with a mystique that seemed more in harmony with the Southern lifestyle and economic pressures.

The authors thus lived vicariously through the fateful day of Richmond's fall, April 3, 1865, as well as the forty-eight months preceding this mortal blow to secession. Some 200 observers made it possible to attempt the formidable task of re-creating, hopefully, in some depth, color and dimension this climactic chapter in American history.

To "meet" this legion of a century past, especially through original source material with all its inherent immediacy, the authors sought the help of others, whether custodians of yesterday's treasure or writers who had previously trod some of the familiar paths.

As always concerned about inadvertently omitting a name or names of those who had assisted, the authors nonetheless wish to thank:

Edward C. Bill, of Princeton, New Jersey, who granted permission to use his father's book as general source material. Alfred Hoyt Bill published *Beleagured City* in 1946. A meticulous researcher, Professor Bill provided a comprehensive bibliography. The thrust of his study, however, was life in this "beleagured city" rather than its inevitable day of reckoning.

Elva J. Bogert, of the Massachusetts Historical Society, who made a diligent search for the elusive letter of Charles Francis Adams, Jr., describing his entry into Richmond, leading his black cavalrymen.

Eleanor S. Brockenbrough, assistant director of the Confederate Museum in Richmond (sometimes called the Confederate White House), where research for the book actually began . . . although as a possibility, the fall of Richmond had been in the back of A. A. Hoehling's mind ever since he published *Last Train from Atlanta* in 1958. Ms. Brockenbrough gave generously of her time in searching the museum's ample files.

Margaret Cook, curator of manuscripts, College of William and Mary.

Virginius Dabney, author and former editor of the *Richmond Times Dispatch*, whose *Richmond, the Story of a City*, published in 1976, is the beautifully written product of untiring research. As questions arose, the authors turned to him, and he never failed to answer—often by return mail.

Gail Jones and Nancy Obersider, curators of the Siege Museum in Petersburg, who through their familiarity with local history and expertise in collecting and stage-setting have made visits to their museum (in the old Exchange building) a stimulating journey into history.

Ross Kimmel, of the Maryland Park Service, who located a photograph of "Gath"—being George Alfred Townsend, the correspondent who later erected an arch to his fellow scribes at South Mountain, Maryland.

Louis H. Manarin, state archivist for Virginia, who happens to be one of the narrowing fraternity of authorities on The War Between the States as it applied to the Old Dominion. It will be noted in the following book index that he edited much of his state's centennial literature.

Mrs. Rembert W. Patrick, of Athens, Georgia, whose husband, then history professor at the University of Florida, published *The Fall of Richmond* in 1960. He died in 1967. The archives of the P. K. Yonge Library, at that university, contain some of his papers but nothing pertaining to this small book, or monograph.

William M. E. Rachal, editor, *Virginia Magazine of History and Biography*, with whom the authors discussed the feasibility of such a book several years ago. This is the publication of the Virginia Historical Society, which makes its headquarters in "Battle Abbey,"

Richmond. Its holdings are considerable, predating the Civil War. Among others who assisted in the research rooms of the society were Mrs. J. A. V. Berry and James Meehan.

Sarah Ringer, Manuscripts Department, Alderman Library, University of Virginia.

Mattie Russell, of the William R. Perkins Library, Duke University, an old friend from previous projects.

Mrs. Carolyn Shelton, of St. Paul's Episcopal Church, Richmond, and others who sought to evoke for the authors testaments to the memory of the Reverend Minnigerode—photographs, sermons, any documents stamped with his distinctive personality. But time in this big city church has sped on swift angel wings. "O lamp of God!" will never ring again in St. Paul's Episcopal Church, downtown Richmond—and if it did, by some miracle, the note would in all likelihood fall sour.

Dr. Peter Walker, Department of History, University of North Carolina, author, student of the Civil War and other subjects, not excluding Russia.

Dr. Carolyn Wallace, director of the Southern Historical Collection, University of North Carolina, among whose predecessors was the late scholar, Dr. James W. Patton. Ellen Neal and Richard A. Shrader are among others who assisted the authors at the Wilson Library, Chapel Hill.

Dr. Bell Irvin Wiley, a friend from *Last Train from Atlanta* research. His assistance is acknowledged further on, after "Books." We note, with sorrow, his recent passing.

Edward A. Wyatt, editorial writer of the *Progress Index*, Petersburg, who corresponded with suggestions well before this book reached the drawing boards.

. . . last but surely not least, appreciation to Mary Huie, of Augusta, Georgia, for her splendid typing.

A Sunday in April

It was sunny, cloudless and quiet in Richmond that Sunday, April 2, 1865. After four days of incessant rain, the soggy earth exuded an aura of spring—of blossoms, of planting, of new life.

This also was the fifth year of the War of Secession, the tenth month of the investment of Petersburg, southern gateway to the capital of the rebellion.

Jefferson Davis, the gaunt, immensely weary President of the Confederacy was occupying, as usual, his private pew in St. Paul's Church, which was but a few minutes from Capitol Square. He had walked this fine morning from his home, which had become known as the White House of the Confederacy.

"No sound disturbed the stillness," noted Sallie Brock, a young resident, "save the subdued murmur of the river and the cheerful music of the church bells. The long familiar tumult of war broke not upon the sacred calmness of the day."

Many times the daily living of Richmond had been punctuated by the nearing rumble of hostile artillery and even the crack of musketry. But the people maintained a childlike trust in the now General-in-Chief Robert E. Lee. Sometimes it seemed that he alone had muted, even made a mockery of the North's battle cry: "On to Richmond!"

The sad-eyed Davis could no longer share—if he ever had—the citizenry's simple faith. On his desk were the dispatches of yesterday, Saturday, and of early this Sunday morning from Lee, telling of the crumbling of his lines south and west of Petersburg after a furious Federal attack at the insignificant crossroads known as Five Forks. The specter of evacuation, which had loomed darkly over the city's spires and chimney pots earlier in the war, had again returned— along with the greater specter of a full retreat of the Confederacy's mainstay, the Army of Northern Virginia.

Midway through the service, Mrs. Josiah Gorgas, wife of the Chief of Ordnance, would recall, "a messenger came into the church and walked quickly to the President's pew. He said something in great excitement. Mr. Davis' face grew pale, but in a moment he controlled his emotion, arose and with his usual dignity of bearing walked out of the church."

In another pew, a young lady, Connie Cary, turned from her *Book of Common Prayer* to watch the head of state "with stern, set lips and his usual quick military tread" virtually march from the church.

"I think," read the telegraphed message from Lee handed Davis, "it is absolutely necessary that we should abandon our positions tonight. . . ."

The President would recall, "I went to my office and assembled the heads of departments and bureaus. . . ."

A young Confederate captain, Clement Sulivane, noted "a strange agitation perceptible" on Richmond's streets as the news seemed to radiate through the walls of the presidential offices in the old U.S. Customs House, now the Confederate Treasury. It spread, germlike, by word of mouth even before the President had begun to ink his signature to the many formal papers necessary to set an entire seat of government into fevered departure.

And, yet, on this bright, beautiful sabbath, disbelief predominated. Was this not another "Sunday sensation rumor"? There had been so many since April 1861 when Virginia passed an ordinance of secession—mortal 1861, which now, to the tired, hungry people of Richmond, seemed light years ago.

Dramatis Personae

Adams, Charles Francis, Jr., Colonel, USA, Fifth Massachusetts Cavalry.

Anderson, Joseph R., Brigadier General, CSA, commanding Governor's Mounted Guard, supervisor of Tredegar Works.

Beecher, Herbert, Corporal, USA, First Connecticut Light Battery.

Benjamin, Judah P., Confederate Secretary of War; later Secretary of State.

Blair, Francis P., Sr., semiofficial peace emissary from Washington.

Blackford, William W., Colonel, CSA, engineering officer.

Boykin, Edward M., Captain, CSA, Seventh South Carolina Cavalry.

Breckinridge, John Cabell, Major General, CSA, secretary of war.

Brock, Sallie (Putnam), young resident of Richmond.

Burnside, Ambrose E., Major General, USA, second commander, Army of the Potomac.

Butler, Benjamin F., Major General, USA, commander of the Army of the James operating against Richmond, May and June 1864.

Cadwallader, Sylvanus, reporter for the New York Herald.

Campbell, Judge John A., former associate justice of the U.S. Supreme Court; Confederate assistant secretary of war; peace emissary.

Cary, Constance ⎫
Cary, Hetty ⎬ Young women of Richmond.
Cary, Jennie ⎭

Chamberlain, Joshua L., brevetted Major General, USA, brigade commander with Grant's Fifth Corps.

Chesnut, James, Colonel, CSA, aide to President Davis; promoted to Brigadier General, April 1864.

Chesnut, Mary Boykin, diarist, Colonel Chesnut's wife.

Christian, Asbury, 19th century historian.

Coffin, Charles Carleton, correspondent for the *Boston Journal*.

Cooper, Samuel, Adjutant General, CSA, oldest general officer in the Confederacy.

Crump, Emmie (Lightfoot), young girl of Richmond.

Crump, Judge W. W., assistant secretary of the Confederate Treasury, Emmie's father.

Custer, George Armstrong, Major General, USA, commander of cavalry division under Sheridan.

Dahlgren, Ulric, Colonel, USA, cavalry raider.

Davidson, Dr. F., Richmond physician.

Davis, Jefferson, President of the Confederacy.

Davis, Varina Howell, First Lady of the Confederacy.

De Leon, Thomas Cooper, writer, of Richmond.

De Peyster, Livingston, Lieutenant, USA, Thirteenth New York Artillery.

Eggleston, George Cary, law student from Indiana caught up in the war.

Ewell, Richard S., Lieutenant General, CSA.

Fontaine, Mary, woman of Richmond.

Fry, James B., Captain, USA, assistant to Major General Irwin McDowell.

Gary, Martin, Brigadier General, CSA, commanding a cavalry brigade.

Gorgas, Josiah, Brigadier General, CSA, chief of ordnance.

Gorgas, Amelia, General Gorgas's wife.

Grant, Ulysses S., Lieutenant General, USA, commander of the Armies of the United States.

Graves, E. E., Major, USA, Fourth Massachusetts Cavalry.

Grey, Nellie (pseud.), woman of Richmond.

Harrison, Burton, aide to President Davis.

Haskell, John C., Lieutenant Colonel, CSA.

Hathaway, Leeland, Sergeant, CSA, convalescent in Richmond.

Hill, Ambrose P., Major General, CSA, commanding Lee's Third Corps.

Hill, Daniel H., Major General, CSA.

Hill, G. Powell, an assistant paymaster in Richmond.

Hill, Henry, Jr., G. Powell Hill's cousin.

Hoge, Dr. Moses D., pastor, Second Presbyterian Church, Richmond.

Hood, John Bell, General, CSA.

Hooker, Joseph, Major General, USA, third commander of the Army of the Potomac.

Howard, McHenry, Captain, CSA, assistant inspector general with Major General Custis Lee's division.

Jackson, Thomas J., "Stonewall," Major General, CSA, Second Corps commander under Lee.

Johnston, Joseph E., General, CSA, commander of the Army of Northern Virginia and later of the Army of Tennessee.

Jones, John B., a "Rebel War Clerk," diarist.

Kean, Robert G. Hill, head of Confederate Bureau of War.

Kilpatrick, Judson, Major General, USA, cavalry commander.

Lawley, Francis Charles, Richmond correspondent, *The Times of London*.

Lee, Robert E., CSA, General-in-Chief of the Confederate forces; also war-long commander of the Army of Northern Virginia.

Lee, Mary Randolph Custis, wife of Robert E. Lee.

Lee, Custis, Major General, CSA, division commander.

Lee, Fitzhugh, Major General, CSA, cavalry commander.

Lee, Fitzhugh Rooney, son of Robert E. Lee and Mary Custis.

Letcher, John, Governor of Virginia.

Leyburn, John, a young man of Richmond.

Liddell, John A., Surgeon, USA, inspector of Medical and Hospital Department under Grant.

Lincoln, Abraham, President of the United States.

Long, Armstead L., Brigadier General, CSA, chief of artillery, Second Corps; staff officer to Lee and his authorized biographer.

Longstreet, James, Lieutenant General, CSA, First Corps commander under Lee.

Lowe, Thaddeus S. C., head of the U.S. Aeronautical Corps.

Lubbock, Francis R., Colonel, CSA, member of Davis's staff.

Mallory, Stephen, secretary of the Confederate Navy.

Martin, George Alexander, Colonel, CSA, Thirty-eighth Virginia Infantry.

Mayo, Joseph, mayor of Richmond.

Mayo, Peter Helms, Private, CSA, Governor's Mounted Guard.

McClellan, George B., General, USA, first commander of the Army of the Potomac.

McDonald, Edward H., Lieutenant Colonel, CSA, Eleventh Virginia Cavalry.

McDowell, Irwin, Major General, USA, commander of the Department of Northeastern Virginia.

McGuire, the Reverend John P., Episcopal minister, resident of Richmond.

McGuire, Judith Brockenbrough, wife of Reverend McGuire, diarist.

Meade, George Gordon, Major General, USA, fourth commander of the Army of the Potomac.

Memminger, Christopher, Confederate secretary of the treasury.

Meredith, Judge John A., member of the surrender party.

Minnigerode, the Reverend Charles G., pastor of St. Paul's Episcopal Church.

Mordecai, Emma, mistress of Rosewood Plantation.

Munford, Thomas, Brigadier General, CSA, commanding Second Virginia Cavalry.

Parker, William H., Captain, CSN, commanding training ship C.S.S. *Patrick Henry*.

Paul, Alfred, French consul in Richmond.

Pegram, John, Major General, CSA, married to Hetty Cary.

Pember, Phoebe, matron of Chimborazo Hospital.

Pickett, George E., Major General, CSA, division commander.

Pickett, LaSalle, his wife.

Pollard, Edward A., assistant editor of *The Richmond Examiner*.

Porter, David D., Admiral, USN.

Porter, Horace, Brigadier General, USA, aide to Grant.

Potts, Frank, Captain, CSA, quartermaster on Longstreet's staff.

Prescott, Royal B., Lieutenant, USA, Thirteenth New Hampshire Infantry.

Pryor, Roger A., Brigadier General, CSA.

Pryor, Sara, wife of General Pryor, diarist.

Quarles, Mann S., youngest teller in the Confederate Treasury.

Reagan, John H., Confederate postmaster.

Reid, Whitelaw, correspondent for the *Cincinnati Gazette;* used the pseudonym "Agate."

Ripley, Edward H., Colonel, USA, Thirteenth New Hampshire Infantry Regiment; garrison commander in Richmond.

Rowland, Kate, young refugee from Alexandria.

Rutherford, John Coles, member of Virginia legislature.

Sayre, Marie Burrows, correspondent of Mary Fontaine.

Schofield, John M., Major General, USA, corps commander under Sherman.

Scranton, Samuel W., Lieutenant, USA, First Connecticut Light Battery.

Semmes, Raphael H., Rear Admiral, CSN, commander of the James River Fleet.

Seward, William H., U.S. Secretary of State.

Sheridan, Philip H., Major General, USA, commander of the Cavalry Corps, Army of the Potomac.

Sheldon, James R., Sergeant (acting Lieutenant), CSA, Thomas Company Rangers, Fiftieth Georgia Regiment.

Shepley, George F., Brigadier General, USA, military governor of Richmond.

Sherman, William T., Major General, USA, commander of the Military Division of the Mississippi.

Simmons, William, Confederate officer evacuating Richmond with his wife.

Smith, William, "Extra Billy," Governor of Virginia.

Stanton, Edwin M., U.S. Secretary of War.

Stephens, Alexander H., Vice-President of the Confederacy.

Stevens, Atherton H., Major, USA, Fourth Massachusetts Cavalry.

Stoneman, George, Major General, USA, cavalry leader.

Stoodley, N. D., Major, USA, Thirteenth New Hampshire Infantry.

Stuart, J. E. B., Major General, CSA, cavalry leader.

Sulivane, Clement, Captain, CSA.

Sublet, Emmie, 13-year-old girl of Richmond.

Taylor, Walter H., Colonel, CSA, Adjutant General to Lee.

Thompson, S. Millett, Lieutenant, USA, Thirteenth New Hampshire Infantry.

Townsend, George Alfred, *New York Herald and World* correspondent.

Trenholm, George Alfred, Confederate secretary of the treasury (succeeding Memminger).

Trenholm, Anna, his wife.

Tucker, Dallas, a young boy of Richmond.

Van Lew, Elizabeth, Northern sympathizer in Richmond.

Walker, Fannie, War Department copyist.

Watehall, Edward T., 14-year-old boy of Richmond.

Warren, Gouverneur Kemble, Major General, USA, commanding Fifth Corps, Army of the Potomac.

Weitzel, Godfrey, Major General, USA, commanding Twenty-fifth Corps, Army of the Potomac.

White, W. S., Richmond Howitzers.

Wigfall, Louis T., Brigadier General, CSA, member of the Confederate Congress.

Wigfall, Louise, his teen-age daughter, diarist.

Withers, Anita Dwyer, Texas girl in Richmond.

Winder, John H., Brigadier General, CSA, provost marshal general of Richmond.

Woods, John L. G., Private, CSA, Company B, Fifty-third Georgia Regiment.

PART

I

★★★★★

"ON TO RICHMOND!"

WE TOOK RICHMOND AT 8:15 THIS
MORNING. I CAPTURED MANY GUNS. THE
ENEMY LEFT IN GREAT HASTE. THE CITY IS
ON FIRE IN ONE PLACE, AM MAKING
EVERY EFFORT TO PUT IT OUT. THE PEOPLE
RECEIVED US WITH ENTHUSIASTIC
EXPRESSIONS OF JOY.

—To Secretary of War Stanton from General Weitzel,
transmitted from City Point, Virginia at 11 A.M.,
April 3, 1865

CHAPTER

1

★★★★★

1861

A People
"Totally Ignorant of War"

From the earliest days of the conflict between North and South there had arisen in the Union a welling cry to seize Richmond. It commenced in April 1861, when the capital of the Confederacy was relocated from Montgomery, Alabama, to the prosperous, architecturally pleasant capital of Virginia.

At first hesitant to rebel, the Convention of Virginia, after an all-night session, passed the Ordinance of Secession on April 17, 1861. Virginia was among the last of the southern states to take that fateful step. In Richmond, the news prompted "grand demonstrations of delight."

"As if by magic," wrote 16-year-old Sallie Brock, "the new Confederate flag was hoisted on the Capitol, and from every hilltop in the city it was soon waving. The excitement was beyond description; the satisfaction unparalleled."

The state's convention had snatched heady words almost verbatim from the Declaration of Independence: "that government is founded on the consent of the governed." The words proved as inflammatory as they had in 1776.

The implications, as with the first gulp of whiskey, could not at the time be measured, and only a few dared express contrary sentiments. One was Elizabeth Van Lew, middle-aged daughter of a Northern-born hardware merchant who added a sour note: "How heavy was the air with treason!" She then postscripted cynically to her journals, "For once the whole idle South had something to do!"

Richmond's exuberance, garishly etched by torchlight parades, cheering, band music and endless speeches by professional haranguers, was echoed in Washington. There the drums beat for a crusade southward that dramatically would crush secession—"secesh," as much of the North offhandedly alluded to the spasm which had seized a third of the nation. "On to Richmond!" was the war cry.

And some 110 miles south, in the nation's "other Capital," was the complementary refrain, "On to Washington!," proving that one city's giddiness was rousingly challenged by that of the other. At least one youthful Southern politician thumped, "in less than sixty days the flag of the Confederacy will be waving over the White House!"

Southern optimism was not wholly groundless. As Sallie Brock wrote, "Richmond was never in a more prosperous condition . . . trade flourishing . . . food abundant and cheap."

The "tocsin" (as coined by Jones, the war clerk) from this square bell tower in Capitol Square was a familiar sound throughout the war, warning of impending danger. This ringing sometimes warned of battle preparations, as happened many times during McClellan's abortive Peninsular campaign, or a cavalry raid; sometimes the alarm sounded merely because the bell ringer was nervous. *From the Authors' collection.*

Citizens had scarcely begun to realize that war, with its long-term implications, had truly come.

A few military organizations already were in existence, their ranks rapidly swollen by volunteers: the Richmond Light Infantry Blues, dating to colonial times; Company F; and the strutting Richmond Greys, whose muster read like a social register of the affluent. With the battalion of the Richmond Howitzers and the Fayette Artillery, sporting a few six-inch naval guns, these companies were the military backbone of Richmond.

On Sunday, April 21, need suddenly appeared to materialize for these peacetime weekend soldiers. Church services were interrupted by the clanging of the alarm bell in the old, square, brick tower on Capitol Square, a signal that danger impended. But it turned out to be only a "Sunday rumor," sparked by the operations far away at Hampton Roads of the unlikely little U.S. steamer, *Pawnee,* falsely reported to be headed up the James. She carried no armament.

The preceding day, Saturday, April 20, far up the Potomac in Arlington, Colonel Robert E. Lee received a telegram from

The five-story Spotswood Hotel, just off Capitol Square, was opened in 1860. Davis, Lee, and many notables lived there at one time or another, and its bar attracted military leaders, politicians, and newspaper reporters. Yet its lifespan was ephemeral. A Christmas Eve fire in 1870 claimed at least eight lives as it reduced a colorful symbol of an era to ashes. *Library of Congress.*

Virginia's Governor John Letcher summoning him to Richmond. The distinguished West Point graduate, who two years earlier had led a company of U.S. Marines to capture the fanatic abolitionist John Brown at Harper's Ferry, had made the choice of state over country and resigned his commission in the U.S. Cavalry. Now he must arrange to move his invalid wife, Mary Randolph Custis, granddaughter of Martha Washington, from their stately mansion "Arlington," overlooking the national capital, to a haven near Richmond.

Guaranteed safe conduct through the confused U.S.–Confederate lines, Lee arrived in Richmond by train on Monday, April 22. He was in civilian attire, his predominantly dark hair covered by a tall silk hat. He was 53 years old; his black moustache lent a hint of past youth and his upright posture provided an illusion of height. He was somewhat under six feet.

Crowds waited at the famed five-story Spotswood Hotel at the corner of Eighth and Main streets to greet the officer. But Lee went at once to meet with Governor Letcher who offered him command of the military and naval forces of Virginia. The appointment was accepted and confirmed in a night session of the same convention that had severed Virginia's umbilical to the Union.

A month later Jefferson Davis, provisional President of the Confederacy, and his family settled into the high-ceilinged, handsome rooms of the same hotel where Lee was staying. The Spotswood was in view of the Capitol, an imposing marble structure which had been fashioned after Thomas Jefferson's beloved Maison Carré at Nîmes. Here the Confederate Congress, as well as the state assembly and convention, would shortly convene.

The presence of two leaders of the stature of Davis, himself a West Pointer, and Lee underscored what was now obvious: Richmond as the capital of the rebellion had indelibly stamped the entire state with the dubious honor of being a principal battleground.

Richmond's recent slow and gracious pace was relegated to antiquity by the hoarse, shrieking whistles of trains bearing the military and their supplies in and out of the city's four principal stations, and by an around-the-clock tramp of boots over dusty streets. Regiment after regiment passed through—mostly green recruits without proper uniforms, if any at all, compensating in ebullience for what all lacked in expertise or even rudimentary military comprehension. This was true as well of units deployed about the several frontiers of Virginia, from the Shenandoah to Chesapeake Bay.

Old flintlocks, similar to those of the revolution, had been converted to percussion cap muskets. As a matter of fact, a survey by the *Examiner* turned up the intelligence that all but ten percent of the sixty thousand state-owned infantry weapons were indeed flintlocks. Those converted could not be rifled, but they did shoot the heavy, tapered "minié balls."

The cavalry supplied its own steeds. As a poor substitute for leather saddles, heavy cloth was often used.

In every church basement and in comparable areas of hotels such as the Spotswood or American, the ladies kept their fingers flying day and night sewing clothes and collecting a grab bag of articles for the troops.

"Lizzie" Van Lew alone refused "to make shirts" for the recruits whom she considered "deplorably ignorant." As to her sisters of Richmond, she dubbed them "bloodthirsty" and assumed that "Charlotte Corday" of French Revolution infamy was their "favorite heroine." She scribbled her treasonable sentiments on sheets of foolscap in her angular, difficult scrawl. These she hid beside her mansion's great marble fireplace since, she noted with pride, her secessionist neighbors had already voiced "personal threats" against her.

The recruits were drilled by Virginia Military Institute cadets at Howard's Grove on the Mechanicsville Pike and at the Central Fair Grounds. The latter, situated two miles west of the center of the city, had been handily renamed Camp Lee. An artillery school banged away at Richmond College, and the Howitzer Battalion loaded its noisy wares on Chimborazo Heights to the east overlooking the muddy James. So exuberant were all spirits that any need for a draft appeared preposterous.

Hastily printed notices on fences and lamp posts attested to the genesis of one new fighting unit after another: "It is proposed to form a company of infantry," or of "cavalry," or "artillery," or even of the less glamorous "home defense" for men over 45.

The city, as if through the machinations of a martial genie, had been converted into one vast armed camp. Citizens, accustomed to being awakened by the rattle and creak of horse carts, now sat up to sleepy-eyed attention by reveille and were lulled to sleep by "retreat" from a dozen leather-lunged buglers. The smell of gunpowder was heavy in the air.

Soon troops from other seceded states converged on Richmond to march along with some 40,000 Virginians: first the South Carolinians, then the Georgians wearing butternut uniforms, Louisiana Zouaves with baggy scarlet trousers, the New Orleans Tigers. Their colors snapped overhead as regiment followed regiment: the Lone Star of Texas, the Louisiana Pelican, the Mississippi Magnolia.

White handkerchiefs waved from nearly every window. Cheers followed them, "the change in Richmond . . . only understood by those who daily witnessed the stirring scenes."

In July, elderly Major General Irwin McDowell, Mexican War veteran and President Lincoln's choice for commander of the Department of Northeastern Virginia, marched away from his Washington camps with about 35,000 men towards nearby Manassas Junction. His aim was to drive out the some 23,000 Confederates occupying that important railhead so close to the Union capital.

On July 21, a Sunday, the first battle of the war, known as Bull Run for the inconsequential creek near which the opposing forces clashed, ended in a Federal rout and reduced supporters of the Union to nearly psychotic despair.

In Richmond the mood was understandably quite the opposite. Many believed that the "backbone of the war was broken," attested Sallie Brock.

One Richmond correspondent demanded instant recognition of the Confederacy since the "Yankees" had been administered a "downright whipping."

President Davis, ascetic and spiritually minded, came home from the field of battle to proclaim a day of fasting and prayer, "for returning thanks to the Most High in giving us victory in the late battle."

The Lord, however, remained impartial. Rain Monday night swept the platforms and the sidings of the Richmond, Fredericksburg and Potomac rail station, at Eighth and Broad streets, close by the Capitol, where relatives awaited the return of the troops. The locomotives and the jolting boxcars ground in through a miasma of smoke, both from the pine logs that fueled the furnaces and from the fumes of the oil lanterns.

The stretchers, borne out one by one, brought home to a people "totally ignorant of war" its stark reality.

All night long the trains rattled in as the rain continued in torrents. Many of the soldiers walked off and into the arms of their wives and families. But others had to be assisted, or carried. Although the Confederate wounded totalled less than 1,600 and the dead one-third that number, this was quite enough to dull the headiness of an exciting new experience: war.

The sudden appearance of the Confederate casualties together with hundreds of Union wounded and prisoners— bandaged, bloody, hurting young Americans—overwhelmed a peaceful city, whose population was scarcely 40,000, one-fourth of which were slaves. Hospitals overflowed. Private homes took in as many wounded as each could accommodate, and their owners summoned those family physicians who were not away in the army.

Among the dead was Brigadier General Barnard E. Bee, of South Carolina, killed at Manassas as he tried to rally his own men. Before he fell, he was heard to exclaim, "Look at Jackson there, standing like a stone wall! Rally behind the Virginians!"

Bee was referring to Brigadier General Thomas J. Jackson—in so doing, he immortalized the latter with a nickname, "Stonewall."

Bee was accorded Richmond's first state funeral for a fallen hero, with a procession winding towards the Capitol to the strains of Handel's "Dead March" from the Oratorio *Saul*. The same solemn music would be heard again along Richmond's streets.

With casualties becoming the city's main preoccupation, the city council passed an ordinance to reimburse private citizens for the cost of medicine, and at the same time provided for the conservation of ice for military purposes. The same dozen members had been meeting at least weekly since war's inception in the handsome City Hall, with its four imposing front columns, on Capitol and Broad streets.

Horses and vehicles, from two-place carriages to larger wagons, were commandeered. Every housewife was urged to cook meals and hurry them to "hospitals." Farmers, by the same token, were asked to cart in their vegetables, posthaste. Medical students suddenly were at a premium, expected to perform all healing arts barely short of surgery.

On a far less noble key, the prisons filled, not only with the captured in battle but with deserters, vagrants, camp followers, gamblers, street walkers, profiteers, con men . . . the whole dregs of war.

With a dramatically increased population and decreased quantities of essential commodities as a result of the blockade of southern ports proclaimed by Lincoln on April 19, the shopping and eating habits of Richmond were altered. Stores closed early to allow male employes to drill and the young ladies to sew bandages and perform their other warborn functions. Those who shopped before the doors banged shut found the prices inching up, week by week. Coffee, already scarce, was adulterated with unlikely berries, even with sweet potatoes and dandelions. It produced a brew, in the appraisal of at least one, "too nauseous to drink," in spite of advertisements to the contrary.

Fresh fruits and vegetables alone remained plentiful, at least during that first summer and fall. Even pineapples and other tropical fruits transported by "our bold privateers" could be found, though at a price.

The great mills and foundries of Richmond, industrial center as well as capital of the Confederacy, were running short of everything. "Rags wanted" notices in newspapers and on walls and fences attested to the paper mills' dwindling supplies. The famed Tredegar Iron Works, belching black, pungent smoke from its furnaces along the James, at the foot of Capitol Hill, was threatened with shortages of iron ore, coal and especially of skilled workers. The Shockoe Foundry expressed the same complaints. The mills, led in magnitude by the Gallego Flour Mill, said to be one of the world's largest, all felt the pinch.

Transportation itself was one bottleneck. The city's four railroads, not allowed the luxury of spare parts or reserve equipment, struggled to keep up with demand. The Kanawha Canal was busier than ever. The rivers were only partially effective arteries since the Union Navy had blockaded the harbors.

Social life in Richmond, however, was near normal. Theaters opened with their placarded marquees and flaring torches for the winter season. At Metropolitan Hall, a song premiered: "God Will Defend the Right." It compensated in enthusiasm for what it may have lacked in musical quality. An anonymous young lady of Richmond had just composed it.

With colder weather, food prices rose. Shoppers were harassed by young hoodlums who stole the ladies' market baskets and, often, their purses. Rock fights between bored little boys were cheered on by idling soldiers.

Frequent fires were attributed to defective flues and overheated stoves. This was the first wartime winter.

In Washington, material shortages were not a problem. President Lincoln sought a "winning" general. By fall he thought he had found one in 36-year-old Major General George B. McClellan, who had attracted Presidential attention by driving the Confederates from northwestern Virginia. Lincoln also appointed a new Secretary of War, able but irascible Edwin M. Stanton who exclaimed to McClellan: "Now we two will save the country!"

Even as the *Richmond Examiner* stridently demanded a great offensive against Washington, a massive military machine was being forged to march on Richmond: the Army of the Potomac.

CHAPTER

2

★★★★★

1862

"A Black Shadow Brooded over Richmond"

On Washington's birthday, Jefferson Davis was reinaugurated president of the Confederacy. He stood, six feet two inches, impressive if thin, on a temporary platform in Capitol Square beneath the bronze equestrian statue of George Washington. His "provisional" inauguration had been on February 18 the previous year in Montgomery.

By his side was Vice President Alexander H. Stephens. The former Georgia congressman, lean, misshapen and far from imposing, had voted against his state's secession. He was a champion of peace and reconciliation and no supporter of Davis. All in all, the two were a curious emotional combination.

Invoking "the favor of Divine Providence," Davis reiterated what he had said many times before: "We are in arms to renew such sacrifices as our fathers made to the holy cause of constitutional liberty."

Few, however, heard his wordy, meandering inaugural. A cold winter's rain slanted across Capitol Square. The "pattering on the carriages and umbrellas . . . prevented the sound of the human voice from reaching our ears," wrote Sallie Brock.

Connie Cary, who had fled Alexandria to join relatives in Richmond, pronounced it a "dismal day . . . depressing to stoutest spirits."

Although President Davis appeared "pale and tired," he continued on to an evening reception at the executive mansion along with his handsome second wife, the former Varina Howell. The house was the old Brockenbrough mansion near the Capitol at Twelfth and Clay, newly furnished by a committee of Richmond ladies. Heavy, richly colored draperies covered the tall windows; fires glowed in Carrara marble fireplaces; a band tooted away on patriotic, sometimes martial strains. Tropical plants brightened the entrance hall, and a cream-colored carpet warmed the President's office.

Varina was gracious, but her husband remained aloof. Davis, who had been Secretary of War under Franklin Pierce, had reason to be grave. News had just arrived of the fall of Fort Donelson, on the Cumberland River in Tennessee. The "unconditional" surrender, to a little known Union brigadier general, Ulysses S. Grant, was a critical wedge suddenly driven into the Confederacy's western defenses.

"Events have cast on our arms and hopes the gloomiest shadows," Davis would lament. The "shadows" would be the

The Davis mansion, popularly known today as the White House of the Confederacy. *Virginia State Travel Service.*

losses of three important states: Missouri, Kentucky and Tennessee. Roanoke Island had already fallen, and the loss of New Bern, colonial capital of North Carolina, was but a matter of time. Even Warrenton, Virginia, forty miles west of Washington, had been captured, projecting a new flood of refugees into Richmond.

Jefferson Davis could not contemplate this last week in February 1862, with much pleasure. Others did—such as Louise Wigfall, 15-year-old daughter of a former United States senator from Texas, Louis T. Wigfall, now a member of the Confederate Congress and with a new commission as brigadier general commanding the First Texas Volunteer Regiment.

The war had caught Louise and her sister in Longwood, Massachusetts, near Boston, visiting a grandmother. Not until

Inside the Davis mansion. *Metropolitan Richmond Chamber of Commerce.*

July 1861 had a way been found to smuggle them through the lines to rejoin their parents.

Wigfall was but one of numerous political generals or officers of other rank—so many, in fact, that the wife of another, Mary Boykin Chesnut, wrote that the Confederacy would be "done to death by politicians." The sharp-tongued Mary was the wife of Colonel James Chesnut, Jr., intelligence officer and aide to the President. He too was formerly a United States senator from South Carolina. Mary had never been wholeheartedly in favor of secession. When her husband resigned his seat in the United States Senate, she had been visiting in Florida. "I might not have been able to influence him," she commented obliquely, "but I should have tried."

In her cynicism, she was seconded by yet another: Sara Rice Pryor, wife of Brigadier General Roger A. Pryor, former newspaperman, diplomat and congressman, who had the ear of Lee. She observed that "this [the war] was the tremendous event which was to change our lives . . . to give us poverty for riches, mutilation and wounds for strength and health, obscurity and degradation for honor and distinction."

Other Richmonders considered secession a sacred cause. Dr. Moses D. Hoge, pastor of the Second Presbyterian Church, supported the rebellion with an ardor scarcely less than that of Jefferson Davis, advising young men that "the best way of showing hatred for the enemy . . . [is] to fight them in the ranks."

Whatever their sentiments, all in the Confederate capital were compelled to live with the historic camp followers of war. Soldiers on leave, full of whiskey and penniless, wandered about seeking shelter. Thieves, pickpockets and "brazen women" terrorized the citizenry, and, as most seemed to believe, "spies were everywhere."

"The enemy . . . knew everything going on within our lines . . . seemed to know what we intended doing in the future, as if the most secret councils of the cabinet were divulged," wrote John Beauchamp Jones, a clerk in the War Department, located in the old Mechanics Institute on Ninth Street. The opinionated diarist had been a journalist in Baltimore and Rutherford, New Jersey, until marriage to Frances Custis of the famous Virginia family made him a convert to the Southern cause. At 51 he was comfortably over fighting age.

He was working for the second Secretary of War, Judah P. Benjamin, who had succeeded LeRoy P. Walker in September. Benjamin, "a short, stout, jaunty gentleman with a sparkling black eye, frank and open, a distinguished jurist," was among the more able in the cabinet.

Martial law was finally declared for Richmond and its environs with passes required to leave or enter. Writ of habeas corpus was suspended. Saloons closed temporarily. The "villain" brooding behind this challenge to civic freedom turned out to be the aging Brigadier General John H. Winder, chief of the Richmond police, and soon to head the Virginia prison system. The snowy-haired general so warmed to his duties that he obtained early notoriety by jailing the editor of the *Whig* for an unfavorable article.

Meanwhile, out of the soldier mob that had broken and fled at Bull Run, "Little Mac" McClellan had forged an army of more than 150,000. It was unquestionably the smartest and best-equipped military machine ever conceived.

His Army of the Potomac, after winter had lost its grip, was transported down the Potomac and Chesapeake Bay in steamers, sailing ships, barges (one especially equipped as a balloon carrier), sloops of war and every available craft that could be loaded at Alexandria and navigate the many shallows of the Potomac. The landbound Confederate forces between Washington and Richmond were outflanked.

In April "Little Mac" took off from his new base, Fort Monroe, with an army about twice the size of his foe. The Confederate defenders of Richmond's approaches, even with stragglers, never counted more than 80,000. The Federals inched from Hampton Roads up the peninsula-like neck of land between the James and York Rivers leading to the beckoning Lorelei—Richmond.

The army's wagons were often mired in the spring mud. Still France's Prince de Joinville, an observer with the Federal forces, thought the "siege" line looked festive, with observation balloons flying, brightly colored signal flags wig-wagging, and bands playing.

The balloons of the Union "Aeronautical Corps" were controlled by a New Hampshire civil engineer, Professor Thaddeus S. C. Lowe. They were tethered to a specially equipped barge that boasted a gas generator, part of the amphibious operation that swept up the York and the James Rivers past Williamsburg and Yorktown.

By early May there appeared every reason to anticipate the fall of the Confederate capital. "With sickening anxiety our hearts were turned towards the little band of men that defended the Peninsula," Sallie Brock wrote.

The "anxiety" of some worsened until translated into one all-consuming impulse—"Flight!" It was at least "distressing to observe how many persons are leaving Richmond, apprehending that it is in danger," in the words of Judith Brockenbrough

McGuire, wife of an Episcopalian minister. Formerly headmaster of the Episcopal High School in Alexandria, the Rev. John P. McGuire now made do with a postal clerk's job.

"But it will not, I know it will not fall," Judith postscripted, as to the fate of the Confederacy's capital.

Two church conventions which were being held in Richmond adjourned, and their delegates encamped on the city's four rail stations. Gambling casinos temporarily locked their doors. The proprietors thumbed back nervously over their lives and decided to donate profits to the wounded, and other charitable causes—some $20,000, it was estimated.

Richmond's peace of mind was hardly improved by the spectacle of Professor Lowe's balloon *Intrepid* hovering just beyond the city's chimney pots. The balloonist could discern activity despite haze and smoke billowing up from the Tredegar Iron Works. He interpreted dust swirls on the exit roads and smoke plumes from locomotives as signs of possible evacuation, and so advised Signal Corps telegraphers.

The Confederate Congress had adjourned, which meant that people as well as their paperwork were enroute to other secessionist States. Much was being shipped by canal boats to Columbia, South Carolina. The Treasury's gold reserve was packed, but remained in Richmond. General Winder, who also controlled passports, could hardly enter his office, so mobbed was it with those desiring to flee.

"Citizens were leaving by hundreds," wrote Sallie Brock, with the understatement that "the hasty adjournment and dispersion of the Confederate Congress had no tendency to reassure us."

The lawmakers were crudely lampooned by cartoons which sprouted like dragons' teeth in shop windows. Fat, frightened congressmen were depicted fleeing with their carpet bags, pursued by long-legged insectlike gunboats as well as snakes and frogs. Endeavoring to protect them were escorts of nicely dressed ladies.

"Baggage wagons, heaped with trunks, boxes and baskets, were constantly rattling through the streets," Sallie continued. "Houses were left deserted . . . but a more alarming feature was noticeable in the ominous-looking boxes that were brought out of the offices of the different departments, containing the archives of the government, and marked for Columbia, South Carolina."

St. Paul's in 1865: "Most of Richmond was in Church that Sunday
[April 2, 1865], . . . a majority within the limited confines of St. Paul's."
Library of Congress.

The same rumors leaped the Atlantic to be circulated in
Great Britain and France. These did not aid the Confederacy's
several foreign business negotiations, such as the building of
merchant raiders in Liverpool. Davis denied all such reports,
and at the same time formulated plans to hustle his family
southward. It included three children, Margaret Howell (also
known as "Polly", 7, Jefferson, Jr., 5 and Joseph Evan, 2
years old.

The President chose this moment for his own baptism.
This solemn Christian rite was performed in the Confederate
executive mansion by the Reverend Charles G. Minnigerode,
the German-born rector of St. Paul's Episcopal Church.

Minnigerode, in spite of lengthy sermons delivered in a
thick German accent, drummed his way into the affections of
his congregation. When the preacher fell seriously short of
English, he would, according to Mary Chesnut, "shout his

battle cry, 'O lamp of God, I come!' " To which they could only echo an "Amen!"

On May 9, during another reception at the Davis's residence, a courier arrived bearing dispatches. As the President passed Varina on his return to the drawing room, she would recall, "I looked a question and he responded in a whisper, 'the enemy's gunboats are ascending the river.' "

Varina and her children boarded a train for Raleigh in the morning. There was no problem in leaving since all the rail lines, except those to Norfolk, were open. Overly solicitous, since he had lost his first wife and, indeed, more recently, a son, Samuel Emory, Davis turned a deaf ear to her protestations. She was, she insisted, "always averse to flight."

Preparations for a possible evacuation continued, as Judith McGuire watched "loads of furniture passing by, showing that people were taking off their valuables."

A Prussian officer with the defending forces, who wrote of his experiences in the *Kölnische Zeitung*, of Cologne, Germany, attested to the "confusion" which he believed "reigned supreme . . . a feverish state of mind bordering on insanity.

"All was crying and noise and confusion . . . all fled who could," according to the foreign-born officer. Public buildings were prepared for burning if McClellan moved any closer.

On May 14, the legislature of Virginia, which had remained—along with the Richmond City Council—in constant session, passed a resolution that concluded, "The General Assembly hereby expresses its desire that the Capital of the State be defended *to the last extremity!*"

The next day Federal gunboats, which included the scrappy little turreted *Monitor* and the cumbersome ironclad *Galena*, were driven back at Drewry's Bluff, just eight miles below Richmond. The fleet could not have steamed unopposed so far upriver had not the *Monitor* already met the *Merrimack* (renamed the *Virginia* by her Confederate appropriators). The latter was scuttled on May 11, Norfolk having been abandoned two days previously, not quite thirteen months after the South had seized that important Federal port and naval base.

Residents of Richmond ventured out to watch the exchange between the forts and the fleet, the guns of which could not be elevated sufficiently to reach the heights. Phoebe Yates Pember, recently widowed and now matron at the newly opened Chimborazo Barracks Hospital, "a sprawling institution perched on a high hill" east of the city, wrote: "The inhabitants crowded the eastern brow of the hill above Rocketts [a port section] and the James River, overlooking the scene and discussing the probable results of the struggle."

Even though the fleet limped off, measurably battered and carrying the bodies of thirteen U.S. Navy dead, Richmond remained shaken. Governor John Letcher scribbled urgent orders for the Home Guard to report for duty. These were the middle-aged men, many of them veterans of the Mexican War, some lame and none in top physical shape, much less "fighting trim." Then Letcher ordered all businesses temporarily closed at 2 P.M. to enable the militia to commence drilling an hour later.

Within hours, the proud Tredegar Battalion, composed of the foundry's workers and former employees, had dusted off faded uniforms, pulled muskets down from mantelpieces and shuffled off for the Capitol's spacious green lawns to drill.

On May 24, Mechanicsville, seven miles east of Richmond, was captured by Federal troops. Early the following Saturday, May 31, units of the Confederate First Corps, commanded by Lieutenant General James Longstreet, a South Carolinian sometimes referred to as Lee's "War Horse," marched out the Williamsburg State Road to meet the "invaders." Bands were playing and colors flying as residents along the way came out to cheer them on.

The armies clashed that afternoon at Fair Oaks, a railroad station six miles due east of Richmond. In fierce fighting that lasted through Sunday, June 1, McClellan was abruptly halted by the same nemesis who routed McDowell at Bull Run— former Indian fighter General Joseph E. Johnston, who was at 56 one of the oldest ranking officers in the Confederate service. Next to Shiloh and Fort Donelson, Fair Oaks (or Seven Pines) became the largest-scale battle yet of the Civil War, with more than 6,000 Confederate and 5,000 Union casualties. The wounded in those numbers predominated, characteristically.

The skirmish lines, which were the outermost claws or tentacles of the armies, brought the sound of battle into the homes of Richmond "so sharp and clear . . . that it seemed the fight must be on the very edge of town . . . windows rattled at every discharge." So spoke a young South Carolinian of letters,

Thomas Cooper De Leon, engaged in duties of a "confidential nature" for Jefferson Davis. Connie Cary, the redhead from Alexandria, shaken by the "hideous clamor," wrote,

> the first guns sent our hearts into our mouths. The women . . . had, with few exceptions, husbands, fathers, sons, and brothers in the fight. I have never seen a finer exhibition of calm courage. All went about their task preparing for the wounded.

Matron Phoebe Pember, leaning out of a window at Chimborazo Hospital, smelled the acrid clouds of burnt powder. She watched the "dense smoke rising," and "with the aid of glasses, dark blue masses of uniforms . . . though how near the scene of action could not be discerned." She slammed the window shut, as if to close out the reality of battle, and hurried back to her wards. Later, she was preparing to return for the night to her room at Secretary of the Navy Stephen Mallory's home "when the pitiful sight of the wounded in ambulances, furniture wagons, carts, carriages and every kind of vehicle that could be impressed detained me."

Among the disabled arriving in Richmond was General Johnston himself, heavily wounded in the shoulder and chest, "unhorsed," by his own laconic statement. Lee was put in command of the Army of Northern Virginia.

The capital of the Confederacy was less than ready for the influx of so many casualties—thousands rather than hundreds. Even Chimborazo could not keep pace with the ambulance trains, disgorging their litters. Phoebe sought to have the wounded distributed to other make-do hospitals in the absence of sufficient surgeons or beds. The ambulatory and the less seriously hurt were placed on the floor, in bed sacks, or simply tucked into their blankets. The nurses dressed minor wounds with what passed for bandages, leaving antiseptic for the stronger-nerved surgeons. Nitric acid, which seared the flesh, was the only and heroic hope against infection.

"Agony!" Sara Pryor splashed the word boldly across her diary. She continued to ink the pages.

> This bloody battle, the incoming wagons . . . laden with the dead . . . every house was opened for the wounded. They lay on verandas, in halls, in drawing rooms of stately mansions. Young

girls and matrons stood in their doorways with food and fruit for
the marching soldiers, and then turned to minister to the
wounded men.

"The ghastly procession of wounded," to Constance
Cary's young eyes, "many . . . so black with gunpowder as to
be unrecognizable . . . limping on foot . . . men in every stage
of mutilation, lying, waiting for the surgeons on bare boards,
bandaged faces stiff with blood and thick with flies. . . ."

The scene extended from houses and hospitals into the
streets, "crowded with ladies offering their services to nurse,"
according to Judith McGuire, a volunteer nurse,

the streets are filled with servants darting about, with waiters
carrying trays covered with snowy napkins, carrying refresh-
ments of all kinds to the wounded. Many of the sick, wounded,
and weary are in private houses. The roar of the cannon has
ceased.

Can we hope that the enemy will now retire?

Not until June 25 was the tide actually turned and then
only when Confederate forces were joined by two divisions
under Major General Thomas J. "Stonewall" Jackson. They
arrived fresh from a series of victories in the Shenandoah Valley
to turn McClellan's mighty army back from the environs of
Richmond. In seven days of fighting, with temperatures hovering near 100° on some afternoons, the Union troops were
pushed from Mechanicsville back down the peninsula to
Gaines' Mill, Savage Station, Frayser's Farm and finally Malvern Hill.

"The slaughter has been terrible" declared Brigadier General Louis T. Wigfall, now an aide on Longstreet's staff, "but
our success glorious."

But again "a harvest of wounded," penned Sara Pryor,
now nursing at Kent and Paine's Warehouse hospital.

"The air was fetid with the presence of the wounded and
the dead" declared Elizabeth Van Lew. From her mansion on
Church Hill, to the east, she had a commanding view of the
city. But the northern-born maiden lady took no part in the
nursing that occupied every other able-bodied female in
Richmond. Rather her innovative brain was seeking positive

ways of aiding the Union—and of more immediate importance, keeping her brother, John N. Van Lew, from being impressed into the Confederate service they both despised.

The scenes in the Army of the Potomac were as sobering as those in the streets and homes of Richmond. George Alfred Townsend, correspondent for the *New York Herald*, darkly moustached and rather a dandy, was at the same time reporting back to his editors:

> *The sickening smell of mortality was almost insupportable, but by degrees I became accustomed to it. The lanterns hanging around the room streamed fitfully upon the red eyes and half-naked figures. All were looking up and saying, in pleading monotone, 'Is that you, doctor?' Men with their arms in slings went restlessly up and down, smarting with fever. . . . Many were unconscious and lethargic, moving their fingers and lips mechanically. . . .*

All in all, similar gory fragments of war coupled with the fact that Lee, like McClellan, had not pressed further for a resolution of the conflict served to make Richmond as bitter as Washington at the waste of the intense fighting of the Seven Days—for what purpose, for *what* purpose?

Lincoln, wholly disheartened, wanted no more of the Peninsular campaign. He was convinced that his commanding general had "the slows," that his vast army was scant more than a personal "bodyguard." On July 9, stovepipe hat, morning coat and black baggy trousers making his lowering countenance all the more grave, the president arrived at McClellan's tent at his new base, Harrison's Landing.

With him was Secretary of War Stanton, no longer any champion of "Little Mac." The two men's mutual disenchantment was reflected in a recent letter from George to his wife, pretty young Nell McClellan, asserting that Stanton was capable of such "treachery and rascality" that Judas himself "would have raised his arms in holy horror."

The campaign was cancelled. McClellan's "earnest remonstrances" that he was "prepared to advance . . . with entire confidence" fell on deaf ears. Lincoln could not understand how his general had fought within sight of Richmond's spires, yet could not take the capital. There was also the persisting

"Gath," George Alfred Townsend. *Maryland Park Service.*

nightmare in the President's mind that Washington, if not guarded by tens of thousands of troops, might be picked off by Lee or even one of his hard-riding cavalry corps.

On the other hand, the tall, sad man from Illinois did not appear to appreciate that the South had already sustained in the war some 70,000 casualties, exceeding a comparable Federal total by fifteen percent—a rate which must sooner or later exhaust the very limited reservoir of Southern young men.

For Richmond—respite, except for the continuing reminder of the summer's slaughter. Funeral after funeral "constantly called to our windows," wrote Connie Cary, "by the

wailing dirge of a military band preceding a soldier's funeral.
. . .The coffin crowned with cap and sword and gloves, the
riderless horse following with empty boots fixed in the stirrups
of an army saddle. . . ."

Some still clung to the conviction, if emotional, that now
the Confederacy would be recognized by foreign countries. So
far, Great Britain and France had accepted only "missions"
from the seceding states, and these primarily for purchasing.

Mary Boykin Chesnut, in Columbia, quoted her husband,
now a brigadier general: "He believes . . . that we are to be
recognized as a nation by the crowned heads across the water,
at last. . . ."

The war moved on. . . .

Successes at the second battle of Manassas and at Chantilly
inspired Lee to move north and "liberate" the people of Maryland. Thrown back at Sharpsburg, or Antietam (a creek), the
Confederates limped home to Virginia where they dug in along
the river bluffs across the Rappahannock from Fredericksburg.

On November 5, McClellan was relieved by Major General
Ambrose E. Burnside, undistinguished save for the fact that he
had lent his name in reverse to the bewhiskered mode. Protesting he was not capable of commanding the Army of the
Potomac, he proved his capacity for self-assessment on December 13 with an ill-conceived attack on Fredericksburg, astride the Rappahannock. He was thrown back by a formidable
combination of Lee, Jackson, Longstreet and J.E.B. Stuart, with
nearly 13,000 casualties.

Once more Richmond was spared. Once more, as well, the
carts bearing the dead and wounded jounced and swayed
across winter's rutted roads to Richmond—a journey of some
fifty miles.

Kate Rowland, another refugee from Alexandria, "saw
them bringing in the wounded. The street was thronged. . . ."

The city's meager corps of ministers were overcome with
wholesale death and the challenge of interment. Some, like
Judith McGuire, themselves read the burial service for their
fallen.

Still more hospitals for the backwash. The Baptist Female
Institute pushed desks to the walls and filled the classrooms
with cots and hand-me-down beds. The YMCA, too, at Seventh and Clay, joined the swelling list of churches, warehous-

es, halls and private homes—now some fifty in number—which were designated as places for the sick, wounded and dying.

So important was the task of nursing—scarcely yet a "profession"—that Jefferson Davis commissioned one, Sally L. Tompkins, a "captain of cavalry." An apparently random choice, the token "captain" managed one of the many "mansion hospitals," the home of Judge John Robertson on Main at Third. She was the only woman ever commissioned by the Confederate government.

Prisons, too, were jammed. Libby, a converted ship chandlery on the James, sent its overflow of Federal officers to Belle Isle, normally reserved for the noncommissioned. Paradoxically, a hard-bitten Yankee from Maine, William Libby, had given the rebel prison its name.

December 1862 passed in Richmond as the second wartime Christmas approached. Dominating all were the many and diverse needs of the fighting forces. As snowflakes whitened the heads and shoulders of those attending, a public meeting was held to raise money for military boots. At the same time, an appeal was printed in the *Examiner* for blankets for the regiments in western Virginia. Some housewives, short of blankets, sheared their imported carpets to bed size and shipped them off, hoping they would not be stolen en route to the front.

All in all, scarcely a hint "of the festival known to plum pudding and robin redbreast stories," Connie Cary wryly observed. She faced Christmas in the drab Clifton Hotel, so honeycombed with subterranean passages, "dark as Erebus," that she thought of it as "the Castle of Otranto." It was a far cry from her Grandmother Fairfax's estate "Vaucluse" in Alexandria where she had grown up, and which was complete with slaves, French governesses and frequent balls. Connie continued:

> Every crumb of food better than ordinary, every orange, apple or banana, every drop of wine and cordial procurable went straightway to the hospitals, public or private. Many residents had set aside at least one room of their stately old houses as a ward, maintaining at their own expense as many sick or wounded soldiers as they could accommodate.

Connie Cary. *Virginia Historical Society.*

> *On Christmas eve, all the girls and women turned out in the streets, carrying baskets with sprigs of holly, luckily plentiful since the woods around Richmond still held its ruddy glow in spots where bullets had not despoiled the trees beyond recall.*

Connie was buoyant and decorative. Recently joined by her equally vivacious cousins, the beautiful auburn-haired Hetty and Jennie Cary, refugees from Baltimore, the girls were gaining a reputation for spirit and had been dubbed "the Cary Invincibles." With Burton Harrison, an ex-Yale man who had come south with them and was now an aide to Davis, Jennie had set "Maryland My Maryland" to music. It was already a popular Confederate marching song.

Christmas Eve seemed as appropriate an occasion as any to sing about this semi-Southern state of divided loyalties. And while the Carys and Harrison bounced the stirring notes off the peeling plaster of the Clifton Hotel by candlelight, Kate Rowland and her sister Lizzie spent a substantial part of the night in the kitchens of Chimborazo, cooking "good things for the soldiers, stewed oysters . . . chickens, ducks, pies," to be washed down with cider and eggnog, enough for four hundred men.

For War Department clerk Jones, hardly able to pay rent for his family, it was an austere observance, as he listened to the traditional Southern version of sleigh bells and carols: "The boys . . . firing Chinese firecrackers everywhere, and no little gunpowder is consumed in commemoration of the day."

Then, New Year's Eve, "the last day of a terrible year," as the *Examiner* pronounced its obituary for 1862.

CHAPTER

3

★★★★★

1863

"It Is All My Fault. . . ."

On the first day of the new year, Lincoln's Emancipation Proclamation went into effect. It was aimed against slavery in those states "in rebellion against the United States."

In Richmond, it was paid no heed. This was a struggle for "state's rights," and what did black servants have to do with it, anyway?

"It was bitter last night," wrote Jones, with stiff fingers, chronicling the commencement of the third year of secession, "and everything is frozen this morning; there will be an abundance of ice next summer, if we keep our icehouses."

Virginia had been whitened off and on since early November, and heat was a luxury. The price of coal and even wood kept soaring. Gas for street lamps was turned off during the daylight hours until 4 P.M. to conserve dwindling supplies. Offices and shops became as gloomy as their occupants' spirits on dark, chill winter mornings. Candles and smoky tapers began to replace oil lamps in private homes. Nocturnal reading was a prime casualty.

An epidemic of smallpox added to the winter's miseries. Malnutrition inevitably resulted from high food prices: flour, $200 a barrel; salt, $2 a pound; beef unobtainable and turkeys as high as $30; hams sometimes going for $350; a room in a boarding house up to $100 a month. . . .

On February 13, windows cracked and chinaware fell off shelves as an explosion rocked the city. A powder works on Brown's Island, in the James, had been blown to atoms, killing thirty-one women and two men. Although a belief persisted that Yankee spies were responsible, ordnance experts suspected the instability of detonating caps which were produced on the island. Only a gaping crater remained.

The winter did not ease. A foot of snow fell one day and the temperature dropped to 10°. The girls at Miss Pegram's diverted themselves by watching the ever-changing scene beyond the school's somber brick walls, sometimes even venturing into the world on the other side to have snowball fights with passing soldiers.

Finally, spring, and with it the release of pent-up emotions. On Maunday Thursday, April 2, some five hundred women and boys gathered in Capitol Square to protest the lack of food. Before the Public Guard, a city battalion with police duties, restored order, windows had been smashed and many varieties of stores, including clothing and jewelry, looted.

Jefferson Davis, Governor Letcher and Mayor Joseph Mayo, who was 78 years old, all took part in efforts to assuage the citizenry. The esteemed Catholic Bishop John McGill added his own entreaties. He fared better than the President, who caught a loaf of bread tossed at him, then waved it as he chided: "Bread is so plentiful that you throw it away!"

Confusion stamped the whole episode. Almost every literate person in Richmond went home to scribble impressions of what had happened. None was in full agreement as to who led the riot, if indeed there was a leader. A tall woman with "a feather in her hat," one wrote; it was an "Amazonian," by the measure of Varina Davis.

The extent of damage, amount of plunder, and exactly how the mob was dispersed were also variously described. Some testified that the guard fired over the people's heads. Still others swore that the participants merely went to their many homes and rooms to eat what food they might have appropriated.

The city council, which had just authorized $20,000 for the destitute, was hurt, shaken and shocked.

At this time, a new adversary of armed secession appeared—Major General Joseph A. Hooker, who had fought well in the Mexican War and with particular gallantry at Antietam, where he had been wounded. Totally despairing of Burnside after the Fredericksburg debacle, Lincoln had appointed the Massachusetts-born Hooker late in January as his third commander of the Army of the Potomac. At 50, big, handsome "Fighting Joe" became that army's oldest general thus far.

With 130,000 men, the Union general commanded a force that outnumbered the enemy at least two to one. On May 1, the armies met at Chancellorsville, ten miles west of Fredericksburg.

In the dusk of the following evening, Stonewall Jackson launched a furious surprise attack, stabbed with rebel yells, that not only turned Hooker's flank but so upset the Union commander's strategy that the next day he called off the engagement.

However, on that same Sunday, May 3, Major General George Stoneman's cavalry did in part succeed in a diversionary raid by galloping to the northern boundaries of Richmond. Mary Chesnut was in St. Paul's when she heard the

Main Street, Richmond, as photographed by the Brady group. *Library of Congress.*

bell in the tower on Capitol Square clanging its now familiar alarm.

"The rattling of ammunition wagons, the tramp of soldiers, the everlasting slamming of those iron gates of the Capitol Square just opposite the church made it hard to attend to the service," she would write.

Before the Federal forces withdrew from Chancellorsville, they had sustained 16,000 casualties, or twenty-five percent more than the Confederates. "The victory at Chancellorsville," mused Sallie Brock, "was again a victory barren of practical results." It seemed to her "remarkable that in the changing fortunes of war" neither side had yet won "a success which might be considered decisive."

But the South sustained a terrible blow in that battle, the mortal wounding of its preeminent general, Stonewall Jackson, shot by his own men in the confusion of the moment. He died eight days later in a field hospital after murmuring words that would become his epitaph, "Let us cross over the river and rest under the shade of the trees." Thus ended the genius as well as the mystique of Jackson.

The prisoners began to arrive, "many sullen," Sallie Brock thought,

> and glanced with angry scowl upon the spectators who assembled on the pavements, at the windows and on the porticoes to look at them. Many seemed humiliated, cowed and depressed, while others were buoyant and cheerful, and laughingly left the ranks to purchase papers, and occasionally a loaf of bread . . . to regale themselves on the march to prison.

Bystanders cried "On to Richmond, boys!" to which they replied "in the Western or Yankee dialect": ". . . got here sooner than we thought . . . didn't think to come this route . . . tired of fighting the Johnnies, anyhow. . . ." Louise Wigfall thought, "3,000 [prisoners] went through on the day that General Jackson's funeral took place."

With or without Jackson, Lee wanted to push ahead. To fill the gap left by Stonewall's passing, he resolved not merely to appoint a new commander of Jackson's Second Corps in the Army of Northern Virginia, but to create a Third Corps. Both would be led by former division commanders under Jackson: Lieutenant General Richard S. Ewell, a native of Washington and a Mexican War veteran, succeeded Jackson; and Major General Ambrose P. Hill, a Virginian and veteran fighter of the Seminole and Mexican wars, directed the new Third Corps. The bald Ewell had lost a leg at Second Manassas.

In June, Lee started northward a second time, with objectives less than lucid. They could, however, have concerned much-needed supplies, especially flour and corn; or a diversion to relieve pressure on Vicksburg, besieged by Major General Ulysses S. Grant; or they could have been conceived simply to elicit new overtures from the peace party of the North. Surely, Lee could have no illusions about assaulting Washington, ringed every few miles with a total of some forty heavily-gunned forts, fourfold greater than Richmond's bastions.

On June 28 Hooker was suddenly replaced by Major General George Gordon Meade, who like A. P. Hill had fought in the Seminole and Mexican wars. Meade had been commander of the Fifth Corps. Three days later, the plans of Lee, whose armies already occupied Hagerstown, York, Carlisle and Chambersburg and were aiming at Harrisburg, were abruptly changed by a singular chance encounter. Units from the Confederate and Union armies converged in Gettysburg, both seeking the same supply source of shoes. The proximity of the two vast armies soon became evident to both.

As a result, three scorching days under a July sun—the first through the third—blazed a stark new chapter in military annals and made imperishable the name of a sleepy southern Pennsylvania town—Gettysburg. The carnage ended only after a suicidal charge by Major General George E. Pickett's division, Virginians all, leaving three-fourths of the 4,500 dead or wounded.

Out of 85,000 Federal troops involved at Gettysburg, 23,000 were casualties, including 3,155 dead; out of 65,000 Confederates, 22,638 were casualties, including 2,592 dead, a proportion the South could in no manner sustain. The course of the war was altered in those three bloody days. Lee retreated but Meade was unwilling or unable to follow up this signal Union victory.

> Down to zero dropped the spirits of the people; down to depths of despairing gloom, only the deeper from the height of their previous exultation. The dark cloud from Gettysburg rolled back over Richmond, darkened and made dense a hundredfold in the transit.

So wrote De Leon in Richmond, at once seconded by Sara Pryor: "The emblem of mourning hung at many a door among our friends in Richmond and Petersburg."

On July 4, one day after the guns cooled in Gettysburg, Philadelphia-born Lieutenant General John G. Pemberton surrendered more than 31,600 troops to General Grant at Vicksburg, allowing the Mississippi, as an exultant Lincoln phrased it, to flow "unvexed to the sea."

Davis, who at first had merely tagged Gettysburg as "unfortunate," now expressed doubts as to the cause of secession. He asked Brigadier General Josiah Gorgas, his chief of ordnance, "can we believe in the justice of Providence, or must we conclude that we are, after all, wrong?"

Lee, according to some who had seen him, had lamented in tears over Gettysburg—"it is all my fault." And to another friend, Brigadier General John D. Imboden, he had repeated, "Too bad! Too bad! Oh, too bad!" Offering to resign, he wrote Davis, "I cannot even accomplish what I myself desire. How can I fulfill the expectations of others?"

Yet the Confederacy minus Robert E. Lee was wholly implausible by the measure of most Southerners. "His army," wrote a young minister, John Leyburn, expressing the sentiments of many, "between us and danger [is] enough to quiet all fears."

In mid-July, Mrs. Lee, long lame, was sent in an especially outfitted freight car to Hot Springs. With her went worries not only for her husband's burdens but for her son, Fitzhugh Rooney Lee, wounded and taken prisoner after the cavalry battle at Brandy Station, preceding Gettysburg. He was a most valuable hostage against Confederate excesses towards Northern prisoners.

Libby and Castle Thunder were bad enough. Captives freshly arrived from Gettysburg pronounced both prisons: "Hell!" It would have been worse yet without Lizzie Van Lew who bribed the guards to allow her to visit with gifts of food, clothing, writing paper and, even, furniture.

She felt she was doing her patriotic duty by "serving my own country within its recognized borders," but in the Confederate capital "Crazy Bet" was considered the number one spy. Her mansion atop Church Hill had become the rendezvous for a trusted coterie of Union supporters, with such fanciful names as "the Quaker," "His Honor," "Abigail," or simply "Mr. Babcock." She often signed the last named to her own communications, written in cipher with invisible ink. She kept the code in her watch case, and placed the messages in the hollow heads of animals flanking the fireplace, to await the next pickup. A regular messenger was an old black man with a cavity in his shoe heels for wadded-up paper. His comings and goings were so regular that Van Lew would quip that her service beat the Confederacy's own postal delivery.

She even had a pipeline to the executive mansion, having placed a former slave, Elizabeth Bowser, as a servant to Jefferson Davis. Lizzie had, before the war, sent the girl to Pennsylvania to be educated.

Meanwhile, the hospitals continued to fill, along with the prisons. Many of the churches, warehouses, homes and other temporary hospitals, so-called, had been combined into larger, somewhat more formalized institutions bearing names such as

Chimborazo, believed to be the largest military hospital in the world, "had mushroomed into a small city—sprawling over some 50 acres, comprising 150 structures, each a ward, maintaining its own dairy herd of as many as 200 head, goats, bakery, and soap factory, which made heavy use of the kitchen's plentiful byproduct: grease." Atop a bluff on the eastern edge of Richmond, Chimborazo cared for some 76,000 sick, wounded and malingerers, or "hospital rats," nearly twice the number of its closest rival in size, the Lincoln Hospital in Washington. *U.S. Park Service.*

Camp Jackson, Camp Winder, Howard Grove, Stuart and, simply, "the Alabama." There were about 150 all told, even though some were limited in their accommodations and not open continuously.

Chimborazo, a community in itself, counted as many individual structures as all of the Richmond hospitals—sprawling over fifty acres, each building a "ward." The unusual complex maintained its own dairy herd of often as many as two hundred head as well as goats, a bakery, and a soap factory, which made use of the kitchen's plentiful by-product, grease.

This hospital plenty, nonetheless, did not hold true for those who comprised the citizenry. "We are in a half-starving condition," wrote Jones. "I have lost twenty pounds, and my wife and children are emaciated to some extent. Still I hear no murmuring."

In an effort to introduce a glimmer of light into an otherwise gray landscape, Connie Cary and other young ladies organized "starvation parties." These featured lively dancing to piano music, although refreshments no stronger than water were served. It seemed sufficient, measured against the stark times.

Not all spirits were so easily elevated, this third war Christmas, "a sad one," wrote Jones, the war clerk. Too, it was "threatening snow . . . my two youngest children, however, have decked the parlor with evergreens, crosses, stars, etc. . . . Candy is sold at $8 per pound. . . . A few pistols and crackers are fired by the boys in the streets—and only a few. . . . No merriment this Christmas."

Although his family went to church that night, Jones stayed home, since "it would not be safe to leave the house unoccupied: robberies and murders are daily perpetrated." He also was readying his garden tools for an early planting, "preparing for the siege and famine looked for in May and June, when the enemy encompasses the city."

Instead of Christmas parties for the troops, the ladies of Richmond decided to bake New Year's goodies. They met in the basement kitchens of the old Ballard House and heated the ovens for pies and cakes. By the time they had exhausted available flour, sugar and other scarce ingredients, thousands of soldiers shivering on the perimeters of the city had benefited from the production of the smoky Ballard kitchen and the toil of many women.

4

★★★★★

1864

"A Dream of Terror"

January 1 arrived in Richmond on a ceremonial note: William "Extra Billy" Smith was inaugurated governor, replacing John Letcher. Jefferson Davis, drawing himself away from his burdens, stood by the side of Varina at an evening reception.

The city was a brazenly different one than three years before, having more than tripled its size to at least 128,000. Refugees, troops temporarily billeted and the tens of thousands of hucksters, camp followers, prostitutes and the less definable "train" tagging along after a war—these could be counted in the new swarms along the dirt streets and byways of Richmond.

Problems normal to such a population explosion were compounded by a creaking transport, even as Cooper De Leon wrote:

> No department was worse neglected and mismanaged [than the Transportation Department]. The existence of the Virginia army wholly depended on a single line, close to the coast and easily tapped. Nor did the Government's seizure of its control in any manner remedy the evil. Often and again, the troops around Richmond were without beef—once for twelve days at a time; they were often without flour, molasses or salt, living for days upon cornmeal alone; and the ever-ready excuse was want of transportation.
>
> Thousands of bushels of grain would ferment and rot at one station; hundreds of barrels of meat stacked at another, while the army starved because "no transportation."

Overcrowding, lack or shortage of food, disease (especially venereal), poor communications, all served to chip away at morale.

The fourth year of the war was soon rung in by the Capitol Square bell. On a cold February night, its metallic insistence awoke all within range. The cause: some 100 prisoners from the 1,100 at Libby, led by eleven colonels, had tunneled out and escaped. Fears entertained by the populace that night, however, were unfounded since the officers were unarmed and wished only to reach Union lines.

Elizabeth Van Lew did her best to aid them, hiding a few in her secret attic room, others briefly in a summer house. By now suspicious, Confederate provosts searched her home, without

Libby Prison, an old ship warehouse on Richmond's waterfront, could accommodate about 1,000 prisoners at a time. After the first year of the war, only Union officers were confined in its bare, cavernous rooms. Conditions were "hell" in the opinion of Libby's unwilling guests, inspiring many to attempt escape. In 1864 Colonel Abel D. Streight and 10 other colonels led 100 fellow officers out through a tunnel. About half were recaptured. *Library of Congress.*

finding her prime hiding place. She wrote of others who had escaped: "Colonel Streight and three of the prisoners . . . were secreted near Howard's Grove. After passing through the tunnel they were led by a Mrs. Green to an humble home on the outskirts of the city."

There Lizzie herself met Streight, overwhelmingly grateful for Van Lew's assistance. Abel D. Streight, commanding the Fifty-first Indiana Cavalry, had been captured in May of the previous year in Alabama. In going to visit the cavalryman, Van Lew had used a favorite disguise: coarse cotton shirt waist, skirt and buckskin leggings, typical attire of the farmwoman.

The escape was worthwhile, although half the officers were recaptured and two drowned, seeking to reach the north bank of the James. There was a rumor that General Winder mined the overcrowded prison and promised earnestly to blow it sky high should another escape be mounted. The thoughtful among Libby's inmates did not much worry. Dozens of Confederate guards would go up with the prisoners.

Conditions, however, remained far from good. The non-commissioned prisoners in Belle Isle became so vocal about their packed-in existence and lack of food that Winder spotted cannon around its rough perimeters. Davis refused, temporarily, to allow flag-of-truce boats through with rations. Exchanges, in response to Washington's increasingly tough position, were also suspended.

A week following the escape, a factory which roasted substitute coffee, but two blocks from Libby, burned to its foundations. It was a loss of $100,000 and a fiery finis to a piece of rebel improvisation. The mysterious blaze had scorched both Libby and Castle Thunder. For a brief time it had appeared that Winder's rumored mines might not be necessary if he wanted to be rid of his Northern guests.

And along the Rapidan and Rappahannock, soldiers blinked at each other across the often ice-filled waters from opposing breastworks and wiped icicles from their beards and eyebrows. They even exchanged rations for tobacco via toy boats when conditions permitted, and they cheered each other in ball games. Rain alternated with snow. More often than not there was mud. The only signal difference in the preoccupations of the two armies was that "Johnny Reb" wondered where his next meal might be coming from, as well as about its composition and quality.

George Cary Eggleston, a law student from Indiana at Richmond College when overtaken by war, would observe that despite all privations, he and his fellow soldiers in gray "schooled ourselves . . . to think we should ultimately win . . . a habit of thinking too strong to be easily broken by adverse happenings."

Cavalry horses of the Army of Northern Virginia were rationed to three pounds of corn a day. By the end of February there was less than one week's supply of bread for their riders, and for most of the infantrymen as well.

More soldiers than ever were disappearing from the lines, making their way homeward, taking a chance on being shot—or hung—for desertion. After all, there were many places to be hidden on a farm, with its various outbuildings, icehouses and the like.

On the last day of the same month of February the tocsin rang again, sending the city forces tumbling out of their beds and nightgowns and into what passed for uniforms. All men on furlough were recalled. A winter's sun rose over a city whose business establishments and offices were closed. The Home Guard, sometimes known as the "Clerks' Battalion," was marching towards the northern outposts of the capital.

There was reason. Youthful Judson Kilpatrick, Federal cavalry major general, was galloping past Spotsylvania Court House, south of Fredericksburg. He was deeply into a raid with several objectives: to tear up rail and telegraph lines, to circulate Lincoln's recent amnesty proclamation and, finally, to pound into Richmond itself and liberate Union prisoners.

The key to the latter spark of daring was 22-year-old Colonel Ulric Dahlgren, who stumped about on a wooden leg since losing his own at Gettysburg. This disability did not much hinder the son of Admiral John A. Dahlgren, ordnance expert and commandant of the Washington Navy Yard. A fearless cavalryman, Ulric was set to dash with five hundred picked, desperate riders through the streets of Richmond, then open the prison gates. "The rebels be damned!"

With more than 3,000 cavalry, "Little Kil" Kilpatrick accomplished much of his mission, then was brought to a dead stop about ten miles north of Richmond at a railroad station named Atlee's. Lieutenant General Wade Hampton's cavalry had eminently succeeded in a bold counterattack.

Unaware of this reverse, Dahlgren galloped on. Ambushed on the northeastern outskirts of Richmond, Dahlgren was defeated by a mixture of local defense forces and regulars, including Company H of the Ninth Virginia Cavalry. He fell, riddled by buckshot, on March 2.

Three days later, the Richmond press published papers allegedly found on Dahlgren's body to the effect that he had planned to "destroy and burn the hateful city" after first releasing Union prisoners. The latter would then aid in killing "Jeff Davis and Cabinet." The authenticity would be disavowed by General Meade, who still commanded the Army of the Potomac.

While Ulric's body lay all day in the York River Railroad Station, his wooden leg was placed on display at the offices of the *Whig*. His remains were finally buried, supposedly in secrecy, in Oakwood Cemetery, resting place for many deceased Federal prisoners. But when Admiral Dahlgren requested the body of his son returned, only an empty grave was found . . . and Confederate authorities were baffled as to what had happened.

Only Lizzie Van Lew knew, and she would not tell. "On the cold, dark and rainy night of April 5," she confided to her diary, she "removed his honored dust to friendly care." With very little assistance, she trundled the corpse in a farm wagon covered over with fruit trees to the farm of a Scotch-born Northern sympathizer, Robert Orrick, eight miles north of the city. And there, in the dead of night, as barn owls looked on, the "honored dust" was again laid to rest.

In the meanwhile, the victor of Vicksburg, Ulysses S. Grant, now a lieutenant general, was given command of the Armies of the United States, and something that none of his predecessors had enjoyed: a blank check to conduct the war as he saw fit.

From his field headquarters at Culpeper Court House, Virginia, well removed from the political cauldron of Washington, Grant proceeded to assemble his fighting force. He started with his commander of the increasingly important cavalry corps of the Army of the Potomac, Major General Philip Sheridan, who had helped win Chattanooga and Chickamauga. His dogged and aggressive spirit was diametrically opposite to that of hesitant generals such as McClellan or Burnside.

The furious western fighter, whose command would also be known as the Army of the Shenandoah, conceived of the cavalry as a hard-hitting, far-ranging, independent fighting body, not as subordinate or merely protective units. Others wearing the blue were of similar mind: "Little Kil" Kilpatrick, Custer, Stoneman, and the late Ulric Dahlgren, among them. Confederate leaders including Jackson, Stuart and John S. Mosby had adhered to much the same philosophy, harking back centuries to the Mongols and their swift, frightening pony hordes.

"My general plan now was to concentrate all the force possible against the Confederate armies in the field," Grant would write. There were really but two: Lee's and Joe Johnston's in Georgia, awaiting an impending southern operation of Major General William T. Sherman. The wiry, red-haired Sherman, who shared part of the honors with Grant for the surrender of Vicksburg, had succeeded the latter as commander of the large Military Division of the Mississippi. It was composed wholly of raw-boned westerners, particularly adept at hacking through forests.

Lincoln, impatient for final victory, had confided in Grant that "all he wanted, or had ever wanted, was someone who would take the responsibility and act." His new commanding general assured the President he would "do the best he could."

Richmond, apprehensive, waited. There was a decision to start moving some of the government offices south, away from an impending scene of renewed battle. The Treasury Note Bureau was the first, its several hundred women clerks told to start packing.

Then, on April 30, tragedy at the executive mansion—4-year-old Joe Davis, "the most beautiful and brightest of my children." by the measure of his mother, fell to his death from the second story back porch. Shaken as few had ever seen him before, Jefferson Davis maintained a "terrible self-control" during the funeral the next day at St. Paul's, which attracted, it appeared to Constance Cary, "every child in Richmond" with "flowers and green leaves" to heap on and about the coffin. Yet, civic grief over the loss of one child was almost at once sublimated by the greater concerns over large-scale resumption of the war.

On May 5, Grant clashed with Lee in a rough, wooded area south of the Rapidan and Rappahannock rivers known as the Wilderness. In spite of tremendous casualties—almost 18,000, including more than 2,000 dead—Grant confused his opponents by pushing right on, undaunted. No Union general on this front had acted in this aggressive fashion after a repulse.

Now, according to Eggleston, the Confederates, some of whom were returning to the ranks after wintering at home, "understood what manner of man" Grant was.

Trying to outflank Lee to the southeast, between May 8 and 21, the Federal troops fought a series of bloody engagements at Spotsylvania Court House. Although Union losses were materially less, the result was as indecisive as the Wilderness assault. Frustrated but still determined, Grant now moved his ponderous army of some 100,000 far to the south, towards the very portals of Richmond. Martial law once more went into effect; schools and stores were closed and all who could leave the city were told to do so. Yet, the general feeling was that Grant would encounter the same difficulties as his predecessors.

During this period, Sheridan was ordered by Grant to "cut loose from the Army of the Potomac" and harass Lee's left all the way from Charlottesville to Richmond. He galloped so close to the Confederate capital that on May 14 Van Lew wrote that she was "awakened by the cannon so loud as to jar the windows. . . . We mingle our hopes, our fears. . . . Oh the yearning for deliverance, . . . the uncertain length of our captivity now reckoned by years, . . . the almost apathy and despair which creeps into our hearts."

Grant reported that Sheridan accomplished much more, that Sheridan passed "entirely around Lee's army; encountered his cavalry in four engagements and defeated them in all; recaptured 400 Union prisoners and killed and captured many of the enemy." Sheridan also tore up rail and telegraph lines and burned ordnance depots and other supply dumps for Lee's army.

On Wednesday, May 11, at Yellow Tavern, a popular if rude spa six miles north of Richmond, Jeb Stuart was mortally wounded in the final hours of Sheridan's slam-bang foray before Richmond, which, Sheridan had boasted, "I could capture . . . if I wanted." The flamboyant Confederate cavalryman was carried bleeding into the city to the home of his brother-in-law, Dr. Charles Brewer. He died the same evening.

There was no time for mourning. Troop trains whistled and rasped northward day and night, as supply wagons trundled slowly behind. Grant was still driving south, and had to be stopped. Van Lew noted on May 27, "we are on the eve of fearful bloodshed. There is a portentous calm."

It ended June 1 when a half-sick Lee met Grant at Cold Harbor, a few minutes' gallop from the old battlefield of Gaines' Mill. The crossroads, capriciously named "Harbor," was but ten miles northeast of Capitol Square. Once more the sound of cannon rolled through the streets of the city, and the bell tower was sounding its alarm.

In this mixed wooded and open-field arena of battle, some 103,000 Federal troops smashed head-on into approximately 78,000 Confederates. About dawn on the third day, Friday, June 3, an assault resulted in the almost unbelievable slaughter

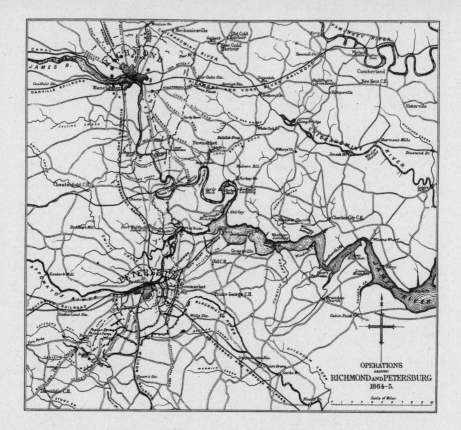

OPERATIONS
AROUND
RICHMOND AND PETERSBURG
1864-5.

of 7,000 Union killed and wounded in the space of an hour.

Lieutenant S. Millett Thompson, of the Thirteenth New Hampshire Infantry, wrote in pain and disbelief:

> Language cannot describe the fearful picture. . . . Rushing in the mad plunge of a battle charge, with muskets in hand and gleaming bayonets fixed, thousands of swords flashing, hundreds of battle flags waving, many hundreds of officers shouting loud their words of command and the men screaming and yelling their battle-cries, all mingled with the shrieks of the poor men who are struck in their wild career—here in ten short minutes ten thousands of them, a thousand men falling in every minute; while along the dense battle lines of more than four miles, huge clouds of gunpowder smoke roll up above the fields and forests. . . .
>
> . . . and in addition to the concentrated fire of hundreds of Union cannon and thousands of Union muskets, there roars, bellows, howls, crashes and thunders the awful and tremendous rebel artillery fire and musketry fire. . . .

Grant himself was shaken at this wholesale sacrifice—now totalling more than 55,000 casualties since the Wilderness only a month before. He would admit, "Cold Harbor is, I think, the only battle I ever fought that I would not fight over again under any circumstances," and postscripted, "I have always regretted that the last assault at Cold Harbor was ever made."

The repercussions of Cold Harbor were felt in Richmond, where Connie Cary doubted "we could stand more of these bludgeonings of fate." Older women who had taken a respite from nursing returned to the hospitals. Among them was Constance's mother who became a division matron at Camp Winder, "in a barren suburb" of the city. "To the nurses and matrons was allotted one end of a huge Noah's Ark, built of unpainted pine, divided by partition, the surgeons occupying the other end . . . the whole camp occupying an arid, shadeless, sunbaked plain, without grass or water anywhere, encircled by a noxious trench too often used to receive nameless debris of the wards."

Connie determined to stay with her mother and help as best she could. To brighten their "rough-boarded" room, she persuaded one of the soldiers to obtain a large flower box. Although later identified as a container for artificial limbs, her "window garden" proved the envy of our camp once she had filled it with ivy, geraniums and sweet alyssum, and covered it with bark.

To the north, Grant, who had promised to "fight it out on this line" if it took all summer, quietly changed his mind, and lines. Able to cloak his initial operations in secrecy, the Federal commander commenced moving his vast army out of Cold Harbor on June 12.

Four days later, he was across the James.

Lieutenant Charles Francis Adams, of the Fifth Massachusetts Cavalry, now would postscript of the Army of the Potomac that it had "literally marched in blood and agony from the Rapidan to the James."

Soon Grant's full force was facing tiny Petersburg, the hub, like Richmond, of four rail lines and, for this reason, a Lorelei beckoning to Ulysses S. Grant. Well before the Wilderness, he had been poring over charts of the whole Petersburg area. He set up headquarters at City Point Landing, eighteen miles down the James from the Confederate capital, about 12 miles to the northeast of Petersburg.

This James River scene is believed to be the dock area at City Point showing several transports and schooners at anchor behind the steamship *Robert Morris*. Mortars, roundshot and iron gun carriages are in the foreground. *U.S. Navy Photograph*.

After one especially futile attempt to storm the city on June 18, Grant, as he had before Vicksburg, resolved upon a siege, although "it bids to be fairly tedious." Now, about 110,000 Union troops faced slightly less than half that number of dug-in defenders.

Nonetheless, early in the morning of July 30, the Federals made a massive effort to knock the Confederates from one sector, known as Elliott's Salient, when they exploded a powder magazine thirty feet below the surface. Pennsylvania miners had been tunnelling for weeks. The Vesuvius-like blast hurled bodies, guns, timbers and chunks of earth and rocks into the air, leaving a crater 170 feet in diameter.

But the Confederates recovered to slaughter their opponents who had prematurely rushed into the newly won position. The toll was 4,000 for the North, about one-third of that for the South. Yet, as Colonel Walter H. Taylor, Lee's long-time adjutant, observed, "Grant had no difficulty in recouping his losses. He had the whole world to draw from."

If Grant could not take Petersburg, he could shell it. And he did.

"The month of August," wrote Sara Pryor, "passed like a dream of terror. The weather was intensely hot and dry, varied by storms of thunder and lightning." One piece of artillery came to be known by residents as "our own gun, fired as if to let us know our places." When the shelling became too heavy, the citizenry retreated to bombproofs, such as the coal cellar of Charles Campbell, who furnished the area with lounges and chairs. Others sand-bagged the first levels of their homes.

As summer moved on, George Alfred Trenholm, of Charleston, succeeded Christopher Memminger as Secretary of the Treasury. Head of the exporting firm of Fraser, Trenholm & Co., Trenholm presided over steamships, wharves, railroads, hotels, cotton presses, plantations, a bank. The company was an important supplier to the Confederacy, from British Enfield rifles to iron and salt. The Madeira wines his wife, Anna, served at her Saturday night suppers became as popular in Richmond as Navy Secretary Mallory's mint juleps. But Trenholm suffered from chronic stomach disorders, possibly, some quipped, from sampling too much of his Madeira.

Richmond itself was not far removed from the sounds of battle. As Phoebe Pember wrote from Chimborazo, "day after day and night after night" the sudden "boom" of cannon rumbled over the city. "In the silence of night alarm bells would suddenly peal out," but so often that the people became accustomed and almost disinterested. So the summer passed.

Then, on September 3, news from Georgia, spelled out in Sherman's telegraphed announcement to Washington: "Atlanta is ours and fairly won!"

The Richmond *Examiner*, pausing for breath in its diatribes against the administration, editorialized with unfamiliar objectivity: "the final struggle for possession of Richmond and Virginia is now near. This war draws to a close."

There seemed to be foundation for such a conclusion. Richmond citizens were subsisting on a ration of dried beans, and corn bread with bacon drippings, or soaked in hot water and sprinkled with salt or brown sugar when available. The latter concoction was dubbed "Benjamin hardtack" for the secretary of war. There was, mused Connie Cary, "no discussion of diets." Yet it appeared to her that no people were "in better physical condition than the besieged dwellers of Richmond when their cause was beginning to feel the death clutch at its throat."

, Added to hunger, there was increasing crime, from burglaries to murder. Hangings of convicted felons increased, but did little to further "law and order." In mid-October, an incendiary fire burned down ten houses on Main Street between Seventh and Eighth Streets.

Surely it was a time for prayer, and Dr. Minnigerode from the handsome pulpit in St. Paul's was among the most vocal exponents. Mary Chesnut noted that every Sunday, he

> cried aloud in anguish his litany, "from pestilence and famine, battle, murder and sudden death," and we wailed on our knees, "Good Lord deliver us;". . . . And on Monday all the week long we go on as before hearing of nothing but battle, murder, and sudden death which are daily events. . . . We live in a huge barrack. We are shut in, guarded from light without.

Sometimes, but not now as frequently as in the past two years, worshippers spotted General Lee. " 'God bless him! God bless his dear old soul!' " Judith McGuire quoted an enraptured parishioner at St. Paul's.

The recent cutting of the so-called Weldon Railroad, running from Petersburg to Wilmington, North Carolina, aggravated scarcities for Richmond and waystops along that important artery. Also known as the Petersburg Railroad, it connected at Weldon with other coastal lines to funnel to the Confederacy cargoes of blockade runners. Now it mattered not whether the adventurous captains made it through the Federal fleet.

Grant was fully aware from his and Sherman's previous campaigns of the overwhelming logistical importance of railroads. He was already capitalizing on a short train line linking City Point with Petersburg. His engineers had extended it to serve his spreading offensive arc around Petersburg's southern perimeters.

"The military railroad connecting headquarters with the camps," wrote Brigadier General Horace Porter, on Grant's staff,

City Point Railroad. General Grant, fully aware of the importance of the railroad in communications and transport, immediately captalized on the short line linking City Point with Petersburg. His engineers extended it to link his headquarters with the spreading arc of Federal camps around the city. Shown is the terminus at City Point with three conventional wood-burning locomotives working on freight and flat cars. Barge traffic and a marine railroad are in the background. From this point, "Unconditional Surrender" Grant and his staff, after bidding adieu to President Lincoln, entrained for the last campaign of the war, the general "wreathed in the smoke of the inevitable cigar." *Library of Congress Photograph.*

was about thirteen miles long, or would have been if it had been constructed on a horizontal plane. But as the portion built by the army was a surface road, up hill and down dale, if the rise and fall had been counted in, its length would have defied all ordinary means of measurement. Its undulations were so striking that a train moving along it looked in the distance like a fly crawling over a corrugated washboard.

The Federal army indeed was providing for itself as though it had come to stay. Major General Godfrey Weitzel's Twenty-fifth Corps, for example, had built log houses, chinked with mud and finished off with canvas roofs. Many boasted stoves or fireplaces. There were churches, supply buildings and tow-

Federal troops in trenches outside Petersburg. Unlike their starving, ill-clad Confederate counterparts, Union soldiers were well fed and clothed. Even during the long winter and rainy spring of 1865, the ingenious Yankees made themselves as comfortable as possible, sometimes "building log houses with mud chinks and canvas roofs. Many boasted stoves and fireplaces." Shown here is a rifle trench, described by "A Recruit before Petersburg," Lieutenant George B. Peck, Second Rhode Island Infantry, as "simply a low parapet—say four and one half feet in length—without banquette, but revetted with turf and fascines. The . . . slopes were not accurately graded, yet . . . sufficiently steep to afford decided vantage to . . . use the bayonet in repelling attack." Noteworthy in this Brady photographic "corps" photograph are the expressions on the men's faces. *Library of Congress.*

ers from which Richmond could be plainly seen. One intrusion in this unique military city, according to Corporal Herbert Beecher, of the First Light Battery, Connecticut Volunteers: he was awakened before dawn regularly by the braying "of at least 3000 mules."

On December 20, Savannah fell to Sherman. The week before, the army of General John Bell Hood, former defender of Atlanta, was decimated at Nashville. Now, General Sherman roared towards the Carolinas like an avenging angel.

There was scant joy in either Richmond or Petersburg this yuletide, with the general outlook so gloomy and with so many households missing one or all of their male occupants. Sara Pryor's husband, for one, was a prisoner in old Fort Lafayette, New York. Like Rooney Lee, he was a hostage for the safety of ranking Federal captives.

Nonetheless, with the good things of life nonexistent or priced out of reach—turkeys, as an example, up to $100 each—the *Whig*, evincing some sort of fragile euphoria, editorialized: "Far from being depressed, there is every reason to feel hopeful."

5

★★★★★

1865

"Darkness over the Confederacy"

Sallie Brock, who apparently did not read the *Whig*, wrote that the new year was

> *ushered in with no better prospects . . . we could at best only look forward to an indefinite continuation of the dire evils which had shrouded our land in sorrow and misery. Day by day our wants and privation increased.*
>
> *The supply of provisions in the city of Richmond was altogether inadequate to the demand and generally of a quality that would have been altogether unappetizing in seasons of plenty.*

On New Year's Day, U.S. Army engineers detonated a massive powder charge to blast final obstacles in creating the Dutch Gap Canal. The imaginative plan of General Butler's aimed at eliminating a perilous bend in the James about halfway between Petersburg and Richmond. The explosion, like that of the ill-fated crater, echoed for miles around. Earth and rocks shot a hundred feet into the air—then settled back to clog much of the area that had been excavated. Discouraged, the engineers abandoned the entire project.

A sleety drizzle fell all day January 1, making the truce prevailing along the front lines more welcome. Trenches, anyhow, had become "perfect mudholes." Operations, especially those of the cavalry, were halted.

And yet, again, "rumors of contemplated evacuation," heard by Jones. He feared "a great panic prevails in the city."

There was reason. Lee had warned both the Confederate Congress, in a secret session, and Jefferson Davis that the defense of Richmond was a "detriment." The enemy, "able to make my plans for me," Lee admitted, sat on a great thirty-five-mile crescent from White Oak Swamp, east of Richmond, to Hatcher's Run, southwest of Petersburg, perhaps 100,000 or more strong—three times that of the defenders. If the Army of Northern Virginia fell, so would the capital. On the other hand, Lee believed he could save his army if Richmond were, in effect, abandoned.

Jefferson Davis would hear none of it. As Lee's Chief of Artillery, Second Corps, Brigadier General A. L. Long wrote: "It was decided that the Confederacy should live or die in Richmond." However, peace feelers went out.

The Confederacy dispatched Vice-President Stephens and Judge John A. Campbell, former associate justice of the U.S. Supreme Court, now assistant secretary of war. Their desires for peace had long been a matter of record. With their aides, the pair journeyed first to City Point, where they waited as guests of General Grant aboard the comfortable converted Hudson River steamer, *Mary Martin*.

After three days, Stephens and Campbell continued on to Hampton Roads where Lincoln and Secretary of State William Seward awaited them on the *River Queen*, a 141-ton former Norfolk steamer now operated by the Quartermaster Department of the Army. Neither of the Confederate commissioners heard what he might have hoped. There could be no armistice, the president emphasized, without unconditional restoration of the Union and total dissolution of the Confederacy. Northern states, even as he spoke, were voting on the Thirteenth Amendment to abolish slavery.

And so, as one observer noted, "the dove of peace departed."

On January 19, in threadbare Richmond, there was a wedding in St. Paul's of some glitter: that of Hetty Cary to handsome John Pegram. The 33-year-old major general had been wounded in the Battle of the Wilderness. For the superstitious, an ominous shadow had hovered over the proceedings: a small hand mirror had been dropped and shattered while Hetty was trying on her bridal veil, the horses had almost bolted while drawing the bridal carriage to the church, her tulle face veil was ripped. . . .

Not quite two weeks later, on February 1, Robert E. Lee was appointed General in Chief of the Confederate forces. Considering the poor morale of the troops, and inability to properly equip and feed them, the honor was somewhat empty. George Eggleston, for one, found no basis for hope "except that Providence would in some way interfere in our behalf." Soldiers of less faith simply deserted. Three hundred of them arrived one day at Union-held Fort Harrison, a former Confederate bastion.

Other defenders of Richmond and Petersburg, however, were more phlegmatic. Captain Frank Potts, an assistant quartermaster on Longstreet's staff, had "never despaired." For one consideration, the First Corps, which Longstreet commanded, was now to the east of the Capital, a fairly quiet sector although

Fort Harrison, a strongpoint in the defense of Richmond, was captured
by Grant's forces. *Virginia State Travel Service.*

it covered eleven miles, starting at Chaffins Bluff. "We had a
comparatively easy time during the winter," he would write.
"Our work was in beating the enemy up occasionally to prevent them from reinforcing their left. . . .

On the other extremity of the front—Hatcher's Run—a
Union assault was parried on February 6. One part of the price
for holding this left anchor of the gravely overextended Confederate lines was the death of General John Pegram, while
leading a cavalry charge. Young Pegram, who happened to be
known by his friends in the exclusive Mosaic Club as "a de-
lightful and artistic whistler," was dead. He had been married
just three weeks. "Like a flower broken in the stalk," Hetty left
the home she had, with exceptional devotion, made for him
near the front, to kneel in the freight car beside the pine coffin
as the train clicked back to Richmond.

Dr. Minnigerode conducted the obsequies in the same
church where the couple had been married. Connie would
write of "the wailing of the band . . . on the slow pilgrimage to
Hollywood Cemetery. . . ."

The war went on. Petersburg continued to be shelled with
regularity, night and day. Columbia, the capital of South
Carolina, surrendered on February 17 against the glow of burning cotton bales, its entire heart, 1,300 structures, reduced to

cinders. Neither side would admit having set the conflagration. The same day, Charleston was evacuated. Wilmington, North Carolina, fell on February 22. This was the port into which blockade runners unloaded "Nassau bacon" and other goodies for Richmonders with cash to pay.

Davis was becoming desperate. He hammered out emergency measures including one to Lieutenant General Richard S. Ewell, charging him with the defense of Richmond.

"Lee," he would recall, ordered him, "about the middle of February," to make preparations for the destruction of cotton, tobacco and such. He continued:

> I immediately sent Major Brown of my staff, to Mayor Mayo with the document, requested him to call a meeting of the Common Council to give their opinions as to the measures proper to be taken. After a free discussion with some of the Council and by their advice, I issued a circular to the merchants and owners of cotton and tobacco, embodying the substance of your order and the law that accompanied it.

Next, at Lee's urging, the President returned General "Joe" Johnston to command the "Army of Tennessee," which included as well South Carolina, Georgia and Florida. Yet it was a questionable favor for the small, goateed Johnston, who had been replaced before Atlanta by Hood. His sphere was now largely Union-held.

Another order involved Rear Admiral Raphael H. Semmes, whose cruise in the raider *Alabama* had furrowed a wake of burned and ransomed Union and neutral merchant vessels from the South Atlantic to Singapore. His depredations were ended on June 19, 1864, off Cherbourg when the *Alabama* was sunk by the heavy steam sloop USS *Kearsarge*. This left him without a command until February 18, 1865, when he was put in command of the James River Fleet.

A native of Alabama and a veteran of the "old U.S. Navy," the red-headed Semmes was as well an international lawyer of known capabilities. His fleet, largely in disrepair and providing almost "prison ship" living accommodations, consisted of three ironclads and five wooden gunboats. The flagship was the *Virginia*, successor to the scuttled *Merrimack*, renamed the *Virginia*.

All eight, manned "almost entirely from the army," were

moored in sight of Richmond. The Union fleet controlled the remainder of the James, at least to strategic Drewry's Bluff.

By the end of February, "it began to be felt" by Phoebe Pember, "that all was not as safe as it was supposed to be . . . the incessant moving of troops through the city from one point to another . . . the scarcity of rations . . ." Some estimated that only one soldier in four wore proper shoes.

Even so, Richmond society went down hard. There were still balls and other social events, even if their frequency was diminished. Damask and lace curtains, even mosquito netting, was cut up and resewn into evening gowns.

With the arrival of March came orders to remove from Richmond all government property that could possibly be spared.

> *First the archives and papers went,* [wrote De Leon] *then the heavier stores, machinery and guns, and supplies not in use; then the small reserve of medical stores was sent to Danville, or Greensboro. And, at last, the already short supplies of commissary stores were lessened by removal—and the people knew their Capital was at last to be given up!*
>
> *Deep gloom—thick darkness that might be felt—settled upon the whole people. Hope went out utterly.*

"The war," the respected Judge Campbell confided, "must terminate in the spring." Lee himself, apparently of similar mind, sent a truce-flag message to Grant proposing a "military convention" to "put an end to the calamities of war." The suggestion had arisen from a prior chat between General Longstreet and Major General Edward O. Ord, commanding the Department of Virginia and North Carolina, succeeding General Butler. The two West Point friends had met earlier to discuss the exchange of prisoners and burial of the dead.

The Federal commandant at once telegraphed Secretary Stanton, who sizzled back a reply the next day, which happened to be the second inauguration of Lincoln. In substance, the War Department ordered Grant not to talk with Lee other than to arrange for the "capitulation" of his army and, in the meanwhile, "press to the utmost your military advantage."

For the second time, in the very early months of 1865, "the dove of peace departed" the capital.

In continuing testament to the depression and defeatism

which was gripping the Confederacy, Lee at this same time held with Jefferson Davis "a long and free conference," as Davis would recall. The President's General in Chief stated bluntly that "the evacuation of Petersburg was but a question of time." In this case, Richmond would have to be given up and a retirement made initially to Danville, 145 miles to the southwest and a subsequent link up with Johnston's forces in the Carolinas.

A few days later, on March 9, responding to the new Secretary of War John C. Breckinridge, Lee wrote that it "must be apparent to everyone" that the military position "is full of peril and requires prompt action."

The appointment in early February of Breckinridge as the Confederacy's fourth Secretary of War was symptomatic of the desperation of the administration for magic solutions. The 44-year-old handsome, moustached major general had proven an effective and intelligent fighter in spite of a more than average thirst for his native Kentucky's bourbon. Vice-President under Buchanan, Breckinridge had been the Southern Democrats' presidential nominee in 1860, winning electoral votes second only to Lincoln's. Although a believer in states' rights, he kept his seat in the U.S. Senate until long after Bull Run—December 1861—and was only expelled then since he had accepted a commission in the Confederate army.

Lee's moment of truth appeared to have arrived. It was not easy to accept, much less to rationalize. Varina Davis, present at most of his comings and goings at the White House of the Confederacy, wrote that the white-haired general looked "dispirited and wretched," adding that he complained, "Congress does nothing to reinforce us."

Her husband appeared in yet worse condition, "quite feeble, but used to remain in his office from 10 A.M. until 7 and sometimes 8 o'clock in the evening without food. If I sent luncheon to him he forgot to eat it and I fell into the habit of going to his office daily for ten minutes to offer it to him."

Davis relied heavily on his former Secretary of War, now head of the State Department, Judah Benjamin. Undoubtedly the most able and efficient member of the Confederate cabinet, Benjamin worked rapidly, endeavoring to clear his desk by 3 P.M. in order to go to the adjacent offices of the President. There he toiled with Davis, often far into the evening.

About the middle of the month, thirteen-year-old Emmie Crump overheard a conversation between her father and

Jefferson Davis, *left*, and Judah Benjamin, *right*. The lean, intense
President of the seceded states depended heavily on his able secretary
of state. Plump, usually sanguine, Benjamin was Davis's opposite in
numerous respects. Fanatically devoted to the Confederate cause, the
chief executive at Richmond did "not expect to survive the destruction
of Constitutional Liberty." Benjamin, a fatalist—and opportunist—
thought it "wrong to weaken one's energy and muddle one's thoughts"
in a situation that appeared "foreordained." *Library of Congress.*

mother that caused her "first feeling of anxiety." This she
considered a "warning of the storm which was to break over
our heads."

> *He was on the eve of starting a mission for the Government
> in his capacity as Assistant Secretary of the Treasury, and being
> thoroughly acquainted with all the interests of our poor languish-
> ing cause foresaw with more clear vision than many others the
> impossibility of holding Richmond much longer.*

About this same time, a foreign businessman who had
been frequently in "the metropolis of the Confederacy" paid

another visit. As soon as he stepped from the train, wiping cinders from eyes and shirt, he was aware of a "deathlike stillness." He elaborated:

> Everyone wore a haggard, scared look, as if in apprehension of some great impending calamity. I dared not ask a question, nor had I need to do so, as I felt too surely that the end was near. My first visit was to my banker, one who dealt largely in Confederate securities, and knew too well the ups and downs of the Confederate cause by the fluctuations of its paper. As soon as he could give me a private moment he said in a sad, low tone:
> "If you have any paper money put it into specie at once."

In mid-March, Fannie Walker, who believed she was the only woman employed in the copying section of the War Department, was handed "a package of letters" signed "R. E. Lee." She would recall:

> Perfect silence soon fell on all, and nothing save the scratch of the pen could be heard. I had not proceeded far when I came to the statement that unless so many troops and provisions for same could be furnished he [Lee] could not hold Petersburg.
> This I knew was an impossibility, and exclaimed: "O, Doctor [Dr. Cooke, who was the chief clerk of the department], if this is so, we are lost!" The reply of the old gentleman (who I suppose was possibly following up the same thought), "Remember, mum is the word," silenced me.

Frustrated at its inability to treat the many emergency provisions urged by President Davis, especially those dealing with finance, Congress adjourned—"fled," Varina Davis scoffed. On March 18, the lawmakers left, setting no date to reconvene, exchanging acrimonious charges with Davis. All sounded to Jones, the war clerk, like "the mere quibbling of politicians, while the enemy's artillery is thundering at the gates." He added that the "bickering" between the legislative and executive branches had succeeded only in "demoralizing the community."

Few in Richmond thought the Congress would, or could, ever return. The bitter fight with that body left Davis "worn and exhausted," his wife wrote, and he "prays without ceasing . . . hopes for better than I can foresee. . . ."

Varina Davis' pen inked it in these words, "darkness seemed now to close swiftly over the Confederacy."

The day following Congress's adjournment, a crumb of hope came from Bentonville, North Carolina, near Fayetteville. Joe Johnston struck a wing of Sherman's army and took a few hundred prisoners before falling back—a few hundred out of a Federal force now numbering no less than 80,000.

On March 21, Jones, the war clerk, observing the appearance of "apricots in blossom," remarked on the "many red flags displayed this morning on Clay Street, for sales of furniture and renting of houses to the highest bidders." Also, he reported that flour was $1,500 a barrel; beef $12 to $15 a pound; butter, $20.

On March 20, a curious sight for Richmond: a parade in Capitol Square of two Negro volunteer companies, with three companies of convalescent white troops. Since they were not in uniform, their appearance was something less than smart. However, although their presence in all-Negro units of fighting forces had been authorized by Congress just before it adjourned, yet the status of the blacks as humans remained ambivalent.

A Georgian, Mrs. William A. Simmons, whose husband was in the trenches, summed up living in Richmond under a notation of March 23, Thursday: "close times in this beleagured city. You can carry your money in your market basket and bring home your provisions in your purse."

On Friday, late in the evening, there arrived at City Point a visitor from Washington, at the invitation of Grant. With his stovepipe hat and long black coat, Abraham Lincoln appeared to Grant's aide, General Porter, like nothing so much as a "boss undertaker." Accompanying him on the *River Queen* were Mrs. Lincoln and his son Tad.

The commander-in-chief was shown by Grant at the outset of their talks an order some days in its formulation but only now ready to be shown in confidence to a very few:

> *On the 29th instant the armies operating against Richmond will be moved to our left, for the double purpose of turning the enemy out of his present position around Petersburg and to insure the success of the cavalry under General Sheridan, which will start at the same time, in its efforts to reach and destroy the South Side and Danville Roads.*

Lieutenant General Ulysses S. Grant's headquarters at City Point in the winter of 1865, according to an engraving from *Harper's Weekly*, April 15, 1865. President and Mrs. Lincoln with their son Tad joined Grant there on Friday, March 24, steaming down from Washington aboard the *River Queen*. Lincoln and his son remained until Richmond and Petersburg were captured eight days later. *U.S. Naval Historical Center Photograph*.

Meanwhile, Lee, desperate to relieve pressure on his lines, ordered a strike on Federal trenches hard enough to drive a wedge or at least disrupt Grant's immediate plans.

At dawn, Saturday, March 25, Lieutenant General John B. Gordon, a moustached Georgian who, along with Jubal Early, had opposed Sheridan in the Shenandoah, launched a surprise attack against Fort Stedman. On the south bank of the James, the strongpoint was no more than a mile from the easternmost backyards of Petersburg.

Some 5,000 Confederates followed woodcutters who swung axes to smash a hole through spiked *chevaux-de-frise* and other barricades. The surprise and the fury of the blow carried the fort, but the Third Division of the Ninth U.S. Army Corps quickly counter-attacked, regained all lost ground and took some 2,000 prisoners.

First telegraphed reports of the initial success arrived as a heady stimulus to the flagging spirits of Richmond. In fact, word was conveyed to the bedside of the dying John M. Daniel, testy, fire-breathing *Examiner* editor, severest critic of the Jefferson Davis administration. Pneumonia bacteria were succeeding where antagonists in some three duels had failed. It was said that even Edgar Allan Poe once challenged him.

But news later that evening confirmed that the Stedman affair was something less than victory. The *Sentinel* simply played down the battle: "There was indeed a grand exhibition of fireworks, but no battle and scarcely any one hurt."

Gordon's supreme effort provoked hardly a ripple at City Point, only seven miles distant. In fact, in a routine message to Secretary Stanton the next day, Sunday, March 26, Lincoln spoke casually of "a little rumpus up the line."

That same Sunday, Lincoln, astride a horse, reviewed several companies of troops. With his top hat and "boss undertaker" apparel, he cut quite a figure, although as a western boy, he was easy on horseback. The president was calm and in good humor until Grant warned matter-of-factly of "one more desperate and bloody battle." The commander-in-chief held up his hands in manifest horror, exclaiming, "My God! My God! Can't you spare more effusion of blood?"

At this time, as several Union divisions were drawn from in front of Richmond to the south in accordance with Grant's order of March 24, the Thirteenth Regiment of New Hampshire Volunteers moved into the position in front of Richmond vacated by the One Hundredth New York. Lieutenant Millett Thompson, who had already written eloquently of Cold Harbor, found the Thirteenth quite thinly spread out and, like so many other units, in earshot of the foe. Often their pickets talked at night.

Sergeant Berry Greenwood Benson, a rifleman with Longstreet's First Corps, for example, noted the "strange tongue" of some of his opposites—probably German as spoken by the Pennsylvania Dutch from two regiments of Major General Godfrey Weitzel's Twenty-fifth Corps. Weitzel, a long-bearded, thin-faced, humorless engineer from Ohio, had meticulously blueprinted Butler's successful New Orleans expedition and for a time served as mayor of the captive city.

Early on Wednesday morning, March 29, Grant, according to Horace Porter, "bade an affectionate good-bye to Mrs. [Julia] Grant, kissing her repeatedly as she stood at the front door of his quarters." Porter thought "she bore the parting bravely, although her pale face and sorrowful look told of the sadness that was in her heart."

The group, which included the President, General Porter continued, then sauntered to the railroad station, which had served the general so well for many months.

Mr. Lincoln looked more serious than at any other time since he had visited headquarters. The lines in his face seemed deeper and the rings under his eyes were of a darker hue. It was plain that the weight of responsibility was oppressing him. . . .

Five minutes walk brought the party to the train. There the President gave the general and each member of the staff a cordial shake of the hand, and then stood near the rear end of the car while we mounted the platform. The general sat down near the end of the car, drew from his pocket the flint and slowmatch that he always carried . . . and was soon wreathed in the smoke of the inevitable cigar.

The train chugged off along its rattling, crooked course, towards its rendezvous with history.

From the heights of Chimborazo, Phoebe Pember listened to whistles of other trains. She surmised they bespoke heavy troop movements aimed at strengthening the Southside railroad, Richmond's sole "artery . . . for the conveyance of food."

With all the struggling, warworn equipment, the Confederacy managed to run several trains a day between the capital and Petersburg. It all depended on how many locomotives that actually worked could be located.

Even this last week of March a new play opened at the Richmond Theater. A benefit performance was scheduled for Metropolitan Hall. But the food stores were half empty while the auction houses were ominously full. In one of them reposed antiques and valuables of Varina Davis—"bric-a-brac" she described them.

Jefferson Davis had decreed his family must quit Richmond. He told Varina that his headquarters "must be in the field, and our presence would only embarrass and grieve, instead of comforting him." Since she was "very averse to flight," she argued and pleaded, but to no avail. He concluded emotionally, "If I live you can come to me when the struggle is ended, but I do not expect to survive the destruction of constitutional liberty."

Keeping a five-dollar gold piece for himself, Davis gave his wife all the gold he had, and something else:

> . . . *a pistol and showed me how to load, aim, and fire it. He was very apprehensive of our falling into the hands of the disorganized bands of troops roving about the country, and said, "You can at least, if reduced to the last extremity, force your assailants to kill you, but I charge you solemnly to leave when you hear the enemy are approaching."*

Then, revealing his profound distrust of the United States, he counselled, "If you cannot remain undisturbed in our country, make for the Florida coast and take a ship there for a foreign country."

She had intended to take along several barrels of flour, but her husband objected, "The people want it, and you must leave it here." She would pack only the gold and her clothing. With her were "my young sister [Margaret] and my four little children, the eldest only nine years old." They would be escorted by Burton Harrison and accompanied by Helen and Eliza Trenholm, daughters of the secretary of the treasury.

Even as Phil Sheridan was advancing toward that menaced rail line, the party started for the Danville station, Wednesday evening, March 29. None really knew if the tracks would remain open through the night.

Peering through the curtained windows of their horse carriages, Varina was aware that "the deepest depression had settled upon the whole city; the streets were almost deserted." Rain began to fall, further dampening the already depressed spirits of the President and First Lady of the Confederacy.

> *With hearts bowed down by despair, we left Richmond. Mr. Davis almost gave way, when our little Jeff begged to remain with him, and Maggie clung to him convulsively, for it was evident he thought he was looking his last upon us.*

Outside of Richmond, the engine, needing parts and worn beyond hope of repair, ground to a steamy halt. And there the train would rest all night. Crackers and milk for Varina's restive children were located after great trouble and expense, costing $100 Confederate.

Others in Davis's social circle had preceded her, some by just a few hours. Louise Wigfall, who had sprouted from a child to a young lady of 19, had sat tearfully by her car window watching "with aching heart . . . the towers and spires" of Richmond fading from her life.

The drizzle of Wednesday night turned into a cold downpour on Thursday, March 30. Jefferson Davis emptied his house of all edibles and packed them off to the hospitals. He then hurried to his offices in the Treasury building and commenced placing his papers in boxes. Those of his servants who had not already fled were certain their master was about to follow their mistress southward.

If the rain was an annoyance and an inconvenience in the city, it was far worse on the battlegrounds: "Roads became muddy, and almost impassable for wagons in many places," wrote Surgeon John A. Liddell, inspector of the Medical and Hospital Department with Grant's forces. Horace Porter found that "whole fields had become beds of quicksand in which horses sank to their bellies, wagons threatened to disappear altogether and it seemed as if the bottom had fallen out of the roads."

Convinced that Sheridan's cavalry was hopelessly mired, General Porter was advised quite the contrary by Little Phil, whom he found "pacing up and down," as "he chafed like a hound on the leash," water streaming from his hat brim all the while. Sheridan insisted he would "strike out tomorrow and go to smashing things." He promised not only to "corduroy every mile" of the road to Dinwiddie that was necessary, but as well obtain enough food from the morass of the countryside to feed men and mounts.

Dinwiddie Court House was about twelve miles southwest of Petersburg, and four miles south of an important highway junction, Five Forks, on the principal White Oak Road. It was but eight miles south of the South Side Railroad, but still twenty-five miles below the ultimate target, the Richmond and Danville Railroad.

On Friday, March 31, about noon, the rain finally slackened, leaving "the roads . . . in a terrible condition from the mud," according to Surgeon Liddell. Even so, Sheridan pushed on towards Five Forks, the western extremity or anchor of Lee's line.

"Hold Five Forks at all hazards!" Lee had ordered Major General George Pickett, division commander under Longstreet, and survivor of the suicidal charge at Gettysburg. Just as spirited as well as reckless as their predecessors, his soldiers swung off to meet their opposites in blue, singing "Annie Laurie" and "Dixie."

They clashed at first with the Fifth Corps of Major General Gouverneur K. Warren, "warmly," by the measure of Dr. Liddell who observed with professional interest the busy stretcher bearers and the "ambulances in motion between the most advanced posts and the division hospital, about two miles in the rear." He thought the "removal of the wounded from the field to these hospitals was accomplished with great expedition."

Sheridan pushed forward, his troops spurred and heartened by singing and band music. Always with a showman's eye, he insisted that his smartly uniformed musicians be mounted on gray horses and keep up with the forward companies. As Horace Porter galloped along with them, he listened to strains of "Nellie Bly."

Not too many miles southward, progressing at a frustratingly slow pace, Varina Davis was enduring a miserable trip: "The baggage cars were all needing repairs and leaked badly. Our bedding was wet through by the constant rains that poured down."

In Richmond, although the city was relatively quiet and removed from the immediate sound of the gathering battle, there were a few such as Elizabeth Van Lew who knew the end was near. She removed from the attic the twenty-five foot flag she had smuggled through the lines and boldly spread it out in the front parlor, checking for flaws and wrinkles. At the same time, she sent a servant up on the roof to see if the staff was well secured and not too rotten from disuse.

There were also those—especially in high places—who, knowing that the end could not be distant, refused to accept reality. Among them was Jefferson Davis. Late into Friday night, under the weak glow of his oil desk lamp, the President of the Confederacy wrote orders, requests, memoranda; including a letter to Lee concerning the difficulty of finding sufficient iron ore and coal to keep the Tredegar Works in production: "There is also difficulty in getting iron even for shot and shell, but I hope this may for the present be overcome by taking some from the Navy. . . ."

The President was concerned as well with the question of raising Negro troops and of funnelling exchanged prisoners back into the ranks. "Your force should have been increased from that source 8,000 or 10,000 men."

An aide might have mused, was the ghost of vanished glory—of the dashing, dauntless Confederate cavalry and leaders like Stonewall Jackson and Jeb Stuart, all gone now, never to be seen again—teasing at the back of his mind?

Davis had heard rumors of a "general engagement on your right last night." He observed that "silence," presumably from Lee's headquarters, led to an "unwarranted conclusion." At the same time he complained that reports, especially from newspaper correspondents, encouraged hope for "better condition and prospect in North Carolina" than actually was the case.

He mused: "The question is often asked, 'Will we hold Richmond?' to which my answer is—*if* we can; it is purely a question of military power. The distrust is increasing, and embarrasses in many ways."

Davis' restless mind was bursting with yet more thoughts to ink for posterity. His pen scratched forward as the clock on the mantel began to slowly chime midnight. It was nearly Saturday morning, April 1.

PART

II

★★★★★

"THE FLAMES OF MONDAY"

6

★★★★★

Saturday, April 1

Saturday dawned pleasant after the Noah's apocalypse of rain. It was still somewhat overcast, a "quiet day, full of dark forebodings," according to Cooper De Leon.

From the more cynical perspective of the "special Southern correspondent" of the *Times* of London, the city, "long familiar with the sights and sounds of war, wore its usual look of unconscious security." The writer was Francis C. Lawley, unobjective drum-thumper for the Southern cause, a bon vivant and darling of Richmond society. Personalities such as Burton Harrison, Cooper De Leon, Colonel Chesnut or the late Jeb Stuart sought him out for hearty evenings of dining, drinking and singing. It was said that he could strike notes of "Rule Britannia" that cracked crystal glasses.

As Jones drew back his frayed, dusty curtains to gaze over a war-worn, drab and dirty city, he obtained the impression that Richmond lay in a state of suspended animation. His mind, as he dressed and shuffled slowly to work, was filled with anticipation of his leave of absence—"to improve my health." He had been plagued in recent months by a feeling of general debility. The leave finally had been approved by the War Department, commencing the very next week. He had the special pleasure of the company of his favorite daughter Anne, and both would be guests at "Mr. Hobson's mansion" in Goochland County, to the northwest, en route to Charlottesville. "I shall look for angling streams, and if successful, hope for both sport and better health."

The area, while swept over by Sheridan, was not necessarily "Union-held." Jones was aware of "vague and incoherent accounts . . . of fighting without result, in Dinwiddie County" and rumors "that a battle will probably occur in that vicinity today."

The only dispatch from Lee he could see on the sketchy morning log was one concerning General Pierre Beauregard's holding operations in North Carolina. There was not much the handsome Pierre could do against Sherman.

Others in Richmond went off to work as usual, though with vastly diminished confidence. David J. Saunders, who had been president of the city council for the past eight years, though scoffed at by editor Pollard as "an illiterate grocer," arrived at City Hall for a first-of-the-month meeting. Eight other members were there, awaiting him. It turned out to be a routine session:

Five thousand dollars was appropriated to keep the Soup House "open for the relief of those who had heretofore participated in its benefits"; a section of the Gas Works ordinance was amended; a citizen asked that a "dangerous" section of a brick wall along Main Street be taken down; the keeper of Shockoe Hill Burying Ground was accused of "failing to clothe some hired negroes and withholding from them money drawn . . . from the City Treasurer for such clothing; and $75 a week was authorized to pay the board [and keep] of several negroes working on the steam fire engine of the Fire Department."

Those who had the time or simple trust to read the *Sentinel* this fresh April Saturday learned that the editors purported to be "very hopeful of the campaign which is opening," and anticipated "a large advantage."

The generally peaceful Saturday morning gave Phoebe Pember no hope whatsoever, as she mused over the "impending crash." Moving about the wards, packed with sick and wounded who seemed to require an interminable time to heal, she knew that duty compelled her to remain since "no general ever deserts his troops."

Later in the day, Richmonders were somewhat surprised when one of Longstreet's divisions, hauled out of the eleven-mile-long line guarding the city from White Oak Swamp to Chaffin's Bluff, tramped through the streets and commenced entraining for Petersburg.

"Genl. L. [Longstreet] and a part of his Staff rode over on horseback [in the evening], but a part were left at the old camp, to await orders, as the change was not regarded as a permanent one," wrote Captain Frank Potts, quartermaster, who remained behind. He, of course, was not aware that the transfer had been occasioned by Lee's belated discovery of a number of Federal divisions slipping off towards Petersburg.

Not far away, near Chaffin's Bluff and Fort Harrison, was a patched up tatterdemalion brigade under the command of Custis Lee. It was composed of some 1,300 local guards from Richmond, chiefly clerks, "augmented" by an artillery group of six battalions so rusty in active service that they scarcely knew a cannon's breech from a muzzle. Yet they all were jaunty in scarlet caps with trim that set them apart from ragged trench-mates, many of whom wore nothing that could be described as a "uniform."

The opposing lines were so close that logs thrown across paths were the only demarcation, and sentries could hear their foes breathing.

Other units were on the move. Captain Edward M. Boykin, stationed with the Seventh South Carolina Cavalry, east of Richmond and north of the James, received orders to dismount and report to the Twenty-fourth Regiment Virginia Cavalry for infantry duty in the lines. He "began to think that a move was intended of some sort, but on the brink, as all knew and felt for some time, of great events, it was difficult to say what was expected."

Waiting on Davis's desk in the Treasury building, perhaps already read, perhaps not, was a warning from Lee that Grant

> *seriously threatens our position and diminishes our ability to maintain our present lines in front of Richmond and Petersburg. . . . I fear he can cut both the Southside and the Danville railroads, being far superior to us in cavalry.*
>
> *This in my opinion obliges us to prepare for the necessity of evacuating our position on James River at once, and also to consider the best means of accomplishing it, and our future course.*

Lee's dilemma was whether to remain and defend cities, or to save the army, perhaps to fight on. But how long, and where? "I should like very much to have the views of your Excellency upon this matter as well as counsel."

But, Lee concluded, he could not leave his post for such "counsel" and proposed that the President or the secretary of war visit him at his headquarters. This was located some two and a half miles southwest of Petersburg, at the home of William Turnbull.

As the day wore on, De Leon postscripted, "the sound of cannon came in mournful cadence from the south, still hope was not abandoned. The miserable have no other comfort but hope."

Along the front lines, Saturday was translated into almost as many meanings, nuances of meanings and realities of the moment as there were soldiers and other participants.

In the foggy early hours, Millett Thompson, of the Thirteenth New Hampshire, perceived an increased tension in fellow fighters:

> We have to exercise the utmost vigilance day and night . . . to be ready at any moment for instant action, if these lines are threatened or assailed, or the enemy appears to be evacuating his works, on our front.

He was simply reflecting the high command's longstanding fears that the enemy would slip away in the night, intact, without opportunity for battle. Grant now knew, however, that Sheridan was moving up with characteristic fire and determination to smash Lee's important right anchor at Five Forks. But just to satisfy himself that all was evolving according to plan, the commanding general asked his trusted aide, Porter, to keep him advised "every half hour or so."

As the sun burned off the mist, the morning turned bright and warm. For the soldiers of Weitzel's Corps, at least, back pay!—up to December 31, last. There was also a further bonus for their spirits: as the morning advanced no attack appeared imminent on this front. The troops relaxed.

"Very quiet along our lines," wrote Thompson, "but General Grant's lines in front of Petersburg are engaged in making a great amount of noise." Indeed the "hideous din" had continued "hour in and hour out" for several days, it seemed to the soldiers.

> At night, from high points along our line, the flashes of the cannon and the bursting shells are distinctly visible far down the lines toward Petersburg.
> The Thirteenth holds a dress-parade at night—the last . . . at the front.

The military telegraph had been snapping out a staccato of commands and reports all through the long, tense night. During the war, the service had literally emerged from the dark ages. Flexible, insulated wire had replaced common bare wire, so it could be wound on spools and placed in a wagon or on muleback. Thus the lines could be strung along the route as rapidly as the animals walked, about two miles an hour.

Telegraph lines, everything sank into the Virginia ooze. Wrote Surgeon Liddell:

> *In the morning the roads were still so muddy and cut up into holes and ruts; that transportation of the wounded over them was much retarded, slow and difficult. But during the day the roads dried rapidly.*

There were a few Confederate ranking officers who went further than Dr. Liddell in their estimation of the day. They manifestly believed nothing would "transpire" as they accepted an invitation from the tough, towering, young cavalry leader, Major General Thomas Lafayette Rosser, to partake of an early Saturday afternoon shad bake at his camp, along Hatcher's Run. Among those who showed up shortly after one o'clock were fellow cavalryman and division commander, Major General William Henry Fitzhugh Lee and George Pickett, who were ordered only the day before to "hold Five Forks at all hazards."

It so happened that "Fitz" Lee—as all knew Fitzhugh—and Pickett held pretty much the center of the Five Forks bastion. Both generals also knew that when the expansive Tom Rosser treated, the whisky flowed. Somehow, his legendary drinking had not impeded his cavalry career.

While the Confederate general officers tore into their shad, Sheridan, with a dismounted division of Major General George Armstrong Custer's cavalry, was pushing Confederate forces from Dinwiddie Court House towards Five Forks. He awaited only the arrival of Warren's Fifth Corps to mount a full-scale attack. "I'm damn tired of the delays in getting infantry up against them. I'm going to strike him with all we have as soon as I get Warren into line."

Never distinguished by his patience, Sheridan now "fretted like a caged tiger," according to Horace Porter.

At four o'clock, still not pleased with Warren's speed, Sheridan struck, and "began to exhibit those traits that always made him such a tower of strength in the presence of the enemy." Spurring on his already legendary horse, Rienzi, (renamed by some Winchester), Sheridan, continued General Porter, in the role of an eyewitness, ". . . dashed along in the front of the line of battle from left to right, shouting words of encouragement and having something cheery to say to every regiment. 'Come on men,' he cried, 'go at 'em with a will . . . They're all gettin gready to run now!'"

This was but partly true since, as Porter pointed out, "bullets were humming like a swarm of bees."

At one point, Sheridan, underscoring his superb horsemanship, jumped Rienzi high over an enemy earthworks to be met by a crouching group of erstwhile defenders, their arms plainly thrown aside. One of them recovered sufficiently to shout to the Union general, "Whar do you want us-all to go to?"

Sheridan reined back his horse. For the first time in many hours the hard lines of his face softened, and he chuckled. Pointing to the rear, he asked, "Are there any more of you? We want every one of you fellows!"

A brevetted major general of but a few hours standing, Joshua Lawrence Chamberlain, brigade commander of the Fifth Corps, added:

> *He pushes on, carrying his flank and rear with him— rushing, flashing, smashing. He transfuses into his subordinates the vitality and energy of his purpose; transforms them into part of his own mind and will. He shows the power of a commander—inspiring both confidence and fear.*

The Maine-born Chamberlain, wounded the previous summer so seriously that he fought a medical discharge, was hit again on March 29, during an engagement on the Quaker Road en route to Five Forks. He had received his field promotion to generalship for rallying his men forward although so badly hurt and losing blood that he could not stand.

While the shad bake was at its convivial height around four o'clock on that warm and pleasant spring afternoon, two couriers arrived to report the enemy approaching on the White Oak Road. Subordinate generals were unable to stem the Union surge. "Fitz" Lee sent orders to Brigadier General Thomas T. Munford, commanding the Second Virginia Cavalry, to "go in person, ascertain the exact condition of affairs."

Munford, with two brigades of cavalry, arrived just in time to take the full brunt of the attack by the whole Federal Fifth Corps: 1200 "carbines" against 12,000 infantry plus "2,000 borrowed cavalry." The force was, at the very least, formidable. "A handfull to a housefull!" Munford despaired. Although he believed that the enemy presented "a glorious target," the defenders "could do nothing but shoot and run . . . like a flock of wild turkeys."

George Alfred Townsend, formerly reporting on McClellan's army for the *New York Herald*, was just back from an indifferent lecture tour in England. Now representing the *New York World*, young Townsend, signing himself "Gath," wrote of Five Forks:

> *Slant fire, cross fire, and direct fire, by file and volley, rolled in perpetually, cutting down their [Confederate] bravest officers and strewing the fields with bleeding men. Groans resounded in the intervals of exploding powder, and to add to their terror and despair, their own artillery, captured from them, threw into their own ranks, from its old position, ungrateful grape and canister, enfilading their breastworks, whizzing and plunging by air line and ricochet. . . .*

The day was lost. Sheridan would reduce his spectacular triumph tersely enough: "Our success was unqualified; we had overthrown Pickett, taken six guns, thirteen battle flags, and nearly 6,000 prisoners. . . . Lee had not anticipated disaster at Five Forks."

Although gunfire was heard plainly in Petersburg and spasmodically in Richmond, unreality persisted in the seat of the Confederacy even as it had for almost five full years. This was apparent especially aboard the James River fleet, still "guarding" the main waterway to Richmond, and on the river itself. True, the canny, war-wise Admiral Semmes knew the midnight hour was at hand, but his advice seemed not to be solicited by the cabinet, surely not by the omnipotent President Davis. "So unsuspicious," Raphael Semmes wrote, "were the Government subordinates of what was going on that the flag-of-truce boats were still plying between Richmond and the enemy's headquarters a few miles below us carrying backward and forward exchanged prisoners."

One of his subordinates, Captain William H. Parker, of the school ship *Patrick Henry* (and a witness, at respectful distance, of the *Monitor-Merrimack* fight) decided upon shore leave this same Saturday afternoon, "not having left the ship for some little time."

Not so averse to meeting the naval secretary, Parker flagged a carriage and "drove direct to Mr. Mallory's house."

He noted unusual behavior on the part of this dignified former member of the U.S. Congress and distinguished lawyer. Parker would write:

> It was then near sunset. I found Mr. Mallory walking to and fro on the pavement in front of his house, with a revolver in his hand. I presumed he had been perhaps shooting at a mark, although I did not ask him. In reply to my question Mr. Mallory informed me that the news that day from General Lee was good, that affairs about Petersburg looked promising.

A relatively few miles to the southeast there evolved an unofficial "race" to get the battle news back to Grant. Sheridan's own dispatch, of course, was sent from the nearest telegraph head, in this case on the very fringe of the action, reaching Grant's headquarters in a matter of seconds. Still, full-dimensional details had to be conveyed in person.

With his own aides fully occupied rounding up Confederate stragglers, General Sheridan's eye fell on the reporter for the *New York Herald*, Sylvanus Cadwallader. He sent the newsman off with a roll of captured colors to Grant's field headquarters. This was temporarily at a picturesque little structure long familiar to the natives, Dabney's Mill.

He made good time and soon was displaying to Grant "a number of regimental and Confederate battle flags." The general then asked the correspondent if he would continue to City Point to take the trophies to Lincoln.

It was Horace Porter, however, who carried the full particulars of the victory to the commanding general. The former found Grant "snuggled in his favorite blue cavalry overcoat and wreathed in clouds of smoke from his cigar." Porter added:

> In a moment all but the imperturbable general in chief were on their feet giving vent to wild demonstrations of joy. For some minutes there was a bewildering state of excitement, grasping of hands, tossing up of hats, and slapping each other on the back. . . . Dignity was thrown to the winds.

As his staff continued to vent emotion, Grant was soberly dictating to his signalman, for immediate transmission to Lincoln, that Sheridan "has carried everything before him, the prisoners captured will amount to several thousands."

The time was now 9:30 P.M., and Grant ordered a massive bombardment of Petersburg.

At the Turnbull house, Lee was in easy hearing of the guns. If that did not keep him awake, the news of Five Forks or a severe recurrence of his rheumatism would have. However, if the shelling was prelude to a general advance, the commanding general preferred to think it would not come until morning, or even later.

At City Point landing, President Lincoln also listened to the thunder of hundreds of cannons and mortars. He met Sylvanus Cadwallader on the lower deck of the *River Queen*:

> As soon as I could convey my orders, he seized the flags, unfurled them one by one, and burst out: 'Here is something material—something I can see, feel, and understand. This means victory. This is victory!'

The barrage was plainly heard in and around Richmond. A couple of hours before midnight it awakened Captain McHenry Howard, an assistant inspector general with Major General Custis Lee's division, defending Chaffin's Bluff. He wrote of "a faint red glare" which illuminated his tent, followed by "a low muttering like distant thunder." He would add,

> The night was very dark and cloudy, the atmosphere damp and heavy, and at another time I might have found it hard to determine whether the sound was the distant roll of musketry or the rumbling of an approaching storm, but under the circumstances there was no difficulty in attributing it to the right cause.

"Mac" Howard was contemplating Sunday as but another wartime day of worship: "I saw no reason why I should not ride to Richmond for the purpose of attending church."

It was without a doubt a sleepless Saturday night in Richmond, although some were busy with personal concerns not directly related to the war. Jones, for one, thought only of packing his bags for the fishing leave in pastoral Goochland County.

In the meanwhile, "Old Baldy"—General Ewell—either stumping about on his wooden leg or, more customarily, riding his horse, was marshalling even the convalescents for the defense of the city. He anticipated that master emergency plans would soon be executed:

> The Ordnance Department offered to furnish barrels of turpentine to mix with the tobacco so as to insure its burning; but this I declined, for fear of setting fire to the city. I sent for the Mayor and several of the most prominent citizens, earnestly urged upon them the danger of mob violence, should we be forced to evacuate and the entrance of the Federal troops be delayed, and begged them to endeavor to organize a volunteer guard force for such an emergency, proffering the necessary arms. I regret to say but one man volunteered.

In the evening, Ewell "received a dispatch from General Longstreet,

> telling me he was going to the south side with two divisions, that Kershaw would be left on the lines, directing me to move whatever troops I could collect down the Darbytown road, and to ride by his headquarters for further instructions. I left my staff to see to the movements and collection of troops (of which only the cadets and three battalions of convalescents from the hospitals were in town), and rode down, but General Longstreet had gone before I reached his headquarters, and I received orders from his Acting Adjutant-General, Colonel Latrobe, to relieve and send forward two brigades left on picket.

In Charlotte, the unexpected appearance of Varina Davis's weary, bedraggled party exploded a chain reaction of apprehension. "What does it mean?" Lydia Johnston wrote Louise Wigfall.

> [The city is in] a state of great excitement . . . at the arrival of the President's family. Everybody seems to think it is the prelude to the abandonment of Richmond. How sad it seems after such a noble struggle as that noble army has made to keep it! . . . These terrible dark hours, when will they be past?

CHAPTER

7

★★★★★

Sunday, April 2
Petersburg

General J. C. Breckinridge:

I see no prospect of doing more than holding our position here till night. I am not certain that I can do that. If I can I shall withdraw to-night north of the Appomattox, and, if possible, it will be better to withdraw the whole line to-night from the James River. The brigades on Hatcher's Run are cut off from us; enemy have broken through our lines and intercepted between us and them, and there is no bridge over which they can cross the Appomattox this side of Goode's or Beaver's, which are not very far from Danville railroad. Our only chance, then, of concentrating our forces, is to do so near Danville railroad, which I shall endeavor to do at once. I advise that all preparation be made for leaving Richmond to-night. I will advise you later, according to circumstances.

R. E. Lee

As Sunday morning, April 2, began in long-harassed Petersburg, citizens who contemplated it as the commencement of a normal sabbath were among the select, noteworthy, and severely deluded minority. "A little after midnight," wrote Horace Porter, "the general [Grant] tucked himself into his camp bed and was soon sleeping as peacefully as if the next day were to be devoted to a picnic instead of a decisive battle."

However, about 3 A.M. a colonel from Sheridan's staff arrived breathless and "bespattered with more than the usual amount of Virginia soil." His report concerned, in general, Sheridan's continuing pressure on the broken components of Lee's left. Grant listened, obviously satisfied, delivered a few orders, rolled over on his bed "and then began his sleep again where he had left off."

Fog hung over the swampy timberland this Sunday morning. It cloaked the folds of terrain pocked with Southern strong points. In the predawn, Federal soldiers crept silently forward through the mist. Suddenly the cannon bellowed into full voice and musket fire ripped through the pines. With lusty cheers, the Union troops rushed forward, tearing away obstacles, leaping others.

Millett Thompson, awakened in his relatively peaceful billet north of the James, reported: "No man here can forget the deep, distant rumble, growl and throb of that . . . terrific cannonade . . . rolling up toward us . . . boding sure death to the Confederacy."

"Everywhere," a reporter wrote, "the masses poured into the works . . . the thin gray line could no longer stem the tide that was engulfing it. . . ."

And, all in all, Surgeon Liddell would pen laconically, "the ratio of killed, in comparison to the number wounded, was decidedly below the average."

About 4 A.M. a tired, dusty Longstreet clomped heavily into the Turnbull House. He wanted to underline in darkest terms the meaning of the rout at Five Forks. When Lee walked outside, he could already see in the distance the lines of advancing blue infantry. General A. P. Hill, who had been sleeping on the floor for want of a bed, or even an easy chair, leapt up, grabbed his aide by the arm and rode off at posthaste. How were his overextended lines holding?

Someone, in dumb awe, watched Lee calmly buckle on his dress sword and walk away from headquarters. He courteously raised his gray hat in response to his staffer's moist-eyed salute.

It was almost over at Petersburg.

On the morning of April 2, Sara Pryor wrote that she and her husband, released from prison in Washington only days before through Lincoln's personal intervention, walked from their house, "Cottage Farm," three miles outside Petersburg, towards Fort Gregg. While pausing to watch a group of laborers spading up earthworks, the fort and opposing Federal artillery suddenly began "belching away with all their might." Her husband exclaimed, "My God . . . they are going to fight here right away! Run home and get the children in the cellar!"

On the Union side, Horace Porter reported that the guns "shook the ground like an earthquake." And the correspondent for the *Boston Daily Advertiser* who signed himself "Wachusett" predicted "Petersburg must be ours within 24 hours."

Impulsive as always, perhaps underestimating the strength of the enemy, General A. P. Hill, with an aide, rode right in to a line of Federal pickets. Desiring to rally his own men, Hill had not allowed for the abnormal confusion in the positions caused by the fog. Federal and Confederate could recognize one another through the mists, however, and upon spotting two soldiers in blue, behind trees, blocking his path, Hill recklessly called upon them to surrender. It was his last command. Ambrose P. Hill fell dead from his horse, hit by a Pennsylvania marksman who had not the slightest idea of his victim's identity.

As the fog cleared, advanced Union signal posts accumulated increasing intelligence about what was happening in Petersburg. From his elevated position, for example, Lieutenant L. A. Dillingham reported "two large fires are now burning in Petersburg and are near the lead works," and later "a column of troops 15 minutes long just moved to our left on road west of the city. Heavy train moving on same road and in same direction. The South Side depot . . . is burned."

The fires probably were from huge tobacco and cotton warehouses, which were fired by the defenders.

The whole city echoed and vibrated from the cannonade. Windows rattled and chinaware tumbled off hundreds of shelves, as if presenting but a confirmation of the doom long anticipated. Shops did not open. There was little or nothing to sell anyhow.

The military was not alone in the evacuation. Citizens with no desire to await their fate in shuttered houses straggled off to the rickety old South Side station on the slim chance one last train just might be attempting to get up steam.

For those, soldier and civilian, who did gain Petersburg's last remaining station, there was indeed a train, heading for Appomattox and the west. But it did not go very far.

During the afternoon, the "special" reached journey's end near Hatcher's Run. A young but unidentified Federal officer with the Fifth Corps leapt into the engine cab, closed the throttle, and held down the whistle for all to hear and applaud.

"This train," wrote General Joshua Chamberlain, "was crowded with quite a mixed company as to color, character and capacity, but united in the single aim of forming a personally conducted southern tour."

Officers and soldiers were detained as prisoners. "The rest we let go in peace if they could find it." There was none at the moment to be found. The Federals were as busy butting their way in on Petersburg and Richmond as the Confederates were in preparing to evacuate. One rebel ploy was to string out the troops, let the bands play loudly, toot their lungs out to make battalions sound like brigades; "every man had orders to act like six."

During the morning, the Federal advance on the Cox Road and the Turnbull house necessitated Lee's abandonment of these headquarters. He rode to the outskirts of Petersburg and set up at the Dupuy house. His erstwhile headquarters by this time had been set aflame by Union artillery.

The remainder of Saturday afternoon, Lee's aide, Colonel Walter Taylor, was busy scribbling his general's detailed plans for hurrying his army out of the trenches and to the west—Amelia Court House, Appomattox, Danville . . . ? None could say surely where. The orders were sober, carefully thought out and surprisingly lacking in overtones of excitement:

> *General Mahone's Division will take the road to Chesterfield Court House, thence to Old Colville to Goode's Bridge. Mahone's wagons will precede him on the same road. . . .*
>
> *General Ewell's command will take the road to Chesterfield below Richmond, taking the road to Branch Church, via Gregory's to Genito Road, via Genito Bridge, to Amelia Court House.*
>
> *The wagons from Richmond will take Manchester Pike and Buckingham Road, via Meadesville, to Amelia Court House.*
>
> *The movements of all troops will commence at 8 o'clock P.M., the artillery moving out quietly first, infantry following, except the pickets, who will be withdrawn at 3 o'clock A.M. The artillery not required with the troops will be moved by roads prescribed for the wagons, or such other as may be most convenient.*
>
> *After all the infantry and artillery have crossed, Pocahontas and Campbell bridges will be destroyed by the engineers. The pontoon bridge at Battersea Factory and the railroad bridges will be reserved for the pickets.*
>
> *Every officer is expected to give his unremitting attention to cause the movement to be made successfully.*
>
> *By order of General Lee*

This in turn inspired further detailed instructions by the generals addressed and their aides down to company commanders and, verbally, by the lowly in the chain of magnitude: the sergeants and corporals.

At dusk, as Lee again packed up preparatory to leaving the Dupuy house, Colonel Taylor approached the general with a strange request:

At the close of the day's work, when all was in readiness for the evacuation of our lines under cover of the darkness of night, I asked permission of General Lee to ride over to Richmond and to rejoin him early the next morning, telling him that my mother and sisters were in Richmond and that I would like to say goodby to them, and that my sweetheart was there, and we had arranged, if practicable, to be married that night. He expressed some surprise at my entertaining such a purpose at that time, but when I explained to him that the home of the bride-elect was in the enemy's lines, that she was alone in Richmond and employed in one of the departments of the government, and wished to follow the fortunes of the Confederacy, should our lines be reestablished farther South, he promptly gave his assent to my plans.

Sara Pryor spent the afternoon, with some assistance, burning those papers and documents she feared would prove "sport for the enemy." The number included even "all my one lover's beautiful letters." After she had put her children to bed and her husband returned from the outer defenses, the door-bell rang. "There stood," she wrote, "Mayor Townes, come to ask if General Pryor would go out with the flag of truce and surrender the city.

" 'Oh, he cannot—he cannot,' " I declared. " 'How can you ask him to surrender his old home? Besides he is worn out, and is now sleeping heavily.' "

Among the first to pull out of the Petersburg defenses was the literate George Eggleston, the Indiana legal student who was becoming increasingly disenchanted with the war. He was sent toward Amelia Court House with a disorganized and demoralized army:

Hardly any command marched in a body. Companies were mixed together, parts of each being separated by detachments of others. Flying citizens in vehicles of every conceivable sort accompanied and embarrassed the columns. Many commands marched heedlessly on without orders and seemingly without a thought of whither they were going.

Forts, guns and entrenchments in their hands, Union forces spent the remainder of the afternoon consolidating their gains. With so much at stake, Grant was taking no chances. At 4:30 P.M. he telegraphed the President at City Point:

> We are up now, and have a continuous line of troops, and in a few hours will be entrenched from the Appomattox, below Petersburg, to the river above.

A jubilant Lincoln almost danced on the decks of the *River Queen* after he read the message. He quickly wrote Mrs. Lincoln:

> At 4:30 P.M. today General Grant telegraphs that he has Petersburg completely enveloped from river below to river above, and has captured, since he started last Wednesday, about 12,000 prisoners and 50 guns. He suggests that I shall go out and see him in the morning which I think I will do. Tad and I are both well and will be glad to see you and your party here.

Walter Taylor was threading through the fearful, milling citizens of Petersburg on his way to the station. Since there was no train, he crossed to a depot at Dunlops.

> . . . on the north side of the river, where I found a locomotive and several cars, constituting the ambulance train, designed to carry to Richmond the last of the wounded of our army requiring hospital treatment. I asked the agent if he had another engine, when, pointing to one rapidly receding in the direction of Richmond, he replied:
> 'Yonder goes the only locomotive we have besides the one attached to this train.' Turning my horse over to the courier who accompanied me, with directions to join me in Richmond as soon as he could, I mounted the locomotive in waiting, directed the engineer to detach it from the cars and to proceed to overtake the engine ahead of us. It was what the sailors call a stern chase and a long one. We did not overtake the other locomotive until it had reached Falling Creek, about three-fourths of the distance, when I transferred to it and sent the other back to Petersburg.

Others, not so fortunate as to find a train or even a locomotive, were also inching their torturous way to Richmond. Among them was the creaking, battle-worn ambulance bearing the blanket-covered corpse of General Hill. His aides and relatives entertained the illusion that somehow, over uncertain roads in pitch darkness along enemy-pocked morasses the cold remains could be delivered to Richmond.

It was a family affair, and the Hills totalled up to a large one. Captain Frank Hill, one of the general's nephews, had returned to the retreating Confederate army. However, Henry Hill, Jr., another nephew of the dead general, had struggled along with the ambulance until about halfway to the capital of the Confederacy.

Then, frustrated at the tedious progress, he left the vehicle in charge of the driver and continued to Richmond, hoping to reach either the house of his father, Colonel Henry Hill, paymaster general of Virginia, or his office in the basement of the old Court of Appeals Building on the southeast corner of Capitol Square. As a matter of fact, at this lonely, emotional hour of the night Henry Hill had no idea whether Ambrose Hill's wife knew of his death, or, for that matter, where she was. The entire population of what remained of Petersburg and Richmond was in a state of flux, with families refugeeing to the homes of relatives or friends outside of the city limits, or farther yet, even as the First Lady, Varina Davis.

This stumbling attempt to bring the body of a fallen military leader back home was conceivably symbolic of the failure of Lee's overwhelming desire for an orderly retreat. It could not be realized on account of the intense pressure on Confederate lines by the advancing Federals and the spread-out nature of the increasingly sparse and now defeated defenders.

Lee this late evening dispatched an officer to President Davis "to explain the routes to you by which the troops will be moved to Amelia Court House, and furnish you with a guide and any assistance you may require for yourself."

As Lee's staff surgeon, Dr. James D. McCabe would write:

> When night came the army breathed freer. The sky was lit up with the glare of the burning warehouses, and the heavy reports of cannon shook the city to its foundations. At midnight the army commenced to withdraw from the trenches, and move rapidly and silently through the streets, towards the river.

A resident, Mary E. Morrison, "said goodbye at midnight" to the troops,

> . . . looking curiously into the faces of those young and old soldiers. . . . The silence, the dead stillness of the last night of

that army at Petersburg, the darkness and the hush, wrapped us as a pall.

With every light extinguished Petersburg was indeed the city of awful night on that eventful 2d of April.

About 11:30 P.M. Lee mounted his horse Traveller and started toward Amelia Court House. His expression was observed to be "impassive." Sara Pryor placed the time after midnight that Lee and his staff "passed the house." "It is said he looked back and said to his aide, 'This is just what I told them at Richmond. The line has been extended until it snapped.' "

In the small city he was quitting—symbolic gateway to Richmond—desolation and apprehension prevailed. In the closed shops and on the tables of some homes lay the *Petersburg Daily Express.* April 1 was the date of this edition of a newspaper which had been luckier than most. Many in the South had been reduced to using junk fiber, even wallpaper, and quick-fading stain from pokeberries and oak balls instead of ink. Among the advertisements was one now of scant interest to refugeeing travelers. It announced the rescheduling, commencing Sunday at 6:30 P.M., of the South Side railroad train to Lynchburg. Also, the defunct paper, the *Petersburg Register,* and its printing plant, at 31 Old Street, would be sold at auction on April 5, Wednesday.

The editors of the *Express,* in this Saturday edition, closed their summary of the war:

> *Our lines are secure against all attacks of the enemy. . . . On the whole all goes well with us and 'ere long we hope to be able to chronicle a glorious victory for our arms and a crushing defeat to the enemy.*

However, seeming to lack confidence in their own rhetoric, the same editors securely locked their doors as they left the offices at 15 Bank Street. They would never put the paper to press again. Remaining only was the familiar pungency of printer's ink and the lesser smell of the paper itself and the ingredients used in its manufacture.

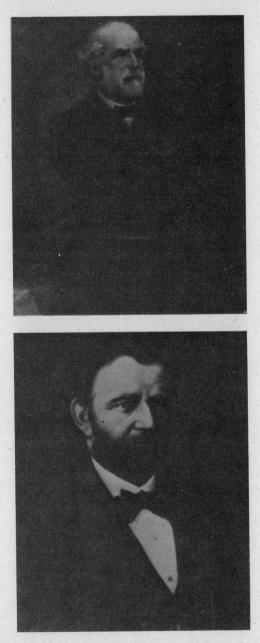

General Robert E. Lee, *top*, and General Ulysses S. Grant, *bottom*.
One abandoned the defense of Richmond, the other won a capital.
U.S. Army photographs.

CHAPTER

8

★★★★★

Sunday, April 2
Richmond

"THE DAY OF WRATH"

Morning

Few in Richmond slept late this Sunday, even though there were no sounds of battle or of other intrusions. While the editors of the *Petersburg Express* were converting fantasy into pompous words, their counterparts on the *Richmond Examiner* were working by candlelight during the first hours of Sunday on an edition to be dated Monday, April 3.

The telegraph key that had spoken its own metallic language throughout the afternoon and evening of Saturday was still. On the blackboard beside it were scrawled fragments of the action that had seared the fields and woodlands near Petersburg, although no clear picture had emerged. With unfamiliar restraint, the editors wrote:

> The decisive battle of the war in Virginia is believed to have been fought on yesterday. . . . This is believed to decide the fate of Richmond. It is not for us to write any particulars as to the future.

With a sense of finality, the newspapermen left the *Examiner* building at Main and Seventh, and walked out into the blackness of a still April night, past the Spotswood Hotel, a block distant, and to their various rooms and homes. Even the distant rumble of artillery that had been heard throughout Saturday was curiously absent.

General Ewell had spent all of Saturday night trying to shore up the ragged defenses of the city. About 2 A.M. Sunday he rode out to take formal command of Longstreet's First Corps. That general and the cream of his command had been ordered south the day before. Ewell knew only desperation must have prompted Lee to pull this trusted general and two divisions to the Petersburg theater. The regular troops left in the northern and eastern defenses of Richmond which Ewell had commanded were sparse, their ranks fleshed out with the old, the much-too-young and the convalescent, short hours out of the city's hospitals.

Yet it was Sunday—and church leave was granted by Ewell to those who sought it. Quartermaster Frank Potts rose before dawn for breakfast since he planned to ride the six miles into Richmond to worship. All horses were lean from want of proper food, so Potts did not expect to make fast time.

Optimism was scarcely a dominant mood in and around Richmond this early Sunday morning, but Potts was an exception. Riding towards the city, the quartermaster accorded the situation a good deal of thought. He "loved the cause" and persisted in taking a positive view despite ominous signs all around:

> *I knew how weak we were in men, though our works were strong, my observation had shown me on what trifles often depended the fate of battles. I could only feel certain we would be victorious. . . .*

About daybreak, the old brick bell tower in Capitol Square vibrated once more to a familiar clangor—"the tocsin," as war clerk Jones recorded the sound with momentary penchant for the poetic. How many times had he faithfully tagged it as a "bell"?

Even the Home Guard had become jaded by frequent alarms, certainly wearied. Some of the clerks, factory workers, street cleaners and retired old men would draw on their threadbare trousers and coats to respond, sleepily taking up their posts in the gray dawn. Many would turn over on their pillows for one more nap. After all, Longstreet's protective corps was just across the James, was it not?

They had reason for their indifference: "Not half a dozen persons in Richmond . . . outside of official circles . . . knew . . . of the three days' fighting that had taken place around Petersburg, and at the distance of only a few hours' ride from the capital." So wrote Edward Pollard, of the *Examiner*.

Even Jones, who worked in the intimacy of the War Department, had to rely on a "street rumor" for his meager intelligence about "bloody fighting yesterday a little beyond Petersburg near the South Side Road, in which General Pickett's division met with fearful loss."

Pollard would add:

> *For months past, the Government had been reticent of all military news whatever; the newspapers had been warned not to publish any military matters, but what should be dictated to them*

from the War Department; and the public was left to imagine pretty much what it pleased concerning the progress of the war. Indeed, the idea current in the streets on this Sunday morning was rather pleasant and reassuring than otherwise; for there was a general impression that Johnston was moving to Lee's lines, and that the combined force was to take the offensive against the enemy. Beyond this general anticipation, the Richmond public had on the day referred to not the slightest inkling of the situation.

Who indeed had an inkling? Certainly not one Confederate officer's young wife, Mrs. Daniel Grey, known to her friends as "Nellie." Assuming her husband was still in the Petersburg trenchworks, Nellie wrote, "There seems to have been in Richmond . . . a singular ignorance concerning our reverses around Petersburg."

Although she had not heard from her husband for more than a week, she did not find the fact disturbing. She had shared his battlefield travels until recently, so knew the vicissitudes of his life. Now she lived with her mother in one room of a small boarding house, the Arlington, and after the hardships of army life could "never remember having more fun. . . .

> *For hungry and shabby as we were, crowded into our one room with bags of rice and peas, firkins of butter, a ton of coal, a small wood-pile, cooking utensils, and all of our personal property, we were not in despair. Our faith in Lee and his ragged, freezing, starving army amounted to a superstition. We cooked our rice and peas and dried apples, and hoped and prayed. By this time our bags took up little room. We had had a bag of potatoes, but it was nearly empty, there were only a few handfuls of dried apples left—and I must say that even in the face of starvation I was glad of that!—and there was a very small quantity of rice in our larder. We had more peas than anything else.*
> *There was hunger and nakedness and death and pestilence and fire and sword everywhere, and we, fugitives from shot and shell, knew it well, but, somehow, we laughed and sang and played the piano (which was crammed into the room of a neighbor, a Mrs. Sampson, along with her husband, two daughters and a son, their coal-box, wood-pile, bags and barrels of provisions)—and never believed in actual defeat and subjugation.*

Ignorance of the true state of affairs extended to much of the military in the Confederate capital, including the ranking officers of the little James River Squadron. Its commander, Admiral Semmes, slept well on the flagship *Virginia*, even as Captain William Parker returned from visiting friends to his school ship, *Patrick Henry*. Like the others, this steamer was at the Richmond port, Rocketts. Some were at pierside, others quietly at anchor, several yards offshore, their presence through the night disclosed only by the yellow glow of their stern lanterns.

Bill Parker, still bemused at yesterday afternoon's spectacle of Navy Secretary Mallory "walking to and fro" in front of his house, carrying a revolver, had the dawning light to guide him through Richmond's largely dark streets. The gas works' reserve was drawing lower and lower, in spite of the city council's efforts to exhume some extra funds.

At the gangway of his ship, Parker paused, his attention arrested by "a company of Home Guards going out in the direction of Wilton. . . . . I wondered at it."

In a moment, they had disappeared around a warehouse, their clomp-clomp-clomp fading into silence. Whatever the mission of these part-time soldiers, Parker had to ready for morning muster.

While the bos'n's staccato piped the men out of their hammocks just as the sun was coming up, others were also commencing their day. Among them were those of various stature, for whom the War Department had become a second home. Postmaster John H. Reagan, for one, had been there "until pretty late Saturday night" with Secretary Breckinridge, returning Sunday "at an early hour."

The head of the Bureau of War, Robert G. Hill Kean, arrived at the same department, at Ninth and Franklin Streets, at 8 A.M. This was his custom. As a member of Richmond's Home Guard, he had been mustered into the Confederate Army during the first days of the war. His present "command" was primarily administrative, supervising clerks such as Fannie Walker.

Kean found others pacing the bare, creaky floors of the austere old "ungainly brick building," formerly the Mechanics Institute. They included, as well as Reagan, Colonel Francis R. Lubbock, governor of Texas in 1863 and a member of Davis's immediate staff, and the ever-faithful Judge Campbell, loyal to the President, if not the cause of secession.

"About 9:30 A.M.," Kean would recall,

> *The messenger from the telegraph office brought in a telegram from General Lee that his lines were broken in three places and he doubted his ability to re-establish them; that preparations should be made to evacuate Richmond at once. Copies sent to President Davis and General Breckinridge at once, and I began to pack the papers and books of the War Office.*

Judge Campbell thought two early messages had arrived from Petersburg headquarters: "One reported an engagement and heavy loss the preceding day; the second reported the disaster and loss to have been more serious and heavy than was supposed at first. . . ."

Yet these critical dispatches were not shared with all the personnel of the War Department. Jones, for one, would write in his diary,

> *I hear nothing . . . at the department; but the absence of dispatches there is now interpreted as bad news! Certain it is, the marching of veteran troops from the defenses of Richmond, and replacing them hurriedly with militia, can only indicate an emergency of alarming importance. A decisive struggle is probably at hand—and may possibly be in progress while I write.*

He concluded, seeming to brush away an unwelcome thought, "There may be nothing in it—more than a precautionary concentration to preserve our communications."

The rest of the city persisted in concert with Jones's ignorance as Sunday morning wore on, "calmly and pleasantly," Pollard observed.

> *The usual crowds were collected at the Post Office and the War Department, asking for news, discussing commonplaces, and idling away the irksome hours of the Sabbath in Richmond. There was not a breath of excitement in the general community.*

Whatever they knew or did not know about the war, the citizens of Richmond were in total agreement on the unusual splendor of this second day of April. Dr. F. Davidson declared that "Sunday was a fair spring day. The trees on the Capitol Square were quickening from bud to leaf. The church bells rang out their monition to cease from labor and invitation to worshippers. Hundreds of women who entered the house of God were in black. . . . The men were nearly all in uniform."

One of the latter, Captain McHenry Howard, the assistant inspector general with Custis Lee's division, was, like Frank Potts, riding into Richmond to church on that "cloudless and lovely" morning.

"Bright and beautiful" thought Mrs. Amelia Gorgas, wife of the chief of ordnance, as she drew her prewar straw bonnet from its tissue wrappings preparatory to attending St. Paul's. Her assessment was seconded in those very words by Jones. "Bright and pleasant," according to John Leyburn.

"As bright a Sunday as had shown in Richmond all spring," noted Cooper de Leon.

"A perfect Sunday of the Southern spring," exulted Connie Cary.

"One of those unusually lovely days that the Spring sometimes brings," wrote another resident, Mrs. Mary Fontaine, to her cousin, Marie Burrows Sayre, going on at some length,

> . . . when delicate silks that look too fine at other times, seem just to suit; when invalids and convalescents venture out in the sunshine; when the churches are crowded as never before. So it was on this Sunday. I have never seen a calmer or more peaceful Sabbath morning. . . .

Secretary of the Navy Mallory, enroute to mass at St. Peter's Cathedral across Grace Street from St. Paul's, found that

> the temperature wooed the people abroad, a pleasant air swept the foliage and flowers of the Capitol grounds, the sun beamed upon its bronze group of conscript fathers . . . and the church bells pealed their invitations. . . . The old city had never, during the war, worn an aspect more serene and quiet. . . .

A young boy, Dallas Tucker, would recall that

> confidence prevailed. A sense of security remained . . . there were no physical portents for superstition to feed on. On the

contrary, the day was as perfect a day as Richmond had ever seen; the budding trees, the flowers of spring, the balmy atmosphere, the clear sky, bright sunlight, all combining to make a spring day of unsurpassed loveliness. . . . It was Sunday, and this, strange as it may seem, added somewhat to its quiet, sweet brightness.

Secretary of State Judah Benjamin positively exuded confidence as he left his residence on Main Street just before 9 A.M. for his daily walk to his office. He was smoking a familiar Havana and twirling his gold-headed cane as if he had not a care in the world. The fresh spring morning appeared to lend added bounce to his step.

One cabinet officer, George Trenholm, didn't care what kind of a day it was. The Treasury Secretary's chronic illness, including neuralgia, had taken a turn for the worse and he was sick at home. Even his personal wealth was insufficient to elicit proper medical attention since the younger doctors were all away with the Confederate forces, and the older ones were too weary and out of touch with advances in *materia medica* to be of much help. His sole consolation: Anna was at his bedside. She happened to be the only cabinet wife still in Richmond.

Fannie Walker, the copyist in the War Department, was spending the day with her mother and sister "who were matrons at Howard Grove Hospital." Otherwise she would have been in her "accustomed seat at dear old St. Paul, of precious memory." As a matter of fact, she was still amused at how she and her friends had passed the time on Saturday: "Even until late in the night we had made merry over various April Fool jokes perpetrated," and now "a brighter Sabbath never shone on merrier or more cheerful hearts."

Only the Reverend Minnigerode himself would etch a question mark across this sabbath:

> *It was Sunday, like that of First Manassas, and the air seemed full of something like a foreboding of good or bad. All expected a battle and I knew that wagons were held in readiness for transportation of commissary stores, ammunition, etc.*

At 10:40, a third message from Lee arrived at the War Department addressed to General Breckinridge.

> *I see no prospect of doing more than holding our position here till night. I am not certain that I can do that. . . .*

As Kean, Judge Campbell and Postmaster Reagan gravely read on, little doubt was left in their minds that the end was, indeed, at hand.

> . . . I advise that all preparation be made for leaving Richmond to-night. . . .
>
> R. E. Lee

"Immediately on receipt of this information," Reagan would recall,

> I started to communicate it to the President, and on the way to the mansion met him and Governor Frank R. Lubbock . . . on their way to church and informed him of the dispatches from General Lee to the Secretary of War.

The postmaster must have been surprised to learn that the pair planned to attend divine services since Lubbock had been at the department and knew what was coming in from Lee. In turn, Lubbock must have told Davis.

Although the President appeared to Reagan to be "distracted," he was as well strangely unmoved as if he simply did not believe or possibly even comprehend what his cabinet member was trying to tell him. Davis, as a matter of fact, had always considered the postmaster "unpolished" and "brusque," which may have rendered what the "uncouth" Texan said less credible.

The President continued on towards St. Paul's, scarcely acknowledging Reagan's presence or his message. Lubbock himself did not seem to share his fellow Texan's alarm. The word nonetheless had leapt from the War Department and was becoming street talk in a slowly rising crescendo.

Captain Howard, also making his way towards church, noted that

> On reaching the city, I was not a little astonished to find it in great commotion. [Maj. Gen. Charles W.] Field's division, which had formed left of the line of three divisions on the north side of the James, had been withdrawn and marched through town early in the morning, being called away in haste to re-enforce the south side, where heavy fighting, it was stated, had

*been and was still going on. Matters were reported to be in a
critical condition there, but there were also cheering rumors that
Joe Johnston had eluded Sherman and was within a few hours'
march of Grant's left flank, and many were buoyant with the
expectation that the day would witness a repetition of the scenes
of 1862.*

Frank Potts, astride his tired horse, arrived in the city to
find "groups gathered around the hotels and public offices,
and fellows there from the right telling what they knew, and
what they did not know; doing as some people used to do at
the Bridge, 'telling lies for scarceness of news.' "

When the quartermaster heard of Pickett's troops and
others "being cut to pieces and cut off from the line" he only
shrugged: "Having often heard such rumors before from
stragglers and demoralized men, I paid no attention to them."

However, after Potts wandered into the Spotswood Hotel
and met a friend from the inspector general's office, he was
confronted with information he had to consider authentic,
being advised,

> *I can tell you nothing good. I have just seen a telegram from
> Gen. Lee to the Sec. of War in which he says his line has been
> broken in three places, and he doubts his ability to re-establish it.
> Should he not be able to do so, preparations must be made to
> evacuate Richmond in conformity with contingent orders already
> given.*

Potts thought this was "news startling enough to satisfy
the greediest news-monger." It was now, he noted, "11 A.M.,
the church bells were ringing, and thousands were on their
way to worship. I didn't go."

As Potts rode off, an old friend, Thomas Connolly, a member of Parliament from Donegal, Ireland, caught up with him to
invite the quartermaster to dinner. To his "regret," Potts had to
"beg off."

In January, the visiting Irish M.P. had stayed with the
Pryors in Petersburg, at Lee's request, although he ate at the
general's mess. Connolly assured Sara that her fare was more
ample than "Uncle Robert's" who, the delegate claimed, had
but two biscuits to share at one dinner.

It seemed, in fact, that most of Richmond was in church that Sunday, and a majority miraculously within the necessarily limited confines of St. Paul's.

"The churches were crowded," Cooper De Leon attested,

and plainly-dressed women—most of them in mourning— passed into their pews with pale, sad faces, on which grief and anxiety had both set their handwriting. There were few men, and most of these came in noisily upon crutches, or pale and worn with fever.

It was no holiday gathering of perfumed and bedizened godliness, that Sunday in Richmond. Earnest men and women had come to the house of God, to ask His protection and His blessing, yet a little longer, for the dear ones that very moment battling so hotly for the worshippers.

Considering it, in retrospect, nobody's business where he went to church, John Leyburn wrote that

at the church which I attended, the text and sermon seemed almost prophetic, . . . 'what I do thou knowest not now, but thou shalt know thereafter'; and the object of the discourse was to render the hearers resigned and contented under even the most mysterious and unwelcome allotments of Providence.

Being the first Sunday in the month, there was communion in the Episcopal churches. Dr. Minnigerode was certainly aware of the cycle for this sacrament:

The beautiful church of St. Paul, in its chaste simplicity and symmetry, was filled to the utmost, as always during the war. Mr. Davis who never failed to be in his pew unless when sick or absent from the city, was there, devoutly following the services of the church.

It was the regular day for the Holy Communion. Nothing had occurred to disturb the congregation, though anxiety was in many a heart.

The President's face was, characteristically, "an impenetrable mask" as he sat stiffly in his regular pew, No. 63, about halfway down the center aisle on the right-hand side. His dress, too, was familiar: Confederate gray trousers and vest,

Prince Albert coat, with his wide-brimmed felt hat on the seat beside him.

Sallie Brock, as if to second the pastor, wrote, "It was again the regular monthly return for the celebration of the sacrament of the Lord's Supper. The Services were progressing as usual, no agitation nor disturbance withdrew the thoughts from holy contemplation. . . ."

Another worshipper, Emmie Crump, had no doubts but what "all was quiet and peace." Judith McGuire, in St. James and of much the same mind, was "hoping for a day of peace and quietness, as well as of religious improvement and enjoyment. . . . The day was bright, beautiful, and peaceful, and a general quietness and repose seemed to rest upon the congregation, undisturbed by rumours and apprehensions."

The Episcopal service being akin to that of the Church of England, St. Paul's often counted visitors from Great Britain among its worshippers. Among them, and regularly, was Francis C. Lawley, correspondent for *The Times* of London. Lawley liked to recall that at St. Paul's "the Prince of Wales attended divine services upon the occasion of his visit." This Sunday his reportorial eye, biased as well in favor of "the fairer portion" of the congregation, observed that the latter "was as usual arrayed with an elegance which has long been an unfailing source of wonder to those who reflect upon Richmond's four years of blockade."

In the modest eminence of the gallery—"a great privilege and liberty"—sat young Dallas Tucker, who normally endured the seemingly endless rites beside his parents in Pew 15:

> *My seat on the front row of pews was on exact line with the President's pew down stairs, so that I not only saw him, but had a full view of the congregation except that portion immediately beneath me. It was inspiring to look down on that throng of beautiful women and fine-looking men assembled to worship Almighty God. . . .*
>
> *The morning service proper had been concluded and Dr. Minnigerode was delivering one of his stirring and fervid communion addresses (for communion was to follow) when the sexton [William Irving] was seen to walk up the aisle. He was a large pompous and swaggering kind of a fellow, whose Sunday costume was a faded blue suit with brass buttons and a shirt with waving ruffles at the bosom and wrists. His supreme delight, aside from*

keeping us boys in order was seemingly to walk up the aisle with a message for some one.

On this occasion his manner was in perfect keeping with his usual consequential air, only it was more so. . . .

Dr. Minnigerode, however, believed at this juncture the "Ante-communion" was being read "and the people were on their knees."

Emmie Crump also recognized the sexton, although she thought of him as "dignified . . . always well dressed and self-sufficient." She watched him until he stopped at the President's pew.

"Gently and respectfully," Dallas Tucker continued, "the sexton touched the President on the shoulder." Sallie Brock believed the man also "whispered to him."

Others, including Sallie and Amelia Gorgas, attested that they did not recognize Mr. Irving since they concluded that the man was "a messenger," probably from the War Department. However, Sallie was conscious of an "uneasy whisper" that "ran through the congregation."

"I happened to sit in the rear of the President's pew," wrote Connie Cary, "so near that I plainly saw the sort of gray pallor that came upon his face as he read a scrap of paper thrust into his hand. . . ."

Dr. Minnigerode paused long enough in his reading to watch the sexton hand something to Davis who "took it quietly, not to disturb the congregation, put on his overcoat and walked out." It was not particularly surprising to the minister since in the war years "the sexton came in repeatedly and called out this one and that one, all connected with the government and military service."

"With stern set lips and his usual quick military tread, he left the church," Connie continued.

"His self-control was perfect," observed Dallas Tucker, mouth agape, leaning over the balcony railing, "and he withdrew from the sacred edifice with a quiet grace and dignity that was not only superb, but well calculated to disarm suspicion and allay excitement . . . his lithe, erect, stately figure . . . disappeared down the aisle."

Davis himself would recall, "The occurrence probably attracted attention, but the people had been beleagured, had known me too often to receive notice of threatened attacks, and the congregation of St. Paul's was too refined to make a scene at anticipated danger."

But, "hardly had Mr. Davis disappeared," noted young Dallas, his heart quickening, "than the sexton came in again and spoke to [Brigadier] General Joseph R. Anderson, who at once went out. This made people look up and shoot inquiring glances at each other."

General Anderson's responsibilities had been varied. Proprietor of the Tredegar Works prior to secession, he was commissioned brigadier general at the outset of hostilities. Commanding the Governor's Mounted Guard, he was wounded during the Seven Days fighting. Although Jefferson Davis subsequently ordered Anderson back to supervisory duties at the important foundry, the general continued to wear two hats, being seen in the War Department almost as much as in the sooty chasms of Tredegar.

Dr. Minnigerode now realized that he was officiating under an increasing challenge, since his congregation had become "very restless."

In St. James a similar script was enacted according to Judith McGuire: "While the sacred elements were being administered, the sexton came in with a note to [Adjutant] General [Samuel] Cooper, which was handed him as he walked from the chancel, and he immediately left the church.

"It made me anxious, but such things are not uncommon and caused no excitement in the congregation."

General Cooper, New Jersy–born graduate of the U.S. Military Academy in 1815, was at sixty-seven the oldest officer in the Confederacy. While he was reading his message, Jefferson Davis, outside St. Paul's, was doing the same thing. What had been handed him was a telegram from Lee, shorter than the earlier one to Breckinridge, but arriving at the same blunt conclusion:

Petersburg, April 2, 1865

His Excellency President Davis, Richmond, Va.:

I think it is absolutely necessary that we should abandon our position to-night. I have given all the necessary orders on the subject to the troops, and the operation, though difficult, I hope will be performed successfully. I have directed General Stevens to send an officer to Your Excellency to explain the routes to you by which the troops will be moved to Amelia Court House, and furnish you with a guide and any assistance that you may require for yourself.

R. E. Lee

Sexton Irving was, in a manner of speaking, wearing a furrow in St. Paul's center aisle carpeting this morning. Next he hurried in and spoke to the Reverend Kepler, assisting the pastor. Minnigerode observed the congregation "begin to stir." It was even more pronounced than that, according to Dallas Tucker:

> *This excitement became manifest. But when the sexton appeared the fourth time, all restraint of place and occasion yielded, and the vast congregation rose en masse and rushed towards the doors.*
>
> *I sat still for a moment, wondering and withal listening to the preacher's earnest appeal to the people to remember where they were and be still.*
>
> *Good Dr. Minnigerode, he might just as well have tried to turn back the waters of Niagara Falls.*

Not yet certain whether to attempt something comparable to such an unlikely feat, Minnigerode spoke to the Reverend Kepler who informed him that the provost marshal wished to see him in the vestry room. There he

> *found Major Isaac Carrington, who informed me that General Lee's lines had been broken before Petersburg, that he was in retreat and Richmond must be evacuated.*
>
> *I returned to the chancel. As I entered, I found the congregation streaming out of the church, and I sprang forward and called out, 'Stop! Stop! There is no necessity for leaving the church,' and most of them returned. . . . I requested the communicants to stay for the celebration. About two hundred and fifty or three hundred remained and some felt as if they were kneeling there with the halter around their necks. . . .*

There was some difference of opinion as to whether Dr. Minnigerode actually had succeeded, as he thought. Connie Cary herself believed he had and that, before dismissing his congregation, "announced to them that General Ewell had summoned the local forces to meet for the defense of the city at three in the afternoon.

"We knew then that Longstreet's regulars must have been suddenly called away, and a sick apprehension filled all hearts," she wrote.

Young Dallas, on the other hand, recalled that the congregation streamed out, not to return, "and I went along with the crowd, excited and alarmed."

Whether some, all or none remained, Correspondent Lawley of *The Times* of London would pen his own cynical postscript:

> *It will be believed that the excitement among those who remained was at its highest, but it was remarked by sly observers that the excellent clergyman, who has endeared himself to his congregation by four years of brave and hearty sympathy with their trials, did not omit to make the usual collection—possibly with the design of impressing upon his congregation that nothing unusual had happened, possibly to give credit to a currency from which all felt that every semblance of value was passing away. The congregation was not slow to disperse, and quickly from mouth to mouth flew the sad tidings that in a few hours Richmond's long and gallant resistance would be over.*

The word was spreading across Richmond, in the phraseology of Connie Cary, "as if by a flash of electricity," and in that of Sallie Brock—perhaps by coincidence—"with the swiftness of electricity." At the Second Presbyterian for example, Dr. Moses Hoge "told his congregation of our situation and the probability that never again would they meet there for worship . . . in the thrilling eloquence of which he is so truly the master, bade them farewell."

Dr. Hoge, who had survived the battlefield and the blockade, had a hard choice: to stay with his flock or flee the conquering armies shoulder-to-shoulder with the Confederate government. He chose the latter.

"The sermon over" wrote John Leyburn,

> *the congregation joined in the Doxology to Old Hundred, accompanied by the grand notes of the organ, and then reverently dispersed. . . . As I was passing out through the vestibule two*

*friends came up, and said they wondered what could be going on;
that there must be something of unusual importance; that the
President and some of the other high functionaries had been sent
for out of church; and that there was evidently some exciting news.*

In contrast to the "excitement" which had prevailed within
St. Paul's, Dallas Tucker watched the congregation spread out
onto the porch "and the pavement beyond . . . ," standing for
the most part in dumb, bewildered silence:

> *Just across the street, in a large house there were a number of
> government offices, and before these, in the middle of the street,
> were several piles of government documents burning their way to
> destruction. I think these burning papers were the first intelligent
> intimation the people had of what was occurring. They told me,
> as they told others, and it was pathetic to see that crowd melt
> away, too full of forebodings and anguish to express the surprise
> and despair which possessed every mind.*

Civilians and officers alike were spurred to instant action.
Captain Sulivane, for one, reported to General Ewell, who had
been ordered to return to the city. Assistant adjutant general
with Major General G. W. C. Lee's division at Chaffin's Bluff,
Clement Sulivane had been detached to the "Local Brigade,"
made up of soldiers detailed to work in the arsenals, clerks
and other government employees. Ewell's instructions to the
youthful Sulivane were to assemble his brigade, "cause it to be
well supplied with ammunition and provisions and await further orders."

Ewell had much on his mind. Custis Lee's division "mostly
composed of heavy artillery, was almost without transportation." Even by "impressing" what spare horses and mules
could be commandeered, Lee would still have to abandon most
of his splendid cannon. Ewell also had to put into action his
standby orders to "destroy the stores which could not be removed" and also to commence evacuating south "the prisoners
from Libby and Castle Thunder."

His two divisions now numbered only some 3,000 each.
The men were weak with hunger. He watched them "eating
raw fresh meat as they marched in ranks."

Frank Potts, instead of going to church, started back

towards camp. En route he "bade farewell to some dear kind friends on Church Hill [where Elizabeth Van Lew lived] and then felt that all my private business was closed and all I could do was needed by my poor country."

Watching the sudden, shocking scenes throughout Richmond as the noon hour struck, Cooper De Leon, like an avenging scribe from the Old Testament, would write:

"The day of wrath had come."

Afternoon

Judith McGuire walked in sparkling sunlight from St. James as the "congregations from the various churches were being mingled on Grace Street. Our children who had been at St. Paul's joined us, on their way to the usual family gathering in our room on Sunday."

Then someone who had "just returned from the War Department" remarked on "sad news—General Lee's lines had been broken, and the city would probably be evacuated within twenty-four hours.

"Not until then did I observe that every countenance was wild with excitement. The inquiry 'what is the matter?' ran from lip to lip. Nobody seemed to hear or answer."

When Leyburn left his church, he saw

> *a bank officer meet another one for whom he appeared to have been in search, and as I passed them I heard a few words indicative of trouble. Just then espying a young man whose connection with the Government ought to make him acquainted with any important intelligence, I asked him what it was that was producing such a ferment. He replied that he was not at liberty to communicate what he knew, but that there had been terrible fighting near Petersburg.*
>
> *"Favorable or unfavorable?"*
>
> *"So far as we have heard not favorable." Then, in a subdued voice, he added, "I'll tell you that I shouldn't be surprised if we are all away from here before twenty-four hours."*
>
> *This was news indeed! No wonder the President hurried out of church, and no wonder bank officers held solemn council.*

President Davis, in terse example of understatement, would write Varina: "I made the necessary arrangements and went to my office, and then to our house, to have the proper dispositions made there; nothing had been done after you left. . . ."

Actually, the President, on reaching his office in the old U.S. Customs House, sent messengers running in various directions to summon those members of his cabinet not already there, as well as the aged Mayor Mayo, former Governor John Letcher, long a confidant, and the present Governor, "Extra Billy" Smith.

Navy Secretary Mallory, who had come directly to the President's office from the Catholic Church, watched silently as the others hurried in. He was particularly impressed with the apparent savoir faire of the squat and bearded Secretary of State Benjamin, in contrast to the nervousness manifested by others. In some cases it bordered on hysteria.

Benjamin's appearance showed he had "completed his plain and unexceptionable (sic) toilet." His conversation revealed that he had "scanned the latest foreign papers." Altogether the secretary displayed

> his usual happy, jaunty air; his pleasant smile, his mild Havana, and the very twirl of his slender, gold-headed cane contributing to give, to casual observers, expression to that careless confidence of the last man outside the ark, who assured Noah of his belief that "it would not be such a hell of a shower after all."

But Mallory, knowing the man behind the facade—intelligent, sensitive; a hard, conscientious worker who put in long hours with the President after his own work was done—had the distinct feeling that Judah Benjamin was "exercised" inside his placid exterior.

The Navy secretary would report that Davis, "in a few words, calmly, solemnly" advised those not already familiar with it of the telegram from Lee. He repeated that the government would evacuate Richmond as rapidly as possible—by evening—and that those state papers which could not be moved must be burned, a process in fact already in execution.

In anticipation, the Louisiana bank branch had earlier hurried specie down to the Danville Depot, a block south of Cary Street, at the end of Mayo's Bridge, about five blocks from the

Capitol. The Richmond banks were following their lead, like tumbling tenpins.

"There were naturally many and serious questions to be discussed," wrote Postmaster Reagan,

> and among them the disposition that was to be made of the public archives. A considerable portion of them, mainly from the executive department, were destroyed.
>
> The most important papers of the Post Office Department had been sent away from Richmond in the care of an employe. There was hardly time for any other consideration; the booming of the guns of the enemy told of the approaching host, and preparations were hurriedly made for the departure of the governmental forces.
>
> The President and the members of the cabinet, with the heads of the bureaus of the various departments, together with many of the clerks, made ready for leaving.

Peter Helms Mayo, twenty-nine-year-old private in the Governor's Mounted Guard, received the word "shortly after twelve o'clock." For the past forty-eight hours he had been desperately busy "superintending the movement of troops by trains between Richmond and Petersburg." He continued:

> Having had no sleep and little to eat during that time, I had hardly retired for a few minutes to adjust my clothes then in poor shape when . . . I was called upon by Major D. H. Wood.
>
> He excitedly informed me that President Davis had just received, while in St. Paul's Church, a telegram from General Lee announcing that Richmond and Petersburg would be evacuated that night.
>
> Major Wood stated further that the congregation of St. Paul's had been suddenly dismissed and that the sad and unexpected news was rapidly extending through the city, which was ablaze with intense and increasing excitement.
>
> He ordered me to report immediately to the War Department to General A. R. Lorton, Quartermaster General. Him I quickly found, and received instructions to have prepared at once a special train to move over the Richmond and Danville Railroad to carry the President, his Cabinet, their effects and horses and further to prepare in quick succession all other available engines and cars to

move from the city the gold and other many valuables of the Treasury and the archives of all the other departments.

The engines and cars were kept in constant use on the road in transporting army supplies and other necessaries. Moreover the railroads from the city were built on different grades and without connecting tracks, so the problem of supplying all the trains needed in this great and sudden demand was a most serious and perplexing one.

Then, too, it was Sunday, and the train crews were much scattered, with no expectation or intimation of any emergency call, as was often the case on the other troop-moving roads. The crews and trains were in number far below what was needed. But the shrill signal, given by the road's old shifting engine, as the engineer had been instructed to give it in certain contingences, summoned the men.

John Leyburn, returning to the friends' house where he was staying, spoke at the dinner table of what he had seen and heard. This "agitated and distressed" the ladies present, "apprehending violence from the dreaded 'Yankees' and contemplating the separation" from their friends who were in the army.

"In a moment the deep pall of uncertainty and gloom was cast over everything."

Leyburn's remarks were lent stark credence when a young man of the family, who worked in a government bureau, arrived breathless to say that he must have his trunk since he was ordered to be gone by 6 P.M. Leyburn continued:

This was the signal for every one of our little company to be on the move to save what he could. Silverware was quickly collected for hiding; watches were gathered up to be sent away; spoons and forks likewise; and every preparation, practicable in the short time and amidst the excitement and confusion, made for the speedily anticipated pillage.

Also at dinnertime but "alone in the parlor" of Waverly Place, a large home used as a hospital, thirteen-year-old Emmie Sublet opened the door for a friend of the family, "Mr. Mc." He led her to a corner and said, "My little friend, did I ever tell you a secret?," to which she replied no. She then would recall:

*"Well, if I tell you one can you keep it?" "Certainly," said I,
laughing all the time thinking he was only jesting. "Well," said
he, "Richmond will be evacuated tonight, and you will see the
Yankees in two days. . . ."*

*I never had such a feeling in my life; I thought I should faint
anyhow. I didn't have any appetite for dinner. Papa, Uncle
George, Mr. Mc. and I were the only ones in the house who knew
it. Mr. Mc. wouldn't let me tell any of them at all. He finished
dinner long before anyone else, came around to me and whispered
in my ear that would be the last dinner he would ever eat with us.*

*I flushed up and the tears would come, so that everyone at
the table noticed it; and I was obliged to leave.*

Mary Fontaine, who had associated the day with a wearing
of "delicate silks" went home to report on the same distress as
experienced by Emmie Sublet: "We ladies were not contented
except in the yard, and all were in the street with troubled
faces. Major Williamson came to prepare to leave; then one by
one the gentlemen hurried up with orders to leave that night."
She continued that the President himself stopped by her
house,

*so bowed and anxious . . . and when he told us he feared
Richmond must be evacuated by midnight, the truth was forced
upon us. We returned to our rooms to prepare those who were to
leave. Mrs. Williamson gave herself to a grief which was terrible.*

Davis was reported as making other calls this early Sunday
afternoon. One citizen happened upon the Chief Executive at
—curiously enough—the African Church. Pushing through a
crowd to listen, he heard Davis say:

*The disasters of today are temporary. . . . We will soon come
back to establish the capital in this city. The ultimate success of
the Southern Confederacy cannot be questioned, but we must
have courage and fidelity. . . .*

The congregation of this particular, segregated house of
worship might well have entertained contrasting hopes.
Among their number was twelve-year-old "Blind Tom," a

sightless pianist whose virtuoso talents had kept him in demand in Richmond society, where classical entertainment was the order.

The church, as Mallory was informed, emptied early and "American citizens of African descent" congratulated each other, shaking each others' hands gleefully. Some seemed already to be watching for the first glimpse of their "friends . . . the Yankees." And this whole episode at the African Church again illuminated in bas relief the mass psychosis affecting Richmond that Sunday.

If there was any consistency this frenetic afternoon, it lay in confusion, uncertainty, unwarranted fright, the very psyche of inconsistency itself. This was true of government, especially in the highest quarters, and certainly in private households. Even a few days later one found it extremely difficult to reconstruct the sequence, personal or public, of the waning hours of April 2, 1865.

For example, the citizen, when he thought back, couldn't swear if, actually, it were some time Saturday that he "got so near to him that I heard every word he said" or early or late on Sunday that he encountered President Davis in front of the African Church. For that matter Dr. Minnigerode decided he couldn't risk a Bible oath as to whether, in truth, he was delivering his sermon or preparing for communion when the sexton arrived with his fateful telegram.

The most orderly lapsed into bumbling confusion, the stoic spirit faltered. Such was the case of Secretary of State Benjamin. About 2 P.M. he was visited by his friend, the French consul, Alfred Paul, who wished to say goodbye. Monsieur Paul, Judah Benjamin's sole contact with his boulevards-loving wife, had become convinced of a Northern victory after Gettysburg, about the same time he languished through yellow fever.

"I found him extremely agitated," Paul would report of Benjamin to the Foreign Ministry in Paris,

> *his hands shaking, wanting and trying to do and say everything at once. He was preparing to leave at five o'clock with the President and his other colleagues. . . .*
>
> *Mr. Benjamin said to me in a trembling voice, "I have nothing in particular to say to you, but I wanted to be sure to shake your hand before my departure. We are going to Danville. I*

*hope that the railroad will not have been captured at the Burke-
ville Junction and that we will be able to pass through. General
Lee insists on the immediate evacuation of the city by the government. It is simply a measure of prudence. I hope that we will
return in a few weeks."*

*"Really?" I cried, carefully watching Mr. Benjamin to try to
discern if he was motivated by a persisting illusion or by a lack of
sincerity, two things which characterize this statesman. "Do you
think you will be able to return?"*

Benjamin assured him he did, adding in response to yet
another question that he was not "sure" whether the army
would evacuate that night. Thinking to himself that "all well
informed people had been sure for an hour," the consul admitted that "Mr. Benjamin is a very reticent man."

When Paul took his leave of the secretary he "persisted in
taking precautions without delay. . . . I knew what was going
to happen during the night. I went to the office of General
Ewell who said to me in his military candor: 'My dear consul,
speak to the provost marshal before he disappears, he will put
a guard detail at your disposition.' "

Paul returned to his carriage to seek out "the agents
charged with guarding the tobacco to give them various instructions. I also had to chase about after the provost marshal."

The provost, whom Paul found rather quickly, wrote in
chalk "on the panel of my carriage" an order to put "at my
disposition a guard detail composed, however, of only thirty-
eight men." The consul grumped that this was scarcely sufficient to protect all the tobacco consigned to the French
government.

And still speculating, without seeming to know officially,
John Jones would write, "An intense excitement prevails at
2 P.M. . . . the excited women in this neighborhood say they
have learned the city is to be evacuated tonight. No doubt our
army sustained a serious blow yesterday."

Relatively minor concerns were assuming disproportionate
dimensions. Back at the White House of the Confederacy,
Jefferson Davis carefully packed a bust of himself and gave it to
a servant to hide "where it should never be found by a Yankee." He did the same with a painting of "the heroes of the
valley." The furniture, manifestly, had to be left behind. He

offered his carriage to a country friend, James Grant. When the latter said he was "afraid" for it to be seen on his farm, the President ordered it driven to the depot and "put on a flat."

Upon his desk was a statement from the auctioneer for the jewelry and other possessions lately disposed of by Varina: the total was $28,400.

The President would take only some bedding and toiletries, such as toothbrushes, comb, hair brush, a minimum of fresh clothing, such as shirts and socks, and a few grocery items as his personal luggage. He would have included his sword had it not been at the arsenal for repairs.

By his testimony and that of others, including Vice-President Stephens and Mary Fontaine, Davis had wandered the Richmond streets at different times during the afternoon. He would recall that "many who saw me" left their residences to ask if it were true that the city was to be evacuated. As he recalled the mood of the people:

> Upon my admission of the painful fact, qualified, however, by the expression of my hope that we should under better auspices again return, they all, the ladies especially, with generous sympathy and patriotic impulse responded, "If the success of the cause requires you to give up Richmond, we are content."
>
> The affection and confidence of this noble people in the hour of disaster were more distressing to me than complacent and unjust censure would have been. . . .

The President was not alone in his distress. General Gorgas, with no bust in testament to personal vanity, nonetheless had packing to do: "It was now impracticable to get the family and our effects ready by the time indicated (8 P.M.), and Amelia concluded at once to remain . . . we began moving all our effects up to Maria's house." ("Maria" was Amelia's sister, Mrs. Bayne.)

Amelia experienced "confusion and despair . . . that she must be separated from her husband and left to the mercy of a victorious army." She was even more anxious to remove herself and her young children from their quarters in the Armory as her husband was of the opinion that the Federals would requisition all large buildings for barracks and offices. Public property was already being moved from the premises.

Trenholm still felt sick. He stopped by the house of his friend Judge W. W. Crump, on Broad Street, overlooking the

Capitol grounds. The assistant secretary of the treasury was still away in Georgia.

In his slow southern drawl, George Trenholm spoke with Emmie's mother in the same "little library" where "a few weeks before" Emmie had heard her father warn of "the storm which was to break over our heads." The meeting was "short but full of intense interest." Emmie elaborated:

> He came to say that the President and cabinet would start at once for some point farther south, Danville, he thought; but the few troops that were here would also leave as the enemy were advancing and would, he supposed, enter the city some time on Monday, or probably Tuesday.
>
> That was the first intimation of the import of the message the President had received in church.

In spite of the news, Emmie did not forget a familiar Sabbath obligation:

> It was then early in the afternoon and I had been accustomed to teaching in the Sunday school of an Episcopal Church for colored people somewhere beyond Leigh Street. D. G. W. Jones was superintendent and Rev. D. Sprigg who edited the Southern Lutheran Churchman took much interest in it. I started as usual, considering my duty and by no means realizing what a state of excitement was prevailing on the streets. I had not gone far before I met friends who sent me home as there would be no scholars or school that day.

Secretary Trenholm had much to worry about besides his bad health and his aches: gold, silver, treasury notes, papers—notoriously incriminating papers. After all, the Confederacy's "hard" security had been appropriated from the U.S. Government: Federal buildings of every size, description and purpose, from customs houses to post offices, docks, ships, trains, wagons, horses, mules, clothing, food, guns . . . the list stretched on and on.

There was a question whether it was faster to burn or to move the damning, perhaps even "hanging" evidence that was at hand, like a haunting clause in a dead man's will.

But quite obviously George Trenholm was in no condition to ready anything for sudden, even leisurely departure. The physical chores were left to employees like Mann S. Quarles, who happened to be the youngest teller in the Confederate Treasury. He recorded the preparations:

> *Instructions had been given for construction of boxes for packing the valuables and papers of the Department, and those were on hand awaiting orders. For several nights myself and others sat up in the Treasury office. We had commenced to pack up vouchers and papers. . . . We were instructed to pack and be in readiness to take an R.&D. train on quick notice. This we commenced to do. A large part of the force went to their respective homes in the city to individually prepare to leave, leaving the brunt of the packing of the coin and really valuable things with but few of us.*
>
> *Observing that no account was being kept of the contents of the respective boxes, I took several large sheets of brown paper, folded same until I had a book of about 6 by 8 inches, with quite a number of pages. On each page of this book I wrote a description of the marks on each box and stated the content of same on such page—then I sealed with a seal used for that purpose retaining the seal in my pants pocket.*

What might be transported obviously had to be guarded. Even before Admiral Semmes himself knew what was going on, one of his squadron members, Captain Parker, received orders inspired by Trenholm but signed by Mallory: "Have the corps of midshipmen, with the proper officers, at the Danville depot today at 6 P.M., the commanding officer to report to the Quartermaster General of the Army."

Baffled, Bill Parker set out to see, once more, the Secretary of the Navy. What, he wondered, was going on?

As he passed the wharves at Rocketts, he met a large number of prisoners on their way to the boats to be sent down to be exchanged. It at once occurred to him that this is what would be done "in the case of the evacuation of Richmond" since such exchanges usually took place at midnight.

> *However I pursued my way up Main Street and in a few moments met a clerk who inquired of me how he could get down to Drewry's Bluff.*
>
> *I told him, and observing him to be excited, inquired if there were any news. "Why, don't you know?" said he with his eyes*

starting out of his head. "Richmond is to be evacuated this evening!"

Parker believed the man. He returned to the *Patrick Henry* and gave orders for all hands to be at the Danville Depot at six o'clock, with the exception of one officer and ten men left to burn the ship. Among the midshipmen, it so happened, were the sons of Breckinridge and Semmes. Parker then resumed his interrupted visit to Mallory.

In the meanwhile, Trenholm had passed the word to Breckinridge who impatiently scribbled off a message to General Ewell: "When the cadets come in please have a strong guard for the railroad depot to report to Quartermaster General."

Mallory confirmed the news to a somewhat breathless Captain Parker, who would write:

> *My command was to take charge of the Confederate treasure and convey it to Danville. Everything was being packed up for carrying off about the departments, though a good many things had been sent away in March in anticipation of this event.*
>
> *In the city those who had anything to do were at work at it, and yet in the midst of all the excitement there was a peculiar quiet—a solemnity; perhaps the pale, sad faces of the ladies aided to bring it about—they knew it was impossible for them to leave, and they prepared to share the fate of their beloved city with the same heroism they had exhibited during the past four years.*

Connie Cary, who never associated herself with "heroism," had, as she hurried home, seen "many pale faces, some trembling lips, but . . . I heard no expression of weakling fear." She continued:

> *Movement was everywhere, nowhere panic. Franklin Street, sending up perfume from her many gardens, was the general rendezvous of people who wanted to see the last of their friends. All over town citizens were aiding the departure of the male members of their family who could in any way serve the dispossessed government. In the houses we knew, there was everywhere somebody to be helped to go; somebody for whose sake tears were squeezed back, scant food prepared, words of love and cheer spoken. Those good, dear women of Richmond, who had been long tried as by fire, might bend but would not break.*

126

Connie accompanied her brother, Navy Lieutenant Clarence Cary, to the railroad station. Although he had steamed safely through many dangerous missions aboard a blockade runner, she

> *saw him off with a heart that for the first time in our war partings felt heavier than lead.*
>
> *His farewell present to me was a ham, of which he unexpectedly came into possession after we had said goodby, sending it to me by a negro tipped with a large amount of Confederate currency, who, to his honor be it said, was faithful to his trust. My brother was aware that in addition to leaving me alone in our lodging [her mother having gone south to nurse a wounded cousin] our larder was nearly bare. I had promised them if an emergency arose to go to my uncle's house, where I presently arrived, my ham following!*

All men in Confederate uniform were in motion this afternoon. Still riding his weary horse, quartermaster Potts was approaching the defense lines east and north of the city. He could not fully rationalize the onrushing events until he met "Headquarters Wagons going toward Richmond," and, finally, back at camp, when he read Lee's orders to abandon defense positions before morning.

"We were," he wrote, "forced to give up the place for which we had fought so long, for which so much precious blood . . . had been shed. Still I trusted in God . . . to extricate us from our difficulties."

Captain Edward Boykin of the Seventh South Carolina Cavalry wasn't so sure. About midday Brigadier General Martin W. Gary's brigade, of which the Seventh was a part, received orders for "the wagon train of the brigade, spare horses and baggage of all sorts that was to go at all—the greater part was to be left—to move into Richmond at once, and fall into the general train of the army on the north bank of the James River."

The cavalry itself was to move out after nightfall from winter quarters between the Williamsburg and Nine Mile roads about four miles from Richmond. Though no public statement was made to the men, all felt that Richmond was to be evacuated.

Sergeant James R. Sheldon, acting lieutenant of the Thomas Company Rangers, Fiftieth Georgia Regiment, thought it was just after noon when the rumor passed down the line "from mouth to ear" that Petersburg and Richmond must be evacuated. The men had spent that bright and tranquil Sunday morning "in placid ignorance of the terrific effort and triumphant assault of the enemy" thirty miles away to the south of their position near Fort Gilmer where they faced General Ord's Twenty-fourth Corps.

Sheldon, from Thomasville, Georgia, who had fought through the war without furlough or ever being hospitalized, now thought he faced his hardest test. The Rangers were to act as rear guard for the regiment as it marched in retreat through Richmond.

Beyond a woods that was neither wide nor dense, Union pickets were watching the Confederate entrenchments. Among them was Lieutenant Royal B. Prescott, Company C of the Thirteenth New Hampshire Regiment, who considered it his good

> fortune to go on the picket line in command of the pickets of the First Brigade, Third Division, Twenty-fourth Corps . . .
>
> We were daily, hourly, expecting an attack from or to advance upon the enemy, and during the afternoon of Sunday, April 2d, we observed a somewhat unusual activity and bustle within the enemy's entrenchments; we could hear their frequent drum-calls . . . and the rumble of their artillery, and many men there were busily loading wagons, which were rapidly moved away as soon as loaded.

Prescott sent word to his brigade commander, Colonel Edward H. Ripley of the Ninth Vermont, of "what was going on within the Confederate lines." Ripley returned orders that the pickets and vedettes should "observe unusual vigilance."

In Richmond, as midafternoon approached, clerk Jones at long last learned:

> It is true! The enemy have broken through our lines and attained the South Side Road. Gen. Lee has dispatched the Secretary to have everything in readiness to evacuate the city to-night. The President told a lady that Lieut. Gen. Hardee was only twelve miles distant, and might get up in time to save the day. But then Sherman must be in his rear. There is no wild excitement—yet. [Brig.] Gen. [James L.] Kemper was at the department looking for Gen. Ewell and told me he could find no one to apply to for orders.

The banks will move tonight. Eight trains are provided for the transportation of the archives, etc. No provision for civil employes and their families.

The latter was confirmed by Fannie Walker. On her way from Howard Grove Hospital, at the corner of Main and Third, she encountered Captain Kean, her superior and head of the War Bureau. Robert Kean, who had "labored hard all day" packing up the bureau records, was also homebound "with as much baggage as he could conveniently carry," according to Fannie, who would write:

In reply to my question whether we should follow, his reply was, "I cannot advise a lady to follow a fugitive government," and with tears in his eyes bade me farewell.

On reaching my home I found my aunt, an employee of the Treasury Department, packing what things she could conveniently carry, preparing to follow with others of her department the next morning. There was nothing left for me but to wait the turn of affairs. Taking my seat at the window, I fell to watching the excited crowds passing, many of the men with such baggage as they could carry making their way toward the towpath, that being considered the safest avenue of escape.

Kean, glancing nervously at his big gold pocket watch, hurried on "to get something to eat and see how my family came on with their preparations to depart by the [James River and Kanawha] canal." His own tight timetable then demanded he leave his family to join the presidential cabinet refugee train.

Preparatory to leaving the Treasury, young Mann Quarles

locked the five or six safes which had old fashioned keys that you inserted in a slot. These keys I placed in the only combination safe we had and threw the combination—but not until each safe was clean of all contents.

Before we left we kept the furnace in the basement of the building . . . red hot with Confederate notes, bonds, papers, etc. until all were destroyed.

We commenced to load the train about 3 o'clock.

When one of Judith McGuire's sons received orders to accompany Captain Parker with his midshipmen, she "began to understand that the Government was moving, and that the evacuation was indeed going on. The office-holders were now making arrangements to get off. Every car was ordered to be ready to take them south."

All in all, she became possessed of a "strange, unrealizing feeling."

Sallie Brock by now had decided the news was no "Sunday sensation rumor." Incredulity by midafternoon turned into "stony, calm despair . . . as the truth, stark and appalling confronted us."

She heard that "thousands of citizens" had already "determined to evacuate the city." But how? The government had commandeered virtually everything available on wheels and already "wagons were driven furiously through the streets, to the different departments where they received as freight the archives of the Government, and carried them to the Danville Depot to be there conveyed away by railroad."

Nellie Grey and other residents of the Arlington had considered news of the evacuation of Richmond a rumor. "At first we did not believe it," she confessed, "but as that spring day wore on we were convinced. The streets were full of people hurrying in all directions, but chiefly in the direction of the Danville depot. Men, women and children jostled each other in their haste to reach this spot. Loaded vehicles of every description rattled over the pavements."

Emmie Crump returned home after her fruitless attempt to teach Sunday school. Winding through increasingly packed and chaotic streets, she found that in her absence her "mother had been advised to remove our silver, my father's private papers, etc. to the house of his sister on Seventh Street." She reasoned that this residence was not

> as liable to be occupied by the incoming enemy as was ours, which was near the Capitol and Governor's house, and not far from the President's house.
>
> One precaution had been taken by my Father which stood us in good stead now; he had sent for an old colored man who had lived with him for many years as his body servant before his marriage, and a mutual attachment had existed ever since; he was a free man, and Father felt he could trust him implicitly, so told him if we were in any trouble to come to our assistance.

We sent for him and gave him many valuables to care for at his house; my sister, two little brothers and myself then carried what we could of silver to our Aunt's house as we were advised to do. My mother made some strong belts and put into them as much gold coin as we could conveniently carry and we wore them under our clothing. Father had left a small amount with her as, of course, our Confederate money would be of no use if Richmond was evacuated.

The city council met at 4 P.M., this time, according to Pollard, "in a dingy room in a corner of the upper story of the Capitol Building." The meeting had been called by Mayor Mayo, "excited, incoherent, chewing tobacco defiantly, but yet full of pluck, having the mettle of the true Virginian gentleman." Less expansive with words, one of the councilmen simply observed that the elderly city father still wore his "irrepressible ruffles."

Between expectorations of tobacco juice, Mayo advised, what every member knew, "of the contemplated evacuation of the City by the Confederate authorities and the withdrawal of the troops from its defence tonight." It was asked that the two city regiments, the Nineteenth and First, of the Second-Class Militia, "be retained . . . for the protection of the City."

It was resolved to be "imperative" that all liquor be destroyed in case of evacuation. A committee of twenty-five citizens was appointed in each ward to carry out the drastic measure, with the provision that "receipts for the same" be given to all owners.

All in all, thought Pollard, "it was a painful contrast to look in upon this scene; to traverse the now almost silent Capitol House, so often vocal with oratory and crowded with the busy scene of legislation; to hear the echo of the footstep; and at last to climb to the dismal show of councilmen in the remote room where half a dozen men sat at a rude table, and not so many vacant idlers listened to their proceedings."

At the same hour, four o'clock, Admiral Semmes was "sitting down to dinner" in the isolation of his comfortable flagship *Virginia.* He entertained not the remotest notion of what had been going on in the city for the last four hours when a messenger from the Navy Department interrupted the stillness of his polished wardroom. The note signed by Secretary Mallory read:

Sir:

General Lee advises the Government to withdraw from this city, and the officers will leave this evening, accordingly. I presume that General Lee has advised you of this, and of his movements, and made suggestions as to the disposition to be made of your squadron. He withdraws upon his lines toward Danville, this night; and unless otherwise directed by General Lee, upon you is devolved the duty of destroying your ships, this night, and with all the forces under your command, joining General Lee. Confer with him, if practicable, before destroying them. Let your people be rationed, as far as possible, for the march, and armed and equipped for duty in the field. Very respectfully, your obedient servant, S. R. Mallory, Secretary of the Navy.

Semmes pushed back his chair, set down his napkin and observed to himself, "This was rather short notice." He added:

Richmond was to be evacuated during the night, during which I was to burn my ships, accoutre and provision my men, and join General Lee! But I had become used to emergencies, and was not dismayed. I signalled all my captains to come on board, and communicated to them the intelligence I had received, and concerted with them the programme of the night's work. It was not possible to attempt anything before dark, without exciting the suspicions of the enemy, as we were no more than four or five miles from his lines; and I enjoined upon my commanders the necessity of keeping their secret, until the proper moment for action should arrive.

The sun was shining brightly, the afternoon was calm, and nature was just beginning to put on her spring attire. The fields were green with early grass, the birds were beginning to twitter, and the ploughman had already broken up his fields for planting his corn. I looked abroad upon the landscape, and contrasted the peace and quiet of nature, so heedless of man's woes, with the disruption of a great Government, and the ruin of an entire people which were at hand!

A glance out of the porthole revealed that the "flag-of-truce boats," which he had noticed before, were still plowing smokily up and down the river. He mused that the returning former prisoners in the north could little realize that "their own fetters had been knocked off in vain."

The whole spectacle made the hard-bitten admiral "sick at heart," but, in the same complex emotion, cross at Lee who "had failed to give me any notice of his disaster or of what his intentions were."

Even so, he rationalized that, as an obedient officer,

> *I endeavored to communicate with him [Mallory]; sending an officer on shore to the signal station, at Drury's Bluff, for the purpose. No response came, however, to our telegrams, and night having set in, I paid no further attention to the movements of the army. I plainly saw that it was a case of* sauve qui peut, *and that I must take care of myself. I was to make another* Alabama-*plunge into the sea, and try my luck.*

General Ewell during this time had scant more leisure for his preparations, but at least he was not forgotten by General Lee who had initiated a series of dispatches to him, the first, at 3:20 P.M. from Petersburg: "It will be necessary for us to abandon our position if possible tonight. Will you be able to do so? Answer as soon as possible."

Almost in the same chain of thought, he sent another:

> General R. S. Ewell:
> *I wish you to make all preparations quietly and rapidly to abandon your position to-night, if necessary. Send back on the line of Danville railroad all supplies, ammunition, &c., that is possible. Have your field transportation ready and your troops prepared for battle or marching orders, as circumstances may require. Endeavor to avoid all alarm or notice of your preparations from getting to enemy. Save all public property. If your artillery or transportation requires horses you must take them in the city.*

Then, in more detail, Ewell was ordered, via Colonel Walter Taylor, to:

> *Move your command to south side of James River to-night, crossing on bridges at and below Richmond. Take the road, with your troops, to Branch Church, via Gregory's, to Genito road, via Genito Bridge to Amelia Court House. All wagons from Richmond will take the Manchester pike and Buckingham road, via Meadville, to Amelia Court House.*

The movement will commence at 8 o'clock, the artillery moving out first quietly, infantry following, except pickets who will be withdrawn at 3 o'clock. General Stevens will indicate routes to you and furnish guides. The cavalry must follow, destroying bridges under the superintendence of the engineer officers. The artillery not needed with the troops will take the road prescribed for the wagons, or such others as may be most convenient.

As he made his own preparations for "scuttling" postal records, John Reagan observed the streets "filled with eager and stolid-countenanced people . . . and everything was hurry and bustle, and preparation." He continued:

Never before had Richmond felt that the doom of capture was in store for her. During four long years, the armies of the enemy had been beaten away from her very gates, but now the sad realization of the inevitable seemed to possess the gallant Confederate citizens. During the years of conflict they had become inured to the rattle of their windows by the thunder of the Federal guns, but now all was suddenly changed.

The chief problem with the citizens, as numbers of them expressed it to me, was whether they should attempt to leave the city or to remain at their homes and submit to the invading army. The question, however, was practically predetermined for them. Limited transportation facilities over the single remaining line of railroad south, and the use of that for the conveyance of such of the archives as could be carried, together with the demands made upon it by the officials of the Confederacy, left but small opportunity of the inhabitants to escape. . . .

Some women, in mingled sorrow and sense of utter frustration, wept, as at a funeral. Only Mayor Mayo appeared calm as he went about his business, in white cravat, spotless waistcoat, and blue brass-buttoned coat, altogether "irrepressible."

Sometime during the afternoon, a proclamation had been made that all who wished might obtain provisions free at the Commissary Department. Refined residents of the Arlington, where Nellie Grey boarded, were sorely tempted. Nellie herself would not entertain the idea at first "in spite of my loathing for dried apples and peas, and a lively objection to starvation. . . ."

But a council was held and it was agreed that no one knew to what straits they might be brought—perhaps actual starvation. Then one resident, Mrs. Sampson, declared she was "bound to have a whole barrel of flour, and she was going for it." Nellie's mother decided that she would accompany her neighbor so Nellie felt she must go too, to protect the older ladies from she knew not what.

We put on our bonnets—home-made straw trimmed with chicken feathers—and started. Such a crowd as we found ourselves in! . . . a starveling mob! I got frightened sick, and mother and Mrs. Sampson were daunted.

The ladies quickly changed course, stopping at the home of their old friend Mrs. Taylor, Colonel Walter Taylor's mother, to enlist as escort her youngest son Bob. He "explained regretfully that he could not serve us. Walter was to be married that day. . . ."

A wedding this Sunday seemed incredible but, Bob explained, "General Lee is going to move the army west . . . nobody knows for how long . . . if Betty is married to Walter she can go to him if he gets hurt."

Somehow the intrepid Mrs. Sampson obtained her barrel of flour anyway, even had it delivered to her room, but Nellie and her mother got nothing.

From the heights of Chimborazo, as the late afternoon sun slanted across a frenzied city, Phoebe Pember watched the spectacle of women lugging hams, bags of coffee, flour and sugar. "Invalided officers" quit their sick beds and took part in this mad "shopping" spree.

What truly impressed the hospital matron was the "immense concourse of government employes, speculators, gamblers, strangers, pleasure and profit lovers of all kinds . . ." and every one of them desperate to flee their home of four years while those who remained to "await the chances of war . . . tried to look calmly on and draw courage from their faith in the justness of their cause."

Phoebe, who had much to do where she was—some 5,000 wounded remained in Richmond's hospitals—had heard that many were leaving for the north from the Fredericksburg depot, a "scene . . . of indescribable confusion." She attributed this state to the vast quantities of personal belongings carried by the passengers who did not know how or where anything "could be replaced."

Amelia Gorgas was strangely not shocked as she watched "poor wretches long strangers to food and clothing . . . [as they] fought for the contents of the commissary stores."

Mallory was impressed with the aura of quiet sadness: "Women . . . clad in deepest black, for all Virginia's daughters mourned the loss of kindred in the war . . . wept in the streets."

There really wasn't much quiet in Richmond. Either Mallory was inside, too busy packing, or didn't really want to accept the confusion which die-stamped the crumbling of a way of life. Most would recall the afternoon as did Judith McGuire:

> *Baggage wagons, carts, drays, and ambulances were driving about the streets; every one was going off that could go, and now there were all the indications of alarm and excitement of every kind which could attend such an awful scene. The people were rushing up and down the streets, vehicles of all kinds were flying along, bearing goods of all sorts and people of all ages and classes who could go beyond the corporation lines. We tried to keep ourselves quiet.*

Like the majority of the citizens of Richmond, the McGuires had little choice. If they refugeed south, where would they go? Nor did she see how, practically, they could "leave the city at all in this hurried way." Like bees which had lost their queen, some of their friends had gone north, others west, just to be in motion. Yet others with ill-founded faith were trying backroads totally unfamiliar to them and which, for that matter, led nowhere.

When the McGuires attempted to "hire a servant to go to Camp Jackson for our sister—we for the first time realized that our money was worthless here." And then the conclusion: "We are in fact penniless!"

Pollard saw much the same sights as the McGuires. "It was late in the afternoon," he would write,

> *when the signs of evacuation became apparent to the incredulous. Wagons on the streets were being hastily loaded at the departments with boxes, trunks, etc., and driven to the Danville depot. Those who had determined to evacuate with the fugitive*

Government looked on with amazement; then, convinced of the fact, rushed to follow the Government's example. Vehicles suddenly rose to a premium value that was astounding; and ten, fifteen, and even a hundred dollars in gold or federal currency was offered for a conveyance.

Suddenly, as if by magic, the streets became filled with men, walking as though for a wager, and behind them excited negroes with trunks, bundles, and luggage of every description. All over the city it was the same—wagons, trunks, bandboxes, and their owners, a mass of hurrying fugitives, filling the streets. The banks were all open, and depositors were as busy as bees removing their specie deposits; and the directors were equally active in getting off their bullion. Hundreds of thousands of dollars of paper money was destroyed, both State and Confederate.

Sallie Brock, although not necessarily a witness, believed that the money was either "buried" or burned in Capitol Square, maybe a bit of both. Destruction, after all, had become the afternoon's suicidal motif.

Back in the city once more, Frank Potts observed the same immolation of the Confederate government and its testament to four wasting years of—what? And to what purpose?

He found, not surprisingly, "the news generally known and the greatest excitement prevailing. Efforts were made to get off public property." His precise quartermaster's mind boggling at the enormity of the task, he continued:

The smallest depot could not have been satisfactorily evacuated in the time given to leave Richmond. Imagine the loss of property and material [materiel], when you know that Richmond was the great workshop of the Confederacy.

In anticipation of this thing all the papers in the offices of the Adjutant General, Quarter Master and Comy [Commissary] General, Treasurer and 1st and 2nd Auditors had been boxed up & ready for shipment. But when the crisis came they could not be moved and most were burned in the square.

De Leon watched agape as other "supplies" were "rolled into the canal." However, already the greatest cornucopia:

Commissary stores were thrown open, and their hoarded contents distributed to eager crowds.

And strange crowds they were. Fragile, delicate women staggered under the heavy loads they bore to suffering children at home; the pale wife clutched hungrily at the huge ham, or the bag of coffee, for the wounded hero, pining at home for such a delicacy.

Children were there with outstretched hands, crying for what they could carry; and hoary-headed men tugged wearily at the barrels of pork, flour, or sugar they strove to roll before their weak arms.

Edward T. Watehall, a fourteen-year-old who had earlier attended the Baptist Church, hadn't heard the developments until he was walking past the President's house. Then it seemed to him "earthquakes and great fires" became analagous to the effect of the news of evacuation. He heard people crying out: "Richmond has fallen! *What* shall we do? There was a wild rush and hurry on all the streets but it was magnified in the crowd that seemed going to the Danville Depot."

There, he had the probably erroneous impression, "trains were leaving every few minutes." He saw soldiers as well as men, women and children "among the citizens going away, and a quantity of gold and money and all sorts of household articles being carried off."

At the commissary warehouse he watched the same spectacle as recorded by De Leon: "You could see old men, women and children snatching for something whether it was useful or not. I made many trips back and forth to carry my pickups home."

Then, in self-justification, Eddie postscripted, "there were any number doing as I did."

Connie Cary, on the other hand, evinced no interest in plunder. The air itself was "full of farewells as if to the dead," and all in all the afternoon had become too much for her sensitivities. She was relieved to find haven in her uncle's home. Although her aunt was ill, the house overflowed with other relatives and friends, clustered together for mutual assurance and fancied security.

There was not a room or a bed to give me, but that made no difference. They insisted on my staying all the same. Up under the roof there was a lumber-room with two windows and I paid an old darkey with some wrecks of food left from our housekeeping, to clear it out, and scrub floor and walls and windows, till all was absolutely clean. A cot was found and some old chairs and tables—our own bed linen was brought over. . . .

Here Connie settled in comparative comfort.

As evening neared and more persons, especially those of government's substrata, prepared to leave, the little dramas of farewell which had been so upsetting to Connie were reenacted on every street. "Numbers," wrote John Coles Rutherford, a member of the Virginia legislature, "were compelled to remain, who would otherwise have gone, because no means of getting off, except on foot." He saw "women and children standing at the doors of their houses looking wistfully out" and before them "galloping of horses and rattling of wheels over the pavements in every direction," and all the while, "Heart-breaking partings . . . terrible distress upon the countenances of some, others showing a forced gayety."

The ladies of Richmond at their doorways had etched a picture in the minds of many men, including Captain McHenry Howard, who had come into the city in the morning but, like Frank Potts, never made church. He described the scene:

> *Bundles, trunks and boxes were brought out of houses for transportation from the city or to be conveyed to places within it which were fancied to be more secure.*
>
> *Vehicles of every sort and description, and a continuous stream of pedestrians, with knapsacks or bundles, filled the streets which led out from the western side of Richmond, while the forms of a few wounded officers, brought home from the battlefields, were borne along the pavement on litters, their calm, pallid faces in strange contrast with the busy ones around.*
>
> *Ladies stood in their doorways or wandered restlessly about the streets, interrogating every passerby for the latest news. All formality was laid aside in this supreme calamity, all felt the more closely drawn together, because so soon to be separated. . . . Learning that movements would soon take place in my own command, I mounted at sundown and galloped back to Chaffin's farm.*

Soldier and civilian were starting to move out of Richmond. William Simmons was one. Like Potts, attached to Longstreet's fragmented First Division, Simmons, who came from Atlanta, Georgia, was more interested in taking his wife to safety than in following the waning fortunes of the military. On attempting to rejoin his regiment, after a Saturday night visit with his wife, he had found that most of the troops had already broken camp.

By late afternoon of April 2, it seemed to him that all who could leave the city were "stampeding." Hitching his horse to the "small family trap," he and his wife loaded up essential household items and joined the throngs heading west.

"As we drove through the streets," Mrs. Simmons recalled, "all were astir at headquarters of the Government, preparing for the exodus, throwing out official papers and records to be burned. Despair was upon the people. . . ."

Evening

At six o'clock, clerk Jones, restlessly wandering out of his office and then back again, encountered "the Hon. James Lyons," a business friend of the Davis family, and asked him "what he intended to do." Lyons replied that

> *many of his friends advised him to leave, while his inclination was to remain with his sick family. He said, being an original secessionist, his friends apprehended that the Federals would arrest him the first man, and hang him. I told him I differed with them, and believed his presence here might result in benefit to the population.*

Walking down Ninth Street on his way back once more to the War Department, Jones "observed quite a number of men—some in uniform and some of them officers—hurrying away with their trunks. I believe they are not allowed to put them in the cars."

At his office Jones learned that Secretary Breckinridge intended to depart at eight o'clock—within the next two hours: "The President and the rest of the functionaries I suppose, will leave at the same time." Then Jones put on his hat and, nervous as a cat, was out on the streets again.

Captain Parker, who had arrived at the depot at 6 P.M.,

> *found the treasure packed in the cars and the midshipmen under Captain Rochelle in charge of it. So far as I know there was about half a million of dollars in gold, silver and bullion; at least*

that is what the senior teller told me, as well as I recollect. I saw the boxes containing it many times in the weary thirty days I had it under my protection, but I never saw the coin.

The teller and his assistant clerks had charge of the money, and the corps of midshipmen guarded and eventually saved it. In addition to the Confederate money, there was also some belonging to the Richmond banks. It was in charge of their officers, and travelled with us for safety. I had nothing to do with it; but, of course, gave it our protection.

"About 6 P.M.," Peter Mayo continued,

we had ready a special and quite a comfortable train for the President and his Cabinet, with cars for their baggage and horses attached thereto. . . . In a short time I had all the other available trains in place, loading them to their utmost capacity with the gold and other valuables of the Treasury and other Departments which I had orders to ship first.

It was impossible to do more than that, notwithstanding the fact that many trains could have been filled with the greatly needed imported and domestic army supplies which had already been received and unloaded: artillery, harnesses, blankets, shoes, clothing, commissary supplies, etc. . . .

The coin and other money valuables were brought to the station in kegs and boxes by four-horse wagons. To guard these treasures in their journey to some more secure place in the South, Captain Parker . . . came with his corps of cadets. . . .

Captain Parker informed me on his arrival that his corps was, almost to a man, without blankets. Seeing the number of bales of blankets that could not possibly be shipped from the station, he urgently applied to me for permission to distribute some of them among his men instead of leaving them for the enemy.

As I had no authority to give this permission, I told him that possibly, as Mr. Breckinridge, the Secretary of War, was with the President at the time in the station, I might get from him the necessary orders. Captain Parker went with me to Breckinridge and, at my request, the Secretary walked through the station with Captain Parker and me.

I was anxious for the Secretary of War to know the real condition of affairs, especially as to the large number of supplies that could not possibly be removed in view of all the trains being required for other purposes.

General Breckinridge told Parker it was all right to take "such numbers of blankets as was necessary for his corps."

At seven o'clock, while standing on the corner of Thirteenth and Main Streets, Eddie Watehall thought he "saw the last Confederate cannons come thundering down the street." Although the hour was yet too early for this to be more than an advance artillery unit, he heard "the driver yelling, 'Is this Virginia Street? Which is the way to the Danville Depot?' They turned into an alleyway and then across the bridge, which had been floored over for this very emergency."

The darkness of the early night was stabbed on Ninth Street by "great piles of paper burning, and by their light I saw some men wearing Confederate uniforms break into Antoni's confectionery. The woman inside asked them not to break the jars, but to take all the candy they wanted.

"As this was private property, I did not try to get any of the candy, as much as I wanted it. I also saw a jewelry store and one or two others broken open, but this was not by the soldiers."

True, the home guard was on duty in the streets, but their capacity for deterrence appeared to be nonexistent.

"Into every house," recalled Sallie Brock,

> terror penetrated. Ladies were busily engaged in collecting and secreting all the valuables possessed by them, together with cherished correspondence, yet they found time and presence of mind to prepare a few comforts for friends forced to depart with the army or the government.
>
> Few tears were shed; there was no time for weakness or sentiment. The grief was too deep, the agony too terrible to find vent through the ordinary channels of distress. Fathers, husbands, brothers and friends clasped their loved ones to their bosoms in convulsive and agonized embraces, and bade an adieu, oh, how heart-rending!—perhaps, thought many of them, forever.

Little girls like Emmie Sublet "didn't go to bed at all, but staid down in the parlor," afraid to go outside, surely to open the shutters. They had reason.

"As night came on," wrote Captain Clement Sulivane, "pillaging and rioting and robbing took place," at the hands of "ominous groups of ruffians—more or less in liquor" who had somehow been materializing in the late afternoon and early evening on the principal thoroughfares of the city. "The police and a few soldiers were at hand, and, after the arrest of a few ringleaders and the more riotous of their followers, a fair degree of order was restored. But Richmond saw few sleeping eyes. . . ."

None of the residents at the Arlington slumbered or even dozed that night. Like lost souls, they "moved about between each other's rooms, talked in whispers," and, in the words of Nellie Grey, "tried to nerve ourselves for whatever might come. . . . People were running about everywhere with plunder and provisions. . . ."

Staring in disbelief at the eerie scenes enacted on the familiar streets of Richmond was Colonel George Alexander Martin, of the Thirty-eighth Virginia Infantry. He was recently routed from his sick bed in the home of a friend by a fellow officer. His mind was still dazed from the news of the evacuation, weak as he was from fever.

"I have no time to lose!" had been Martin's only thought as he sprang from his couch. He must "try to join" his men and share whatever fate awaited them. He hurried into his uniform, buckled on his sword and revolver and started walking rapidly toward the business part of the city. The sights were like part of a delirious dream.

> The panic was extreme, men, women and children were hurrying to and fro, Commissary Stores were being removed or destroyed. Wagons, drays and other vehicles were loading, or being driven swiftly through the streets, creating a rumbling and confused noise, and their drivers were cursing and shouting, men were hallooing, women screaming, children crying, horses neighing and engines whistling. The streets were blocked with human beings, beasts and inanimate things subservient to their use. The liquors had been liberated, to prevent the intoxication of the Government employees and others, and inundated the adjacent gutters. . . .
>
> Alarming reports were in circulation—that the Federal Army had broken through the Confederate lines, and were trying to cut off the retreat of our Army, which was in full retreat towards Danville or Lynchburg, that a part of their Army was marching in force on Richmond and would soon arrive there, that mobs and disturbances were threatened in the City, incited in part, by too free use of Government whiskey, that fires had been discovered in some parts of the City, kindled by incendiaries, and

*that the bridges leading from the City would shortly be burned,
thereby preventing all exit from the same, and various other
sights and reports were seen and heard, too numerous to describe.*

Colonel Martin quickly concluded that his only hope of
intercepting his command in its retreat was the train. He hurried away toward the Richmond and Danville Station.

De Leon was witness to much the same scenes:

> *As the excitement increased, fierce crowds of skulking men
> and coarse, half-drunken women gathered before the stores.
> Half-starved and desperate, they swore and fought among them-
> selves over the spoils they seized. Orders had been given to
> destroy the whiskey at once; but, either from lingering tender-
> ness, or from the hurry of the movement, they were only partially
> obeyed.*
>
> *Now the uncontrolled swarms of men and women—
> especially the wharf rats at Rocketts where the navy storehouses
> were—seized the liquor and became more and more maddened by
> it. In some places where the barrels were stove, the whiskey ran in
> the gutters ankle deep; and here half-drunken women, and chil-
> dren even, fought, to dip up the coveted fluid in tin pans, buckets,
> or any vessel available.*

Meanwhile, the city council met again to be "assured" by
Secretary Breckinridge that all pickets would be withdrawn
from Richmond's perimeters by 3 A.M. in the morning, that the
city would be evacuated "about night," and that "a committee
of prominent citizens should attend the mayor with a flag of
truce to the intermediate line of fortifications and that there he
might hand over the city to the United States authorities."

Thus, it was small wonder that clerk Jones at this time
encountered a distraught Judge Campbell "in 9th Street, talking rapidly to himself, with two books under his arm. . . . He
told me that the chiefs of bureaus determined which clerks
would have transportation—embracing only a small proportion of them, which I found to be correct."

At the Danville station, proportions were far from small.
The drama in progress William Parker found "hard to describe." The President's train was slated to depart at 8 P.M.
preceding Parker's. The latter, containing so much Confederate
treasure, was scheduled as "the last out of the city."

Davis himself, however, while his baggage was being loaded, waited in a station office, supposed to be that of the head of the railroad. The President, as a matter of fact, confided to those pacing the rough wooden floors with him that he was really biding time, hoping "for better news," that is, the junction of Lee's and Joe Johnston's armies.

He continued to be plagued by worries of his personal possessions and servants, several of whom had broken into his whiskey stores. Neither his carriage or horses arrived, although station attendants promised they would be loaded on "the next train." He wrote Varina, although with little certainty of where she was or, for that matter, if his letter would ever reach her:

> I sent a message to Mr Grant that I had neglected to return the cow and wished him to send for her immediately. Called off on horseback to the depot, I left the servants to go down with the boxes and they left Tippy—Watson came willingly, Spencer against my will, Robert Alf V. B. & Ives got drunk—David Bradford went back from the depot to bring out the spoons and forks which I was told had been left and to come out with Genl Breckenridge.

Studying the throngs still pouring down the streets toward the station, Parker was increasingly certain that none else dared second the President's wish for better news. He wrote:

> Both trains were packed – not only inside, but on top, on the platforms, on the engine–everywhere, in fact, where standing-room could be found; and those who could not get that "hung on by their eyelids." I placed sentinels at the doors of the depot finally, and would not let another soul enter.

That few succeeded Parker believed to be a tribute to his midshipmen, "their training and discipline showed itself conspicuously . . . cool and decided in their replies, prompt in action, and brave in danger. . . ."

Despite their efforts Secretary Mallory suspected that some ladies and "artful dodgers" did manage to get aboard.

John Leyburn, escorting a relative who wanted to go "up the country" to be reunited with his family, was among those who attempted to get past the barrier of midshipmen, who said he must have a pass from the Secretary of War.

One of the trains, with much belching of smoke and grinding of wheels, moved off and someone shouted "There goes the President and his cabinet!" Since it was only about 10 P.M., however, Davis was still in the depot office.

Leyburn's friend, meanwhile, had found a way past the "Argus-eyed sentinels," but then, a new difficulty:

> *We could find no admittance into the cars.*
>
> *There were numerous trains—all, I believe, rough box cars—waiting their turn to go. One after another of them we applied to, but in vain. One was the Treasury Department, another the Quarter-Master's Department, another the Telegraph Department, and so on. Most of them contained ladies as well as gentlemen.*
>
> *"Can't we get in here?"*
>
> *"No! Impossible! We're crowded to suffocation."*
>
> *Passing on to another: "Won't you just let one gentleman in here? His home and family are up the country, and he is anxious to get to them."*
>
> *"No, no! We're too full already. This car is marked for 14,500 pounds, and we have 18,000 in it now. We'll break down before we get five miles."*
>
> *We were about giving up in despair, when there hove in sight a man with a lantern, escorting two gentlemen, whom he evidently intended to put into one of the cars.*
>
> *"Now," said I to my friend, "be on the alert, and when he pushes those two up I'll push you immediately following, as if one of the party." We did so, and succeeded. They found out the ruse, it is true, and I heard them berating my friend as an intruder; but having "nine points of the law," he held his ground.*

Leyburn saw his relative off, and also those on other trains as they "rolled away."

Meanwhile, as Captain Parker endeavored to maintain some semblance of order at the depot, his superior, Admiral Semmes, had important and demanding if wasteful work ahead. With night's "friendly curtain between the enemy and myself," Semmes got up steam and his little squadron soon was thumping up to Drewry's Bluff, eight miles below Richmond.

"It was here," he observed,

I designed to blow up the ironclads, throw their crews on board the wooden gunboats, and proceed in the latter to Manchester, opposite Richmond, on my way to join General Lee.

Deeming secrecy of great importance to the army, in its attempted escape from its lines, my first intention was to sink my fleet quietly, instead of blowing it up, as the explosions would give the enemy notice of what was going on. . . .

And while Semmes was preparing to anchor at Drewry's Bluff, Lieutenant Colonel John Cheeves Haskell was ending a visit there with a friend, Major Hamilton Gibbs. He left about 10 P.M. to return to Richmond, with several objectives in mind. One was to replace his new $1,250 boots which he had entrusted to his captain, who had proceeded to get himself—and the boots—captured by the Federals, along with a battery of British Armstrong cannon.

"Everything," Haskell found, as he rode through the darkness into Richmond,

was in the wildest confusion . . . the low characters of the town had broken into everything, gotten a lot of whiskey and were looting the town, being aided to a considerable extent by the soldiers who had broken through all discipline.

As I rode by the principal jewelry store I saw an old woman crawling backwards out of a window. One of the mounted men rode up and whacked her with the flat of his sword when she tumbled out with a yell, and her lap full of plunder from Mitchell and Tylers (the leading jewelers of Richmond) show cases poured over the sidewalk.

At another store, a party was beating in the door which burst in only to show the owner standing there armed and firing on his assailants. One of them fell, but instantly the poor fellow fell, shot to death.

Jewelry stores, even as Eddie Watehall had noted earlier in the evening, had become a prime target for theft. Certainly, as Potts phrased it, "that night in the streets of Richmond beggars description." He added,

Tens of thousands of suits of clothing were thrown from the Clothing Bureau to the howling mob. Flour, Bacon, Sugar and Coffee was fought for by thousands of poor women (among whom

distinguished for their energy, were many of our countrywomen.)
Around the depots of the Subsistence Department the stores of the
Medical Purveyor were thrown open, and property invaluable to
us was destroyed in an hour. . . .

Madness seemed to rule the hour!

The Simmonses, urging their horse forward, were blocked
in their journey across Richmond every few feet by the mob.
He had reason to conclude that only his officer's uniform and
sidearms prevented the appropriation of his horse and buggy
or, worse yet, his wife. She in turn was at once fascinated and
horrified by the scenes about her.

"The stores were thrown open by the merchants," she
recalled,

and dry goods, shoes, provisions were pitched out into the
streets to be eagerly snatched up by a wild crowd of hungry and
needy ones. In Stockoe [Shockoe?] Square, in the lower part of
town, a large stock of tobacco held by the Gov. was ordered to be
burned, and as we passed men were bringing more material for
the bon fire and chairs, tables, desks were broken up and piled
high in front of the ware-houses.

The Simmonses were leaving by horse cart. Many other
types of transportation were being used to escape the city,
according to Correspondent Lawley. "On horseback, every
description of cart, carriage and vehicle, in every hurried train
that left the city, on canal barges, skiffs and boats, the exodus
of officials and prominent citizens was uninterrupted."

"The road and the canal were the only avenues of escape
by public conveyance," wrote Captain Charles M. Blackford,
most recently attached to the War Department, and now retreating on horseback.

The canal was filled with boats extemporized into packets
and loaded with people—gentlemen, ladies, children and
servants—all seeking, very foolishly, some safe place, and seeking
it in a direction in which safety was not to be found.

I had not traveled more than a mile when I overtook a
flat-bottomed open boat full of people for Albemarle and among
them I found Mrs. Kean and a number of acquaintances. I kept
with them near all night. . . .

Canals were more important than roads, especially to a metropolitan area like Richmond, and carried at least the volume of traffic of railroads. Many fled the city prior to its fall in canal boats of every description. A group of refugee slaves may be living on the barge in the foreground. *Library of Congress.*

Richmond's activity found its equally febrile complement in the Confederate works outside the city limits. Only the pickets remained as one company after another dragged wearily westward as surreptitiously as possible in obedience to Lee's order. The pickets were relieved regularly, perhaps with more deliberate noise and confusion than normal, and their fires continued to stab the blackness.

Just after dark, Gary's Brigade moved out from its position immediately behind the outer line of Confederate works. Martin Gary was a hard-bitten cavalryman of the old school leading remnants of the Seventh South Carolina, the Hampton Legion, (sharpshooters, of whom Gary had been colonel), the Twenty-fourth Virginia, and a part of the Seventh Georgia (dismounted). The brigade was halted on the Charles City Road where they found the infantry already gone.

"It was all out now," according to Captain Edward Boykin. "The army is in full retreat. . . ."

The cavalry brigade had orders to wait until 2 A.M. when "we were to move on to the city, acting as 'rear guard,' and burn Mayo's Bridge."

Accordingly, the infantry pickets were replaced by "our dismounted men" and the soldiers of Gary's Brigade settled down to wait.

We built big fires of brush wood, to give light and warmth, and deceive the enemy. It was cold, though in April; the men, as usual, light-hearted and cheerful round the fires, though an empire was passing away around them; some, with an innate consciousness of the work before them, when they heard that the halt was to be for two or three hours, wrapped in their overcoats, with the capes drawn over their heads, were soon sound asleep, forgetting the defeat of armies, the work of yesterday, the toil and danger of to-morrow, in some quiet dream of a home perhaps never seen again.

Although out of sight and hearing of the welling turmoil within the capital of the Confederacy, those in opposing Federal ranks nonetheless felt a presentiment: "The very air seemed to whisper of great events," in the words of Lieutenant Millett Thompson, of the Thirteenth New Hampshire.

"The night was one of intense anxiety and expectation in the Army of the James," reported Lieutenant Samuel W. Scranton, of the Connecticut First Light Battery, encamped so close to Richmond that its spires could be seen in clear weather. He fully expected "when the sun rose" that his battery would "take a dangerous position in the great game of military strategy by assaulting the works in the front and try to capture Richmond itself."

Thompson listened to the familiar artillery fire from the south, "its deep throbs rolling continuously . . . up the misty valley of the James." He was among others who remarked on the enemy's picket fires, "burning as usual along his lines on our front, and with undimmed brightness; but all was very quiet on our own lines." As an afterthought, he added that "Lieutenant Prescott goes out tonight in command of our 1st Brigade picket and vedette [mounted sentries] lines . . . a very careful, prompt and efficient officer being required."

And as Royal B. Prescott spotted his pickets and vedettes in and around their little semicircular rifle pits he warned each to observe "especial vigilance" and make "instant report . . . of any unusual movements occurring within the rebel lines."

From his own lonely post, Prescott noted tattletales of "unusual activity . . . their religious meetings were continued longer than usual, their singing and praying were louder, their pickets and camp fires kept burning later," all, he surmised, "employed to deceive us as to their intentions."

There had, for that matter, been a sort of musical contest between opposite bands—those of Weitzel's and Longstreet's armies—this climactic Sunday evening. As Thompson made mental note, "Dixie vies with Hail Columbia, America with My Maryland, and the Star Spangled Banner dips full notes with the Bonnie Blue Flag. All very fine, but exceedingly deceitful."

The correspondent for the *Philadelphia Inquirer*, listening to this strange symphony, wrote, "The Rebel bands played vociferously and persistently in various parts of their lines; probably half the bands in the Rebel camps had been called into requisition in the game of attempted deception.

"Weitzel followed the example set him; he set all his bands to work upon our National airs, and the night was filled with melodious strains, conflicting somewhat, however, in their political significance." All, the reporter added, was part of the enemy's "great show . . . to make himself appear as much as possible like six."

One thing about the bands: when the brass gave out the notes, the men did not eat. Most musicians doubled as cooks—or vice versa—and carried food, in back packs, to soldiers in the front lines "oftentimes a long way under fire." They also served as nurses, ancestors of future armies' combat corpsmen.

Some time before midnight, the bands grew quiet. "A silence," noted the *Philadelphia Inquirer's* correspondent, "complete and absolute, brooded over the contending lines." Prayer meetings voiced their concluding supplications. The muted obligato of the artillery dwindled to nothing.

Most of the Thirteenth New Hampshire did "turn in," but under arms, with orders to move out at daylight, like, Thompson added, "the night before a battle . . . best framed for dreaming wide awake."

If Union soldiers were dreaming, wide awake or otherwise, neither Confederate soldiers nor sailors had time for such indulgence. While Semmes's lieutenants were preparing to open the seacocks of their small fleet, the admiral observed

the whole horizon on the north side of the James glowing with fires of burning quarters, materiel, etc., lighted by our own troops as they successively left their entrenchments!

Concealment on my part was no longer necessary or indeed practicable.

Having determined to burn the fleet, Semmes set officers and men to work

like beavers. There were a thousand things to be done. The sailor was leaving the homestead which he had inhabited for several months. Arms had to be served out, provisions gotten up out of the hold, and broken into such packages, as the sailors could carry. Hammocks had to be unlashed, and the blankets taken out, and rolled up as compactly as possible. Haversacks and canteens had to be improvised.

How to be rid of a "Navy," even if it amounted only to eight rusting, tired ships? How to move the forces in the Richmond area over unfamiliar roads to Danville? From Lee's provost office a new and urgent message to Major R. P. Archer, in Richmond:

Major:
    Is there any one here who could act as a guide on the roads leading to Danville? General Ewell desires one to report to him immediately. He wishes to know your opinion as to the best routes. Are there boats in Michaux Ferry or Cartersville? General Ewell would like much to see you about this if you can go to his office.
                                Very respectfully,
                                Isaac H. Carrington

At the Danville Depot, "one after another the trains rolled off," according to John Leyburn. "The guards dispersed; and the depot was forsaken and desolate."
Colonel George Martin lost all track of time as he watched train after train depart, too weak even to try to fight his way aboard.

My waiting at the Station was tedious and painful but at last my patience was rewarded by being enabled to obtain a place on an open freight car attached to the train that left the depot about midnight (the last, I think, that left Richmond on that Road).

Martin stretched his aching body gratefully on the floor of

the flat car "without anything else beneath me, or above, except the vault of heaven, which spread out as it seemed to me, a vast pall, ready to receive in its folds the devoted band of patriots, who, for four years, had struggled under its canopy."

Sergeant Leeland Hathaway, of Kentucky, who had been an adjutant with General John Hunt Morgan at the time of his capture, had remained in Richmond as a semiconvalescent after his exchange as a prisoner of war. To a considerable extent, Hathaway closed his eyes to the looting and disorder. As he would write,

> Nothing except the habit of four years of discipline and restraint prevented a general stampede.
> It was a proud sight that day to see this battered remnant . . . ragged ranks . . . of that immortal Army of Northern Virginia as it filed through the streets of Richmond on its first hopeless retreat.

As Hathaway himself left, he assisted an injured friend, Captain G. M. Coleman, even though "I had difficulty in getting him away . . . his physician and many of his friends advised him to stay."

However, Hathaway, none too strong himself, half carried him onto "one of the last trains" and then swung aboard himself.

None was absolutely sure when the "cabinet special" chugged out—somewhere between 9 P.M. and midnight. Lawley of the *Times* thought it was as early as 8 P.M. General Gorgas, however, was certain it was later than that—maybe even 3 A.M.—since he believed it was nearing midnight when he left his wife, "still standing like a brave woman over the remnants of her household goods."

He also found "all was still and orderly on the streets" as he made his way with an aide down Cary Street to the Danville Depot. Passing one of the Armory gates, he encountered a sentry on duty as usual: "Everything promised an orderly evacuation. I had given directions that nothing in my control should be burned lest fires might be general and innocent inhabitants suffer."

Secretary of the Navy Mallory, on the other hand, left orders for the James River Squadron to "go up" before morning and all naval operations east of the Mississippi were to cease.

He believed it was about 11 P.M., as did Anna Trenholm, when the President and cabinet took their seats in the waiting train, "frightfully overcrowded," according to Postmaster Reagan, and its occupants "oppressed with sorrow for those we left behind us."

Almost at once the train moved out across the James, only to grind to an anticlimactic halt in Manchester on the south side of the bridge. Mallory thought that the cabinet members were "very depressed," not only because they were fleeing the capital but because the Federal lines were, every hour, nearing the tracks and there was the dread of a "gobble" by Sheridan's cavalry. Deep down, all close to Davis believed that as Yankee prisoners they would be tried and hung, and quite possibly not even tried.

At the same time the secretary of the navy thought that the evacuation had been ably organized. Everything was aboard to set up the government in short order "in a half-dozen log cabins, tents, even wagons." Only the office buildings of Richmond and, sometimes, its parlors were lacking as a proper womb for the affairs of state.

With a jolt the train started up again to sway and rattle across the dark, uncertain countryside. Possessing no inclination to sleep or even doze, Mallory was afforded ample opportunity to study his fellow passengers.

Reagan appeared the most sad and anxious as he sat "whittling a stick down to nothing." A conscientious administrator, he had watched his mail service reduced to nothing. Communications within the Confederacy had become almost nonexistent—ruptured not alone by the enemy but by incompetence at lower levels until little remained of the postal department but a relative handful of clerks marking time in shabby offices notable only for their disrepair.

The postmaster's eyes were "bright and glistening as beads," and Mallory wondered if they actually saw anything.

Aging Adjutant General Cooper sat in pale silence amidst packages of office records, a few aides at his side.

Ex-governor Lubbock talked incessantly as if he felt bound to "make an effort."

Judah Benjamin's optimistic good humor had returned following his "agitated" meeting earlier with the French consul. Perhaps the presence of his good friend, the Reverend Moses Hoge, calmed him. The two were making plans to share a room in Danville. Many thought it a strange friendship, but there were those who believed that Hoge was the only man Benjamin really trusted.

To Stephen Mallory's observant eye, Benjamin's rather olive complexion did seem "a shade or two darker than usual." But the secretary of state placidly "munched a sandwich" as he proudly exhibited his coat and pantaloons made from "the old shawl" which he claimed had already warmed him through three harsh winters.

Secretary Trenholm, suffering from both chronic neuralgia and a stomach ailment, had been taken to the depot in an ambulance. He had kept his wife close by his side to nurse him. Nor had he neglected to bring along abundant supplies for the "inner man," including a generous amount of "old peach" brandy which he shared with this traveling companions, hoping to elevate, even momentarily, their sagging spirits.

"I was the only lady," Anna later recorded in her diary, "and there were about 30 gentlemen including the President and suite. . . . Mr. Trenholm was quite sick from the effects of the morphine as well as the pain in his head."

Probably the President himself appeared to be the most undisturbed of all. "No man who saw Mr. Davis on that trying occasion," it occurred to Postmaster Reagan, "but was impressed with his calm and manly dignity, his devotion to the public interest, and his courage."

The War Bureau chief, Robert Kean, could not agree with either Mallory or Reagan that there was anything efficient or dignified about the flight of the Confederate government. A consistent critic of President Davis, he brooded bitterly as the train puffed its erratic way towards Danville, blaming the whole fiasco on Davis whom he considered "peevish, fickle, hair-splitting . . . a man with a passion for detail and a grandiose reluctance to delegate authority."

In this dismal hour of his life, Kean found some amusement in remembering the assessment of a friend in regards to Jefferson Davis, in which he characterized him as "a mule" but probably "a good mule." Kean thought his friend would now agree that the President had turned out to be "a jackass."

As the curiously mixed trainload of the leaders of a broken government steamed through the blackness, Richmond neared the midnight hour. John Leyburn, still entranced at the vanished spectacle of departure, including Parker's "gold train," finally started for home, pausing to watch "one of the batteries from below . . . carrying torches and cheering, I suppose to keep their spirits up. They moved off over the bridge."

Judge Campbell, who would remain in the city, noted, "before midnight the trains had gone and all the public buildings were empty. The only sounds came from the march of troops and the passage of wagons across the streets and bridge."

A few with phlegmatic emotions, such as young Leyburn, "went to bed and slept soundly." Dallas Tucker did the same, "feeling little or no concern."

At the Crump home "everything was quiet," although Emmie was certain that "anxious fears" must have filled her mother's heart. Emmie nonetheless "slept the sleep of youth and inexperience."

But Connie Cary, drawn out again from her attic eyrie by the night's excitement, thought "hardly anyone went to bed. We walked through the streets like lost spirits until dawn."

She was one of many who shared the mood of abject hopelessness as expressed by clerk Jones: "I remain here, broken in health and bankrupt in fortune, awaiting my fate, whatever it may be. I can do no more. If I could, I would." The prophecy he himself had written in 1859 in a novel, *Wild Southern Scenes,* was like an apocalypse confirmed:

> *It was the night of the evacuation. For hours, the Federal troops, for all that now defended the South and the government of the United States were thus denominated, had been defiling over the long bridge into Virginia. . . . It is the cavalry of the Valiant, the rear guard of the army, abandoning the city.*

9

★★★★★

Monday, April 3

Midnight

I now pronounce you . . ."
The candles flickered in the parlor of a private residence on West Main Street as Dr. Minnigerode completed the nuptials of Walter Taylor and Elizabeth Selden Saunders, the daughter of a deceased Federal navy officer. The handsome colonel on Lee's staff had arrived in Richmond shortly before midnight "without further incident" and hastened at once to the home of Lewis D. Crenshaw. There his fiancée and the already overtaxed rector of St. Paul's waited.

In characteristic understatement, the handsome, heavily bearded bridegroom would observe, "The occasion was not one of great hilarity, though I was very happy; my eyes were the only dry ones in the company."

There was life, and there was death, in these early minutes of Monday, bright and starlit. Long delayed at the Manchester end of Mayo's bridge by a crush of refugeeing citizens, the ambulance bearing the body of A. P. Hill finally creaked up to the basement of the old Court of Appeals Building where yet another family member, Assistant Paymaster G. Powell Hill, waited. His cousin, Henry Hill, Jr., had preceded the ambulance, but had neglected to mention that the remains were without benefit of coffin.

If Henry had, Powell probably would not have registered anyhow. He had been frantically packing his uncle's Paymaster General records all afternoon and evening and had only moments before returned to his damp, ill-lit office from seeing them off on a canal boat. The latter vessel as well "conveyed the Governor and cadets out of the city."

"Extra Billy" Smith, as a matter of fact, had left his wife behind in his handsomely furnished gubernatorial office, thankful to save his own neck on which he seemed certain the North had placed a tempting premium.

Since "time was pressing us closely, as we were expecting the entrance of the Federal troops into the city," Powell and Henry Hill hurried out in search of a coffin. They found "stores on Twelfth, Thirteenth, Main and Cary Streets . . . broken into, and in many instances sacked and fired." The well-known Belvin's furniture store "had been opened at both ends." The Hills entered from the rear "hoping to find a representative to whom we could apply for a coffin." There were no clerks in evidence.

The two men then selected a coffin. It was small but probably large enough, they guessed, to contain the short frame of General Hill. They carried the pine box to a nearby office and then started back for the ambulance, still the repository for Hill's body.

Their efforts to ready a relative for proper burial proceeded against a noisy backdrop of hungry mobs snatching at every bit of clothing or household goods they could find.

"O, the horrors of that night!" wrote Fannie Walker who, unable to sleep, watched from her window:

> The rolling of vehicles, excited cries of the men, women and children as they passed loaded with such goods as they could snatch from the burning factories and stores that were being looted by the frenzied crowds; for to such straits had many been brought that the looting was not confined to the "poor white" or rabble. Delicately reared ladies were seen with sheets and shawls filled with goods, provisions, etc., even to boxes of tobacco.

Fannie was visited by a neighbor who showed her at least a dozen boxes of tobacco, "a foot or more square," that she had carried "from some factory on Cary Street to her home on Franklin." Fragile though she was, she told Fannie that the prospect of her blind husband and children starving and suffering "nerved her to her work."

Peeking through half-shuttered windows like Fannie Walker and many other ladies, Emmie Sublet noted "our troops were passing through the city the whole night, and our friends dropping in one by one to bid us farewell, perhaps many of them forever."

Family members occupied themselves hiding their jewels in the parlor, "such sewing of bags, pincushions, pads and every conceivable way of hiding things you never heard of in your life."

Cousin "Vic" who was staying with the family "hid her watch in a ball of cotton and commenced to make a sock to make it look as natural as possible. I took ten gold dollars and covered them as green buttons and sewed them on my green *mouselain*."

There was all sorts of visiting. Some time after midnight Judith McGuire's sister walked into the house. She was accompanied by two convalescent soldiers who had escorted her from Fort Jackson. Their presence brought it home to Judith that the sick and wounded soldiers could not go with the others but must wait around to be captured. Still the thought could not dim her joy at being reunited with her sister:

> We collected in one room, and tried to comfort one another; we made large pockets and filled them with as many of our valuables as we could suspend from our waists.
> The gentlemen walked down to the War Office where a telegram had just been received urging haste in evacuation, as by 3 A.M. the work should be completed. The public offices were already forsaken.
> Union men began to show themselves; treason walked abroad. A gloomy pall seemed to hang over us. . . .

Another woman of Richmond, Mary Fontaine, returned late to "our rooms to prepare those who were to leave. . . . All through that long, long night we worked and wept and bade farewells, never thinking of sleep. In the distance we heard the shouts of soldiers and mobs as they ransacked stores; the rumbling of wagons, and beating of drums, all mixed in a confused medley."

Amelia Gorgas toiled into the early morning hours to get her household belongings together, but even with the help of her ten-year-old son and two faithful servants most of the furniture and carpets remained. The wagon which her husband had left was piled high and the two servants made "Herculean efforts to leave nothing for the Yankees. . . . In their panic they deposited on the top of Gamble Hill a sewing machine, a mirror, and a stand of shovel, poker, and tongs."

La Salle Pickett, the wife of the luckless general, postscripted common feminine sentiments, writing, "fear and dread fell over us all. We were cut off from our friends and communication with them was impossible."

Minutes after midnight, a group of armed guardsmen and husky teamsters commenced carrying out orders from the city council. The latter had no way of knowing at the time that what seemed wholly reasonable, if desperate, procedures would have a directly opposite result than intended. The order was to destroy liquor supplies to keep the intoxicants from thirsty soldiers, stragglers and the riffraff which had been harassing Richmond since late afternoon.

To be disposed of were an estimated three hundred barrels of whiskey and any number of cases of the heady stuff in bottles.

In short order, the barrels were being rolled noisily into the streets and their heads knocked off until, as one observer recorded, "a miniature whiskey Niagara poured continuously down in a current almost strong enough to have swept a man off his feet." Another wrote, "The gutters ran with a liquor freshet and the fumes filled and impregnated the air. Fine cases of bottled liquors were tossed into the street from third story windows, and wrecked into a thousand pieces."

While one citizen, with bitter humor, speculated that enough of the distilled spirits had flooded into the James to provide "a big drink to the finny inhabitants of the river," too much survived the scuttling efforts. Bottles refused to shatter. Gallons remained in the casks or collected in ruts in the streets. Quite enough survived to reach the gullets of thirsty soldiers and others—the very ones for whom the liquor was supposed to be denied.

They raced off, laughing hysterically, with bottles under their arms. They scooped up the beverage in saucepans, pitchers and canteens. Twos and threes struggled off with partially filled barrels. Some cupped hands, others knelt down and lapped up the fiery stuff like dogs, from puddles and gutters.

Wrote Nellie Grey, "barrels and boxes were rolled and tumbled about the streets. . . . Barrels of liquor were broken open and the gutters ran with whisky and molasses. There were plenty of straggling soldiers about who had too much whiskey; rough women . . . and many negroes were drunk. The air was filled with yells, curses, cries of distress, and horrid songs."

"From that moment," concluded a sober citizen, "law and order ceased to exist: chaos came and a Pandemonium reigned." The entire, unreal scene was amply illuminated, according to Correspondent Lawley, "by the glare of vast piles of burning papers [which] turned night into day."

W. S. White, of the Third Company, Richmond Howitzers, entered the city at about the commencement of the drunken orgy to encounter "crowds of men, women and children of every hue and size" thronging the streets "in dense masses, bearing away upon their shoulders all kinds of commissary stores. . . ."

What disturbed White's orderly mind, however, was the spectacle of "beastly sots . . . wallowing literally in the mire of inebriation" as they

> *drank deeply from this reeking, seething, poisonous stream; and the fumes thereof ascending, mingled with the curses of strange women, of reeling, staggering, drunken men, of Federal prisoners marching through the streets and shouting forth their jibes and jeers at the downfall of the Southern metropolis. . . .*

He was surprised to observe "all the private dwellings . . . yet lighted up" which told him "of the anguish, the suffering, and the pain of parting then taking place; for from nearly every dwelling, a loved one was going forth from the home, and was leaving all behind him."

Not just the Richmond Howitzers, but all the Confederate forces in or around Richmond were hurrying westward. Sergeant Sheldon, among them, and the Thomas Company Rangers moved behind the Fiftieth Georgia "so quietly and steadily that the enemy in our front was not aware of our withdrawal for some hours. Thousands began that march with empty haversacks and as little in their stomachs. . . . Near the dead of night, we entered the thoroughly demoralized city of Richmond."

As the regiment passed down the principal streets, the sight appeared to Sheldon a "revelry of confusion." The troops themselves, ambulances, ordnance and artillery wagons filed through in a steady though orderly stream. The rest was chaos:

> *Tumultuous masses of humanity augmented by numbers of army stragglers took advantage of the turmoil and hiatus in the government as a license for looting, pillage and anarchy.*
>
> *Men and women madly rushed in and out of buildings and warehouses loading themselves with plunder, only to be thrown down for another load of something more tempting. . . . Gutters and even side-walks [were] streaming rivulets of liquor. Government warehouses were gutted, and here it was discovered that millions of rations were being hoarded for some mysterious reason*

and clothing, shoes, and blankets galore while the faithful, hungry and ragged men had been doled scanty feed and less clothes for months.

Why?

Some avoided the city entirely. McHenry Howard and fellow officers had spent a harrowing night trying to combat "the proverbial carelessness of soldiers," since "every now and then a hut or a pile of brush at the bluff, or in the woods in the rear would blaze up, throwing a lurid glare far and wide," creating an "imminent danger of drawing the enemy's fire."

But, "shortly after midnight," all was ready "for the final and delicate operation of withdrawing the troops." Field's division was well on its way, to be followed by Kershaw's; now Custis Lee was in motion, leaving only pickets, "with orders to withdraw just before day and rapidly overtake the main body. . . . To the relief of all no notice seemed to be taken of our movement. . . ."

The troops departed so stealthily that a few were left behind. Sound asleep in his blanket beside a tree was Private John L. G. Woods, of the Fifty-third Georgia, Sims Brigade. Enlisted at seventeen, Johnnie Woods had fought through the Seven Days, Antietam, and Gettysburg. Now, although a drummer in the regimental band, at twenty-one he hardly qualified for the tag "boy."

His fellow bandsmen, exhausted from their evening concert, slept on around him as the regiment pulled out.

But those not as phlegmatic or as weary as the bandsmen were kept awake in great measure by the sound of trains, even though the Danville Depot itself was shut down. There were, however, switching yards around the city and its environs. The line to Fredericksburg remained open and, to Petersburg, partially so.

As Phoebe Pember listened, "The scream and rumble of the cars never ceased all that weary night, . . . perhaps the most painful sound to those left behind." As the matron of Chimborazo rationalized, while most of the city was "flying," the suburban areas were quiet and even unaware of what was happening in the center of Richmond.

On the other hand, Emma Mordecai, fifty years old, slept, to "awake again, and slept again" at Rosewood Plantation, in Henrico County, four miles from the city. She heard "the

whistling of engines and the rolling of cars" on the Danville
line as she tossed between waking and dozing. News of the
evacuation had reached Rosewood only late in the afternoon.
She was overseeing her brother's plantation in his absence, as
well as caring for his frail wife Rosina and their young
daughter Augusta. Her cousin Caroline had been paying a brief
visit when a young Confederate officer walked out to warn her
of the evacuation, that she might return to Richmond "before it
was too late."

    All tried to persuade the young Augusta to accompany
them to town where she would be more protected from
marauding Yankees, of whom so many lurid tales had reached
their ears. But Augusta would not leave her mother and now
lay sleepless beside her in a downstairs bedroom.

    In Richmond, the pace of "flying" accelerated. The Sim-
monses rode past the last clustered homes on the western
reaches of the city. The roads were rutted and cut by the long
lines of heavy artillery. In their small wagon, they were forced
to dodge "from side to side to escape being crushed by heavy
teams. . . . In the thick darkness I could not see the form of my
husband as he walked at the horse's head or lifted a wheel out
of the ruts."

    Vying for space in the miserable, ill-tended road was a
motley collection of civilians. Their appearance challenged the
descriptive powers of Colonel William W. Blackford, an engineering officer formerly with Jeb Stuart. Blackford had come
along partly as a kind of bemused shepherd:

> *Our wagons were packed up, and we moved off upon the
> great final retreat. . . . A great stream of people they poured out,
> filling all the roads leading westward. These columns we encoun-
> tered as we proceeded on the retreat and a pitiable spectacle they
> presented.*

He especially recalled the "naval brigade," a tatterdemalion group, not connected with Admiral Semmes's squadron,
but with Mallory's own Navy Department:

> *The sailors did well enough on the march, but there were the
> fat old captains and commodores, who had never marched any-
> where but on a quarter-deck before in their lives, limping along
> puffing and blowing, and cursing everything black and blue.*

Then came a perfect army of bureau clerks, quartermasters, commissaries, and ordnance officers all dressed in fine clothes and uniforms, with white faces, scared half to death, fellows who had for the most part been in these bombproof offices ever since the war began and who did not relish the prospect of smelling powder now, nor of having to rough it a bit like ordinary mortals in the field.

Then there were citizens in broadcloth, politicians, members of Congress, prominent citizens, almost all on foot, but sometimes there were wagons and carriages loaded with them. Some ladies too might be seen occasionally and generally they were calmer than the men.

And all the while Blackford mentally cursed the President of the Confederacy, a man for whom he had never entertained any admiration: "Why Jeff Davis should have preferred to be kicked out of Richmond to evacuating it in a dignified manner I suppose he himself does not know. It was the egotistical, bull-headed obstinacy of the man no doubt."

To Eggleston, well west of Petersburg, "Everything seemed to go to pieces at once":

The best disciplinarians in the army relaxed their reins. The best troops became disorganized, and hardly any command marched in a body. Companies were mixed together, parts of each being separated by detachments of others.

Flying citizens in vehicles of every conceivable sort accompanied and embarrassed the columns. Many commands marched heedlessly on without orders, and seemingly without a thought of whither they were going. Others mistook the meaning of their orders, and still others had instructions which it was impossible to obey in any case.

To make matters worse, Eggleston heard that a supply train, which was supposed to rendezvous with the retreating forces, had been diverted to pick up officialdom in Richmond. This meant that "the interests of the starving army . . . [were] sacrificed to the convenience or the cowardice of the President." He believed as well that the "precious cargo of food" had been "thrown out" at Richmond.

Joining the refugeeing multitude was Quartermaster Potts and his unit, which crossed Mayo's Bridge about 1 A.M. Standing on the opposite bank, he took one long last look "on our

Capitol in Confederate hands." Then with "direful forebodings for our future," he rode away with the retreating army "along the line of the Richmond & Danville Railroad."

In the city they were leaving behind, much remained to be done, both in private and public matters—including burial of the dead and the continuing destruction of what was deemed to be valuable Confederate property. When the Hills had carried the general's very rigid if not especially heavy corpse into the vacant office, they decided it was only proper to wash his face and remove his gauntlets, still covering his stiff hands and fingers.

Morbidly curious, these two kinfolk wanted to find "where the fatal ball had entered." Powell Hill "discovered that it had shot off the thumb of his left hand and passed directly through his heart, coming out at the back."

That was enough. The pair then "hastily" lowered the body into the coffin "which was rather small, and putting it in the ambulance, left the city by way of Fourteenth Street and Mayo's Bridge, slowly and sadly wending our way through Manchester and up the river to my father's refugee home. He had refugeed from Culpeper County."

"Sometime after one o'clock of the morning of April 3," Peter Mayo wrote, "the shipment of the Treasury valuables and archives of the various departments was completed as far as possible." Parker with his naval cadets had left aboard this important train. Mayo's orders were to join the army, but

> seeing that there was nothing else that I could do in the city and that the last of the troops defending Richmond under General Custis Lee were crossing Mayo's bridge to join General Lee, I left the railroad station and went up town to bid farewell to my wife, my little baby and my sister, then living in a small house on Grace Street between Third and Fourth Streets.

For the past hour or so, until after 1:30 A.M., a drama had been ensuing between Mayor Mayo, his representatives and their counterparts on General Ewell's staff. Not until midnight had the mayor learned of Ewell's standing orders to destroy the four principal tobacco warehouses: the Public Warehouse (containing stores belonging to England and France), situated at the head of a rectangular area known as "the Basin," adjacent to the Petersburg Railroad Depot; Shockoe Warehouse, on the east side of the Basin and side by side with the Gallego Flour

Mills; and Dibrell's Warehouse and Mayo's Warehouse, both on Cary Street, close by Libby Prison. All of the "immense" warehouses were a relatively few blocks from the Capitol itself.

It was, in Pollard's paraphrasing or recording of Mayo, a "reckless military order which plainly put in jeopardy the whole business portion of Richmond."

James A. Scott and others delegated by the mayor met with a Major Melton, of the War Department's adjutant general's staff. He proved adamant and would not listen to the plea that the burning warehouses might destroy the city itself, labelling the remonstrance "a cowardly pretext on the part of the citizens, trumped up to endeavor to save their property for the Yankees."

One of those ordered to carry out the burning was Lieutenant Colonel R. T. W. Duke, of the Second Battalion, Virginia Reserves. He had just arrived back in Richmond at 2 A.M. after visiting a friend on Sunday at his home nine miles south. Since he missed the last steamer, *Wilton*, he had hiked all the way back.

He found that several of his aides had already made preparations for the burning, even as Mrs. Simmons had noticed on her way out of the city. Colonel Duke directed the officers "to fire these buildings, then pass over the river to Mayo's Bridge and follow the army." Then, "being dead tired, I threw myself down to rest, fell asleep. . . ."

The flames rapidly licked up the walls of the four substantial, well-filled warehouses, their contents so linked with the South's economy. The ever-restless Judge Campbell, making his rounds to the War Office, the Treasury and finally down to the canal, looked up to see "lights in the Shocco [Shockoe] tobacco warehouse resembling lamps at the distance, but in a little time there was a blaze of light and flame."

Eddie Watehall, also on the prowl, watched "crowds of men and women throwing bags of flour out of one side [of the Gallego flour mill] while the other side of the warehouse was burning."

Cooper De Leon learned that at this time the "burning party" was also "putting the torch to every armory, machine shop and storehouse belonging to the Government" until "one lurid glare shot upward . . . then another, and another."

La Salle Pickett, who believed Secretary Breckinridge himself was still remonstrating against this broad-scale official incendiarism, wrote: "A fresh breeze was blowing from the south; the fire swept on in its haste and fury over a great area in an almost incredibly short time. . . ."

At 2:30 A.M., against the glare of mounting flames, Mayor Mayo and his "committee," heavily weighted in favor of the judiciary, started out in what was described as a "shabby" carriage, flying a white flag of truce and drawn by a horse not unlike others still remaining: weary and hungry. Included were Judge John A. Meredith; Judge W. H. Lyons; Judge W. H. Halyburton; William H. MacFarland, president of the Board of Visitors of the Virginia Military Institute; and Loftin Ellett, a citizen of Richmond. The cadets from VMI had been barracked in the Alms House since Sheridan burned the institute in Lexington.

The pale, solemn group of six headed through the milling wilderness of people towards the "outerline of fortifications." They had been authorized by the city council "to meet the Federal authorities to make such arrangements for the surrender of the city as may best protect the interests of the citizens." And while they moved slowly past flaming buildings, other "burning parties" were at work.

"It was," wrote Admiral Semmes,

> between two and three o'clock in the morning before the crews of the ironclads were all safely embarked on board the wooden gunboats, and the ironclads were well on fire. My little squadron of wooden boats now moved off up the river by the glare of the burning ironclads.
>
> They had not proceeded far, before an explosion like the shock of an earthquake took place, and the air was filled with missiles.

It was the incandescent finish of the CSS *Virginia*, Semmes's flagship, on which hours before he had been enjoying his Sunday dinner—meeting the same fate, by the Confederacy's own hand, of her earlier namesake, which had fought the little *Monitor* to a draw. With curious objectivity, Raphael Semmes mused, "The spectacle was grand beyond description." Then he analytically rationalized what was happening:

> Her shell rooms had been full of loaded shells. The explosion of the magazine threw all these shells, with their fuses lighted,

into the air. The fuses were of different lengths, and as the shells exploded by twos and threes, and by the dozen, the pyrotechnic effect was very fine.

The explosion shook the houses in Richmond, and must have waked the echoes of the night for miles around.

He was quite correct, as virtually every resident and soldier on the perimeters would attest. Judge Campbell wrote that the blast "shook the buildings and aroused the slumbering population."

The noise to Sallie Brock was "like that of a hundred cannon at one time. The very foundations of the city were shaken; windows were shattered more than two miles from where these gunboats were exploded, and the frightened inhabitants imagined that the place was being furiously bombarded."

Judith McGuire, as had Semmes himself, likened the concussion to an "earthquake in our midst. . . . The house shook and the windows rattled . . . a loud sound like thunder. We knew not what it was, nor did we care."

Constance Cary counted four distinct explosions, "making the windows of my garret shake." John Leyburn, exhausted from his long vigil at the depot, was awakened "from profound slumbers by a tremendous concussion," only to fall asleep again.

Mary Fontaine believed that not only was glass shattered but that "new houses crumbled beneath the shocks . . . involuntarily, I closed the shutters and then everything became still as death." John R. Southall, a Richmond resident of Church Hill, near Elizabeth Van Lew, "was nearly thrown out of bed" by the blast.

In the Federal lines facing Richmond, the night, which had become "cloudy and dark," passed "uneventfully," by the measure of Colonel Edward H. Ripley of the Ninth Vermont, until "a column of flame suddenly shot high in the air in the direction of Richmond, quickly followed by another and another. Then came the subdued hum of noises far away toward the doomed city."

Fancifully, as he knelt down and pressed his ear to the ground, "the low supernatural rumbling seemed as though its interior was alive with the busy motion of its myriad of dead. Still, strangely, no sound came from our immediate front."

Lieutenant Prescott, one of Ripley's subordinates, recorded that the "concussion" was so "terrific" that

> the earth shook where we were, and there flashed out a glare of light as of noonday, while the fragments of the vessel, pieces of timber and other stuff, fell among my pickets, who had not yet moved from the position where they had been posted for the night watch.

Fortunately, the troops all ducked these nautical airborne missiles. Prescott added that Lieutenant Colonel Bamberger, of the Fifth Maryland, was almost thrown from his horse, when it "reared and plunged" at the noise and shock.

Acting division officer Colonel Bamberger, after quieting his mount, ordered Prescott to advance his pickets, "but to use utmost caution."

At General Weitzel's headquarters an aide-de-camp, Lieutenant Livingston de Peyster of the Thirteenth New York Artillery, heard the explosions about 2 A.M. and saw a "vast blaze in the direction of Richmond." He mounted a signal tower about seventy feet high but still could not decide whether it was Richmond that was burning. General Weitzel sent out a company to try and capture an enemy picket. They returned about 3 A.M. with a prisoner of the Thirty-seventh Virginia Artillery, confused and claiming he had no idea where his general or his command were.

A few minutes later a deserter came into camp announcing that the city was being abandoned. On his heels was a Negro standing upright in a buggy and driving his horse at full speed past pickets and guard as he shouted, "Dey is runnin' from Richmond. Glory! Glory!" Or so Union soldiers quoted him.

Dragged bodily from his makeshift chariot, the man confirmed the news which soon spread all along the Union lines. General Weitzel gave orders to the troops to move out at daylight.

Also east of city, near Fort Harrison and the Varina and New Market turnpikes (across which the lines of the Twenty-fourth Corps stretched), Private Charles Hotchkiss, of the First Connecticut Light Battery, went on guard duty at 2 A.M.

"I soon noticed," he would recall, "something unusual along the rebel lines; large fires on our front and off toward Richmond, with explosions and some heavy firing on our left."

He hesitated for a time to awaken Captain Clinton, but

> as things were getting more lively, especially toward
> Richmond, I finally called the Captain and told him I believed
> Richmond was on fire and troops leaving the city. Well, the
> Captain jumped for his duds and was out in a moment. Assembly
> was blown; and although we could not move without orders from
> headquarters, still the boys began to pick up their traps.

Some of the soldiers climbed the trees from which they
could plainly see that "flames and smoke were rising in the
direction of the city." Lieutenant Samuel W. Scranton, of New
Haven, described the scene:

> Great dense masses of smoke rose in curling columns and
> lost themselves in the clouds. In the midst of these circling,
> eddying columns great black objects rose fifty or a hundred feet in
> the air, and then from out of the darkness would flash a bursting
> shell every few seconds, making the most beautiful and startling
> display of fireworks. . . .

The distant, dramatic manifestations made General Weitzel "most impatient" to swing into motion.

Captain Edward Boykin, of the Seventh South Carolina
Cavalry, was also becoming impatient. Two A.M. had passed
and still the "dismounted men" of Gary's Brigade who were
acting as pickets had not come in. Boykin thought that the
cavalry brigade with its one company of artillery were the only
Confederate troops left north of the James. The men, wide
awake now and shivering in the chill predawn, were endeavoring to keep the horses quiet. Finally General Gary gave the
order to move on towards Richmond. Boykin thought it was
nearly four o'clock and they must reach Richmond before
daylight:

> We could wait no longer, and moved off slowly. In a short
> time after we started a tremendous explosion took place toward
> the river, lighting up everything like day, and waking every echo,
> and every Yankee for thirty miles around. It was evidently a
> gunboat on the river at "Drewry's Bluff." Two others followed,
> but did not equal the first. . . . She burst like a bomb-shell, and

told, in anything but a whisper, the desperate condition of things.

Gary's Brigade quickened its pace.

The retreating Confederates, moving south and west, were quickly made aware of what was happening. Frank Potts, "a few miles from town saw the flashes and heard the explosions of our ironclads in the river and the magazines along the lines."

The blasts combined with the spreading fires and the rivers of whiskey to spawn a night of havoc. "A mob of both sexes and all colors soon collected," wrote General Ewell,

> *and about 3 A.M. set fire to some buildings on Cary Street, and began to plunder the city.*
>
> *The convalescents then stationed in the Square were ordered to repress the riot, but their commander shortly reported himself unable to do so, his force being inadequate. I then ordered all my staff and couriers who could be spared to scour the streets, so as to intimidate the mob by a show of force, and sent word to General Kershaw who was coming up from the lines, to hurry his leading regiment into town.*

Lieutenant Colonel Edward H. McDonald, with the Eleventh Virginia Cavalry, who had also been at St. Paul's on Sunday, was given a buggy to share with a governmental clerk to ride out of the city. But he had been long delayed by the congestion in the streets and at the entrances to the bridges.

"Such harrowing scenes as were created I hope never to witness again," he would write. "These drunken soldiers were fighting among each other and plundering the town. . . . To stop the riots many persons were shot in the streets."

Yet nothing seemed to help much. The night continued a "saturnalia," as La Salle Pickett labelled it. Having "enwrapped" the Shockoe warehouse, the flames, she elaborated,

> *on the wings of the wind . . . were carried to the next building and the next . . . leaped from house to house in mad revel.*
>
> *They stretched out burning arms on all sides and embraced in deadly clasp the stately mansions which had stood in lofty grandeur from the olden days of colonial pride. Soon they became*

towering masses of fire, fluttering immense flame-banners against the wind, and fell, sending up myriads of fiery points into the air, sparkling like blazing stars against the dark curtain that shut out the sky.

A stormy sea of smoke surged over the town—here a billow of blackness of suffocating density—there a brilliant cloud, shot through with crimson arrows. The wind swept on and the ocean of smoke and flame rolled before it in surges of destruction over the once fair and beautiful city of Richmond.

The terrified cries of women and children arose in agony above the roaring of the flames, the crashing of falling buildings, and the trampling of countless feet.

Piles of furniture and wares lay in the streets as if the city had struck one great moving day, when everything was taken into the highways and left there to be trampled to pieces and buried in the mud.

Government stores were thrown out to be destroyed, and a mob gathered around to catch the liquors as they ran in fiery rivers down the streets. Soon intoxication was added to the confusion and uproar. . . ."

This reminded Mrs. Pickett of 1781 "when the British under [Benedict] Arnold rode down Richmond Hill and, invading the city, broke open the stores and emptied the provisions and liquors into the gutters, making even the uninitiated cows and hogs drunk for days."

The few firemen who were available had only two steam engines and four more or less worthless hand pumpers at their disposal. They also feared reprisals from those "who had executed the order to burn the buildings." Some said that significant lengths of hose had been sliced by the retreating soldiers.

The fire raged on, Mrs. Pickett continued,

the sea of darkness rolled over the town, the crowds of men, women and children went about the streets laden with what plunder they could rescue from the flames. The drunken rabble shattered the plate-glass windows of the stores and wrecked everything upon which they could seize. The populace had become a frenzied mob, and the kingdom of Satan seemed to have been transferred to the streets of Richmond.

The fire revealed many things which I should like never to have seen and, having seen, would fain forget.

The most revolting revelation was the amount of provisions,
shoes and clothing which had been accumulated by the
speculators who hovered like vultures over the scene of death and
desolation. Taking advantage of their possession of money and
lack of both patriotism and humanity, they had, by an early
corner in the market and by successful blockade running, bought
up all the available supplies with an eye to future gain, while our
soldiers and women and children were absolutely in rags, barefoot
and starving.

At the very least, mused Colonel Martin from his flat car
which had barely progressed from the city limits, the fires
"kindled in various parts . . . lent a horrid glow to the surroundings."

Dawn

All that remained of the Confederate Navy sailed up the James
towards Manchester beneath the burning bridges. Aboard one
of his wooden gunboats, Admiral Semmes, who had contrib-
uted so much to the early morning's pyrotechnics, watched

a glorious unclouded sun, as if to mock our misfortunes, now
rising over Richmond.
Some windows, which fronted to the east, were all aglow
with his rays, mimicking the real fires that were already breaking
out in various parts of the city. In the lower part of the city, the
schoolship Patrick Henry *was burning, and some of the houses*
near the Navy Yard were on fire. . . .
But higher up was the principal scene of the conflagration.
Entire blocks were on fire here, and a dense canopy of smoke,
rising high in the still morning air, was covering the city as with
a pall. The rear-guard of our army had just crossed, as I landed
my fleet at Manchester, and the bridges were burning in their
rear. The Tredegar Iron Works were on fire, and continual explo-
sions of loaded shell stored there were taking place. In short, the
scene cannot be described by mere words, but the reader may
conceive a tolerable idea of it, if he will imagine himself to be
looking on Pandemonium, broken loose.
The population was in a great state of alarm. Hundreds of
men and women had sought refuge on the Manchester side, in the
hope of getting away, by some means or other, they knew not

how. I was, myself, about the most helpless man in the whole crowd. I had just tumbled on shore, with their bags and baggage, 500 sailors, incapable of marching a dozen miles without becoming foot-sore, and without any means, whatever, of transportation being provided for them.

Ruefully, he reflected, he did not possess so much as "a pack-mule," such lack being underscored by the spectacle of "a current of horsemen" retreating past him. Worse yet, the cavalrymen jibed at him:

It was every man for himself and devil take the hindmost. Some of the young cavalry rascals—lads of eighteen or twenty—as they passed, jibed and joked with my old salts, asking them how they liked navigating the land, and whether they did not expect to anchor in Fort Warren pretty soon? The spectacle presented by my men was, indeed, rather a ludicrous one; loaded down, as they were, with pots, and pans, and mess-kettles, bags of bread, and chunks of salted pork, sugar, tea, tobacco, and pipes. It was as much as they could do to stagger under their loads—marching any distance seemed out of the question.

As I reviewed my "troops," after they had been drawn up by my captains, who were now all become colonels, I could not but repeat to myself Mr. Mallory's last words—"You will join General Lee, in the field, with all your forces."

Yes; here were my "forces," but where the devil was General Lee, and how was I to join him? If I had had the Secretary of the Navy, on foot, by the side of me, I rather think this latter question would have puzzled him.

But there was no time to be lost—I must do something.

Ewell would report, somewhat prematurely,

by daylight the riot was subdued, but many buildings, which I had carefully directed should be spared had been fired by the mob. . . . A party of men went to burn the Tredegar Works, but were prevented by General Anderson's arming his operatives and declaring his intention to resist.

The small bridge over the canal on Fourteenth Street was burned by incendiaries, who set a canal boat on fire and pushed it under the bridge. This was evidently done in hopes of embarrassing our retreat, and General Kershaw's Division passed the bridge while on fire at a "double quick."

Young Eddie Watehall, watching this episode, thought it "entirely accidental." However, he overheard Ewell say, "The first one that puts a torch to this bridge except by my orders I wish shot down." As Watehall saw it, three men in the boat had been "helping themselves to all they could find." He figured they did not know the contents when a "box of powder" they casually tossed into the boat "struck against something and exploded."

In fact, it was Eddie's impression that the boatmen labored diligently, if futilely, to extinguish the blaze. The youth, from more of a distance, also observed "a large coal of fire fall on the steeple of the Presbyterian Church," which "burned so slowly that I am sure it could have been put out if any one could have gotten to it. This church [not that of Moses Hoge], though it stood in a thickly populated part of the city, was the only thing that burned in that neighborhood." Watehall continued:

> The gas was cut off at the works, and there was no light; so people burned paper to see how to pillage and threw the lighted paper on the floors. I saw as many as ten or fifteen of these lights on the floors at once.

"As the night wore away," wrote Lawley,

> the tramp of Kershaw's division and of Custis Lee's local militia was heard in the streets, and it was felt that as the last men were now withdrawn from the north side there was no longer anything to interpose between Richmond and the enemy.

The reporter wasn't entirely correct, however, since other units were still leaving the city, some over bridges half ablaze.

Designated as a rear guard, the Thomas Company Rangers of the Fiftieth Georgia Regiment were among the last troops across Mayo's Bridge. Sergeant Thomas Sheldon thought that had the company delayed many minutes, they would have been unable to cross at all since the bridge had already been fired. Still, he remembered that the Rangers "marched with firm tread, sadly and silently though rapidly across Mayo's Bridge over the James River . . . and bade farewell forever to the Confederate Capital."

"Forward, Third Company!" rang the command of W. S. White's unit of the Richmond Howitzers as they marched over Mayo's "away from all we cherished and held most dear on earth. . . . We lingered not to participate in or witness the shamefully disgraceful proceedings . . . but in silence and sorrow we marched on. . . . No woman's hand waved us a parting adieu . . . no maiden's eye sparkled a farewell and a hope for the future. . . ."

Arriving at dawn, too, was Private Woods, the drummer from Georgia who had fallen asleep. A good soldier, he had run all the way from his deserted encampment—after being awakened by the explosions—carrying even his drum along with haversack and canteen, "I had no idea of being captured by the Yankees." He had paused to watch

> one of the most beautiful scenes, and yet one of the saddest . . . the sight of all the vessels on the James River, Confederate and private, floating down the river on fire, cut loose from their moorings, drifting steadily, silently and serenely, without a pilot or a flag. On they floated until they burned to the water's edge.

Young Woods, "being strictly temperate," was horrified beyond ability to express himself at the scenes in Richmond: "I turned away in disgust on seeing some of the boys . . . make hogs of themselves." Nonetheless, "having drawn no rations for the retreat," hunger quickly overcame his moral restraint, and he merely "turned into one of the doors of the commissary house."

His haversack was bulging when he heard a cry of "fire!" followed by screaming women and children and "a mad rush for the only door. The stampede was general, the mass being excited to frenzy. Men, women and children, citizens, soldiers and stragglers, all in frantic disorder, struggled for the only exit. Fairly in the streets again, I paused a moment to look back on the struggling mass, and then came a warning cry that almost dazed me: 'The bridge is on fire!' "

It was true, but Woods made it across anyhow, as sparks fell around him.

The "sun rose on Richmond," Sallie Brock wrote, to present

> such a spectacle . . . as can never be forgotten . . . the fire was progressing with fearful rapidity. The roaring and hissing and the crackling of the flames were heard above the shouting and confusion of the immense crowd of plunderers who were moving

*amid the dense smoke like demons, pushing, rioting and swaying
with their burdens to make a passage to the open air.*

*From the lower portion of the city, near the river, dense
black clouds of smoke arose as a pall of crepe to hide the ravages of
the devouring flames, which lifted their red tongues and leaped
from building to building as if possessed of demoniac instinct, and
intent upon wholesale destruction. All the railroad bridges, and
Mayo's Bridge, that crossed the James River and connected with
Manchester, on the opposite side, were in flames.*

The "lofty Petersburg Railroad bridge, about a mile long,"
according to John Leyburn, was now "long lines of flame."

All in all, Sallie concluded, "the horrors of the final conflagration, when the earth shall be wrapped in flames and melt
with fervent heat, were, it seemed to us, prefigured in our
capital."

"A scene more awful and at the same time sublime I never
witnessed," wrote Lieutenant Colonel John W. Atkinson, of the
Confederate artillery.

And even "some twelve miles distant," McHenry Howard
turned to marvel at a "dense black volume of smoke . . . rise
and hang like a huge pall over the country in the direction of
Richmond."

"Like a pall over the zenith," echoed a witness directly
underneath it, Jones the war clerk.

"A sea of flame," wrote Leyburn.

The smoke was, in fact, so thick that, to Emmie Crump,
"the sun looked as if in eclipse."

Pollard was particularly awed by the melee around the
commissary depot, "at the head of the dock" where

> *hundreds of government wagons were loaded with bacon,
> flour and whiskey, and driven off in hot haste to join the retreat-
> ing army.*
>
> *Thronged about the depot were hundreds of men, women
> and children, black and white, provided with capacious bags,
> baskets, tubs, buckets, tin pans and aprons; cursing, pushing,
> and crowding, awaiting the throwing open of the doors and the
> order for each to help himself.*

At sunrise they moved in and "a rush that almost seemed
to carry the building off its foundation was made, and hun-

dreds of thousands of pounds of bacon, flour, etc. were soon swept away by a clamorous crowd."

Even at this relatively late hour Dr. F. Davidson thought he saw "a man . . . with a torch" still firing warehouses, though virtually all of such buildings were now ablaze. Nellie Grey, who had sat at her window most of the night, also saw soldiers running down the streets, some with balls of tar, some with torches:

> As they ran they fired the balls of tar and pitched them onto the roofs of prominent houses and into the windows of public buildings and churches. I saw balls pitched on the roof of General R. E. Lee's home.

Inside of Mary Fontaine's shuttered house a "dreadful silence" predominated, while

> immense fires stretched their arms on high all around me . . . I shuddered.
> I watched those silent, awful fires. I felt that there was no effort to stop them, but all like myself were watching them, paralyzed and breathless. After a while the sun rose . . . a great red ball veiled in a mist. . . .

As Connie Cary from her garret window described the same scene "a smoke arose that shrouded the whole town, shutting out every vestige of blue sky and April sunshine. Flakes of fire fell around us, glass was shattered, and chimneys fell, even so far as Grace Street. . . ." John Jones tiptoed over streets virtually paved with "pulverized glass." He was not alone. On Shockoe Hill, Judith McGuire also walked over roads of glass shards:

> It was then daylight and we were standing out upon the pavement.
> The Colonel and B. had just gone. Shall we ever meet again? Many ladies were now upon the streets. The lower part of the city was burning. About seven o'clock I set off to go to the central depot to see if the cars would go out. As I went from Franklin to Broad Street, and on Broad, the pavements were covered with broken glass; women, both white and coloured, were walking in multitudes from the Commissary offices and burning stores with bags of flour, meal, coffee, sugar, rolls of cotton cloth, etc.;

coloured men were rolling wheelbarrows filled in the same way. I went on and on towards the depot, and as I proceeded shouts and screams became louder. The rabble rushed by me in one stream. . . .

Indeed, who, as a participant, "will ever forget that bitter night?" asked Cooper De Leon:

> *Husbands hastily arranged what plans they might for the safety of families they were forced to leave behind; women crept out into the midnight, to conceal the little jewelry, money or silver left them, fearing general sack of the city and treachery of even the most trusted negroes. . . . So men went forth into the black midnight, to what fate they dreamed not. . . .*

He rode by "a well-remembered porch" where his friend Styles Staples was about to depart. "Two weeping girls" clung to him as he kissed them and then "hurled himself into saddle. . . . There was a black frown on Staples' face as he rode up by me; and I heard a sound—part sob; more heart-deep oath—tear out of his throat. . . ."

De Leon listened, through the commotion, to the "muffled roll of distant wagons and, here and there, the sharp call of a bugle:

> *Now and again, the bright glare, above the smoke round the whole horizon, would pale before a vivid, dazzling flash; followed by swaying tremble of the earth and a roar, hoarsely dull; and one more ship of the little navy was a thing of the past.*
>
> *Later still came to the steady tramp of soldiers—to be heard for the last time in those streets, though its echo may sound down all time! The last scene of the somber drama had begun; and the skeleton battery supports filed by like specters, now in the gloom, now in the glare of one of the hundred fires.*

While the "fire raged like a devouring demon . . . beyond human control," according to another observer,

> *people . . . dragged their goods into the street only to [have them] trampled or burned there. . . . Wagons and carts were loaded with goods and carried away; some employed wheelbarrows, others carried their arms full, dropping what they had to seize more.*

Women were tugging at barrels of flour and children were straining themselves to move boxes of tobacco. The sidewalks were strewn with silks, satins, bonnets, hats, clothes, fancy goods, shoes, groceries, and merchandise of every description. . . . Property owners stood helpless and looked on; some were stunned by the awful sight, others wept and wrung their hands. . . .

During this same period, ever since midnight, Grant's Ninth Corps had been observing the fires in Petersburg and telltale sounds, or lack of sounds, in that direction. At 4 A.M., according to Horace Porter, "a few skirmishers" had been captured, who readily confirmed that the defenders had fled.

"At an early hour this morning the rebels kindled some immense fires in the city [Petersburg]," wrote the correspondent for the *Boston Daily Advertiser*, "which illuminated the sky for hours and must have destroyed many buildings. The magazines in the batteries north of the city were blown up and a long chain of fires extended as far as we could see." Like other reporters, he thought of Petersburg as the "Cockade City," so dubbed because of the hats its soldiers wore in the War of 1812.

In the predawn, excitement had welled in the Union lines facing the Confederate earthworks. The "Federal troops were all astir," another reporter noted, "knapsacks were being slung, blankets rolled, and every preparation made for an immediate advance." The *Advertiser* correspondent continued that "regimental bands all along the lines played their most joyful strains" as cheers went up from the many camps.

Word was spreading that Petersburg had already been surrendered to Colonel Ralph Ely, Second Brigade commander, First Division, Ninth Corps (under Major General Orlando B. Wilcox). General Porter put the time at exactly 4:28 A.M. Others pegged it earlier, some later, and there was even doubt as to who had the honor of accepting the capitulation.

This was not surprising since advance Union patrols were swarming into the city's streets in the dark, making it impossible for Mayor W. W. Townes and his surrender party even to leave the city proper. Added to the confusion was the fact that other city councilmen were wandering, on their own, trying to surrender the fallen city and vital rail junction. Sylvanus Cadwallader, *New York Herald* correspondent, could attest to the latter.

Arriving on horseback in Petersburg ahead of most of the Federal soldiers, Cadwallader encountered "a procession of old men, in homespun, butternut clothing, coming towards me on the sidewalk, bearing an improvised flag of truce that looked suspiciously like a dirty linen table cloth." With "sober gait as if attending a funeral," they approached the reporter and "their spokesman began a pompous official address" to surrender the city.

Cadwallader, tired and "impatient," considered the performance "the most ridiculous event of my life." Not amused at all, he lectured the party that their collective desires were "many months" too late, in fact Northern troops were already in the city, and the matter of surrender had become one of cold semantics.

But "the old men" persisted, asking, "was property not to be respected and the rights of unarmed citizens observed?" Cadwallader, now mostly interested in breakfast, turned and rode away "from their questionings and protests."

Already some two hours out of Petersburg, Sergeant James W. Albright from Greensboro, of the Twelfth Virginia Artillery, would observe,

> *Such a march! Much of our stores and supplies were aban-doned on the road for want of transportation. The march was slow and tiresome, and but little firing to give the least excitement.*
>
> *We travelled all night and scarcely made ten miles. Saw many old friends.*

He too heard "terrific explosions towards Richmond."

Back in that city Peter Helms Mayo wrote that sometime before dawn he was on his way

> *to join the army, which could only be done by crossing Mayo's bridge to Manchester. Before reaching the bridge I stopped in the railroad station to take a last look. There I found everything in confusion and uproar.*
>
> *Many of the goods and supplies were being taken away by the citizens and the city was in the greatest state of consternation. In some places the liquor had been emptied from barrels into the*

gutters and caught fire, and was running down the streets in liquid flames, creating great terror.

With him, as they rode on horseback, was the bridegroom of a few hours, Colonel Walter Taylor, and Colonel John S. Saunders, now the latter's brother-in-law.

"Looking back with sad hearts on the city in flames," added Mayo, the trio continued on. Taylor found "universal gloom and despair" the dominant mood, since "at the next rising of the sun" the "detested Federal soldiers" would probably be in the city.

When Colonel McDonald, accompanied by the clerk, finally led their buggy out of the capital, he encountered a "broken-down wagon loaded with shoes. I proposed to my companion that we should help ourselves as they might prove a substitute for our worthless currency."

They helped themselves to "some ten pairs." Very quickly they were able to barter the much-sought-after footwear for riding horses and food. Now McDonald could make the kind of progress he had hoped for.

Just before dawn, "a terrific explosion" shook the whole city of Richmond. The fires had spread to the arsenal back of the Alms House—or it had been deliberately set—and it went off in a roaring tower of flames as if in affirmation of the Biblical prophecy of the end of the earth. The noise, it appeared certain to John Leyburn, "might almost have awakened the dead. The earth seemed fairly to writhe as if in agony, the house rocked like a ship at sea, while stupendous thunders roared around."

Correspondent Lawley believed that the blast shook

every building in Richmond to its foundations. . . . As the first streak of dawn heralded the day . . . a vast column of dense black smoke shot into the air, a huge, rumbling earthquake-like reverberation rent the ground, and the store of gunpowder garnered in the city magazine passed out of existence.

To Emmie Sublet, it was

perfectly awful, and lasted I suppose about two minutes. . . . I thought the house would be jarred to the ground. It broke the windows and I declare it sounded as if a shell had bursted in the house; three times as loud as any thunder I ever heard in my life.

The climax of the night of fires and explosions in Richmond was the predawn eruption of the arsenal (or "magazine"): "the earth seemed fairly to writhe as if in agony, the house rocked like a ship at sea. . . . A vast column of dense black smoke shot into the air, a huge, rumbling earthquake-like reverberation rent the ground . . . the rattle as of thousands of musketry. . . . [It was] like a blaze of day!" A day or a few days later, Brady's photographers found only walls to record on their glass plates. *Library of Congress.*

> *Lizzie, Virginia, Manie, Maggie and Julia came running in our room trembling like aspin leaves, and screaming at the pitch of their voices. I never could have imagined anything so frightful and awful to hear. As mamma says, "ears never heard such a noise before."*
>
> *Although it was so frightful I couldn't help laughing at Lizzie to save my life. You know she is the most excitable poor creature I ever saw.*

Emmie Crump was shaken from her sleep to find herself standing in the middle of her room. Through the windows dawn's light paled before the lurid flames of bursting shells, "the fearful sound . . . louder than any cannon I ever heard." The reaction of Emmie and her sister was perhaps curious: they must rescue their spring bonnets "left at the store to be pressed into a newer shape, having been worn the previous year."

Dallas Tucker was awakened from his deep slumber by a "tremendous shock." He thought at first it was an earthquake "which rocked the house and rattled the windows." Then he got out of bed and observed the same weird spectacle which others had this morning, as

> the sun rose [and] shone with fiery redness through a dense blackness, which at first we took to be heavy clouds, but soon saw was in reality a great volume of smoke passing over the city from south to north.
> Richmond was on fire.
> My first impulse as this became a settled fact, was to go and see for myself what was happening in the lower part of the city. I was deterred, however, from carrying out this impulse at once by certain household duties. I had to go to market. . . .

Clerk Jones, too, was shaken into consciousness from his troubled sleep by "two tremendous explosions, seeming to startle the very earth, and crashing the glass throughout the western end of the city." Curiously, he had labelled it hitherto "a quiet night with its million of stars."

Fannie Walker, who had not "dared to lie down or think of sleeping," was actually walking downstairs when the magazine went up, "and before I knew it I found myself flat. Glass was falling all around . . ."

Capping all, the explosion, Phoebe Pember wrote, sent "shells exploding and filling the air with hissing sounds of horror, menacing the people in every direction."

"Formidable," was the restrained tag of French Consul Paul.

It awoke "most effectually" the "dead tired" Colonel Duke who had organized the tobacco warehouses burning. He then "threw my blanket over my shoulder, sword and haversack on one side, and canteen, with a little brandy, on the other. I struck out for Mayo's Bridge, some one or two miles distant." Duke, despite what he said, must have remained more than half asleep since he believed "the streets were quiet and apparently deserted."

Although four miles from the city, the house of Emma Mordecai was "jarred to its foundations by the report of an explosion." Already in a state of consternation thinking about her distant loved ones, Emma "jumped up, horror-stricken, and groped my way downstairs, and got in bed with R. and A.—all terrified and trembling together."

Just prior to the explosion, Ewell had ordered Captain Sulivane to take his command to Mayo's Bridge at the foot of Fourteenth Street. It was, Ewell advised him, the only bridge over the James remaining. All others had been destroyed by the retreating Confederates. Clement Sulivane was to guard Mayo's until General Gary of South Carolina, with his cavalry, was safely across. In spite of Sulivane's continuing efforts to assemble the local brigade and militia, the battalions "melted away as fast as they were formed. "Now that he had a handful, perhaps two hundred, to protect the bridge "to the last extremity," the cataclysm erupted virtually over his head, a scene of "terrible splendor."

Incendiaries or fragments of bombs had ignited several buildings so that Richmond and Manchester across the river

> *were like a blaze of day. . . . Three high arched bridges were in flames; beneath them the waters sparkled and dashed and rushed on by the burning city. Every now and then, as a magazine exploded, a column of white smoke rose . . . instantaneously followed by a deafening sound. The ground seemed to rock and tremble as with the shock of an earthquake. . . . Hundreds of shells would explode in the air and send their iron spray down far below the bridge.*
>
> *As the immense magazines of cartridges ignited, the rattle as of thousands of musketry would follow, and then all was still for the moment, except the dull roar and crackle of the fast-spreading fires.*

And all had become still, too, in the smoking ruins of the adjacent Alms House where at least a dozen elderly residents had perished. The VMI cadets temporarily billeted there had been ordered out late Sunday morning for many emergency duties.

From "several miles distant on the Amelia Court House road," McHenry Howard heard the explosion, followed by that of what he assumed was the last ship of the James River Squadron: "In the early gray of morning while the command was resting for a few minutes, a sudden bright light drew the attention of everyone to the direction of Drewry's Bluff. A magnificent pyramid of fire, shooting hundreds of feet into the dusky air, and a dull explosion. . . ."

General Gary's cavalry, approaching Richmond from the southeast, had just reached the intermediate line of Confederate works, where the Charles City and New Kent roads met. Colonel Boykin was certain no man could ever forget the sight:

> The sun was just rising, and an ugly red glare showed itself in the direction of Richmond that dimmed the early sunshine.
>
> At this point the General determined (though expecting the enemy's cavalry every moment) to occupy the works, and wait for the dismounted men. The guns of the battery that accompanied us were placed in position, and our men dismounted and occupied the lines on the right and left of the road. In about a half hour's time, and to our great satisfaction—for it seemed a hard case to leave the poor tired fellows to be gobbled up—a straggling line of tired men and poor walkers, as dismounted cavalry always must be in their big boots and spurs, showed themselves over the hill, dragged themselves along, and passed on before us into the city. We followed on, went down the steep hill by the house where General Johnston's headquarters were about the time of the retreat from Yorktown, and got into the river road, and so had the enemy behind us. It was here he might have cut us off from the city and secured the bridge.

A sleepless but characteristically alert General Grant read a telegram Weitzel had sent at 5:25 A.M., "continued explosions and fires in enemy's lines. Large number of deserters. All report evacuation. I will move at daybreak."

In or just beyond Richmond, all were watching the molten end, as the *Chicago Tribune* would editorialize, of "the modern Babylon."

"The flames of Monday" had arrived.

8:00 A.M.

For some not in the immediate vicinity of the fire, or astride the direct routes of retreat, it was breakfast time as usual. Outside of Manchester, Paymaster Powell Hill and his cousin Henry arrived at the home of the former's father. They left the ambulance containing the general's remains, and walked through the gate to the house. Powell had believed that the deceased's

> *wife and children had already reached there with the sad news.*
>
> *I found the family at breakfast and totally ignorant of the sad changes that had taken place within the past forty-eight hours. The General's family had not arrived, and the condition of his remains was such as to give us serious doubts as to the practicability or advisability of attempting to convey them so great a distance across the country in an ambulance (more than one hundred miles to Culpeper).*
>
> *We decided then and there to give his remains temporary burial, and at some future day remove them to his native county and place him by the side of his parents. The grave was hastily dug, and, with the assistance of my father's butler, I made a rough case to receive the coffin.*

Early as it was, breakfast was also being partaken of—by some—in Petersburg. Sylvanus Cadwallader had checked into Jarrat's Hotel, from the dining room of which he could watch "Union cavalry . . . swarming through the streets, soon followed by infantry." To one of the officers who entered the old hostelry, the *New York Herald* correspondent quipped that "this celebrated rebel stronghold" had already been surrendered "to me."

Then, "without a minute's delay," he commenced his dispatch—which would conclude, "God be praised who gives us victory, we are in Petersburg!"

His story was not an exclusive one. The *New York Tribune* reporter was also scribbling at fever pace his own account:

> *On passing through the city I saw most of the stores closed, and a few people in the streets. The Ninth Corps was the first to enter and some of its flags were hoisted upon the Court House [about in the center of the city.]*
>
> *Some large fires were to be seen in the street—one of a large tobacco warehouse near the Jarrat House.*
>
> *The depot of the Norfolk Railroad was also on fire, and the tram bridge over the Appomattox was reduced to a few charred beams.*

He saw women "waving something white. . . . On the faces of some were real smiles . . . and no doubt on those of others the smile dissembled a bitter heart. . . ."

Sara Pryor, "as the dawn broke," saw Federal pickets entering silently, watchfully. Finding no resistance, they threw their muskets over into the yard and hurried downtown to plunder!

> I awoke my boys. "Get up, boys! Dress quickly. Now remember, you must be very self-controlled and quiet, and no harm will come to you."
> Immediately the door of my room was thrown wide open, and Robert ushered in three armed, German-looking soldiers.
> "What do you want?" I asked.
> "To search the house," they answered.
> "You will find nothing worth your while. There is my shawl! I have just run in from the lines. Here are my children."

The soldiers assured Sara they did not want her "clothes," only her "prisoner." With that, her husband, "fastening his collar," appeared and was "marched" off.

In her pique of emotion she accused her servant Robert for having "betrayed" his master, then ordered him to leave the house. "Strangely to say" he left, for the sin of having let in the Union soldiers. But Sara Pryor's troubles were scarcely over, she suspected, since others of the occupying force were gathering outside the back picket fence.

Surgeon Liddell, early in the city, had already ascertained that the enemy had left "149 of his badly wounded" at one principal Petersburg hospital. This inspired him to issue an order that "no houses in Petersburg should be used for hospital purposes or even for temporary accommodation of the wounded belonging to the Army of the Potomac." His reasoning: There probably were other sick and wounded Confederates left behind in the city.

The Navy was finding exit no less arduous than had the Army. After firing and abandoning his wooden gunboats, Semmes and his crewmen hiked into Manchester, "blinded by the dust kicked up by those vagabonds on horseback," the retreating cavalrymen who had jibed at him earlier.

> When we came in sight of the railroad depot, I halted, and

inquired of some of the fugitives who were rushing by, about the trains.

"The trains!" said they, in astonishment at my question; "the last train left at daylight this morning—it was filled with the civil officers of the Government." Notwithstanding this answer, I moved my command up to the [Manchester] station and workshops, to satisfy myself by a personal inspection. It was well that I did so, as it saved my command from the capture that impended over it. I found it quite true, that the "last train" had departed; and, also, that all the railroadmen had either run off in the train, or hidden themselves out of view.

There was no one in charge of anything, and no one who knew anything. But there was some materiel lying around me; and, with this, I resolved to set up railroading on my own account. Having a dozen and more steam-engineers along with me, from my late fleet, I was perfectly independent of the assistance of the alarmed railroad-men, who had taken to flight.

A pitiable scene presented itself, upon our arrival at the station. Great numbers had flocked thither, in the hope of escape: frightened men, despairing women, and crying children. Military patients had hobbled thither from the hospitals; civil employees of the Government, who had missed the "last train," by being a little too late, had come to remedy their negligence; and a great number of other citizens, who were anxious to get out of the presence of the hated Yankee, had rushed to the station, they scarcely knew why.

These people had crowded into, and on the top of, a few straggling passenger-cars, that lay uncoupled along the track, in seeming expectation that someone was to come, in due time, and take them off. There was a small engine lying also on the track, but there was no fire in its furnace, no fuel with which to make a fire, and no one to manage it. Such was the condition of affairs when I "deployed" my "forces" upon the open square, and "grounded arms,"—the butts of my rifles not ringing on the ground quite as harmoniously as I could have desired. Soldiering was new to Jack; however, he would do better by-and-by.

Meticulously, the former cool scourge of the merchant sealanes hauled "those wretched people" out of the cars. To their "plaintive appeals," he replied that "it was better for an unarmed citizen to fall into the hands of the enemy than a soldier with arms in his hands."

He then coupled the cars and seated his crews inside them—the hard boards were still preferable to standing. Next, the engine: he ordered his marines to chop up the nearest picket fence "in front of one of the dwellings." An engineer and a fireman, picked more or less at random, were "detailed" for the locomotive "and in a very few minutes we had steam hissing from its boiler."

Now, in a gesture of magnanimity, Semmes invited the civilians back aboard and "with the triumphant air of a man who had overcome a great difficulty and who felt as if he might snap his fingers at the Yankees once more, I gave the order to 'go ahead!' "

The little engine started "at a snail's pace," crept along with its burden and then came to "a dead halt" just outside of the station. Now, the otherwise unconquerable Raphael Semmes would note in understatement, this was "a predicament!"

By more conventional train, Lawley, of the *Times*, departed some time after 6 A.M. for Fredericksburg, saying his adieus to "Mr. Connolly, the member for Donegal, who had passed a month in Richmond, and was upon this eventful morning still undecided whether to follow General Lee's army or to strike northwards like myself."

Richmond's *bon vivant* of the press corps figured he would go on to Washington and then New York before returning home to London. The balding, patrician Briton realized now that he had lavished his emotions along with his prose on the losing, and, even more humiliating, wrong side.

Watching from an ever-shortening distance outside of the Richmond limits, Major General Alex S. Webb, Chief of Staff of the Army of the Potomac, hurried a message, "Save the bridges!" This was at once seconded by another general officer: "The bridges crossing the river can be saved by a little effort. I have the fire engines at work for this purpose. . . !"

But the bridges were all beyond saving, even though individual Confederates, soldier and civilian, still would claim the dubious honor of being the last across the crackling structures. Some burned more slowly than others, inspiring the supposition that the citizenry had organized bucket brigades to combat the flames.

At 7 A.M. Ewell himself believed "the last troops had reached the south side," leaving only burning and charred bridges in their wake. From the heights of Manchester he watched the flames of Richmond—of early Monday—and was especially surprised to see the eruptions from "one of the large mills" that he had hitherto considered "fireproof."

Ewell would shortly include in his report the interesting observation that "the burning of Richmond was the work of incendiaries, and might have been prevented by the citizens." This from the pen of good soldier Ewell, who had obediently carried out orders to put major warehouses of the Confederacy's capital to the torch . . . and in the face of a brisk southerly wind.

Captain Boykin certainly had remained in the city some time after the commanding general with the short—or convenient—memory. With his cavalry brigade, he had galloped through Rocketts after daylight, remarking on the "peculiar population . . . gathered on the sidewalk," the dirtiness of the women and children, and the "scoundrelly looking men, who in the general ruin were sneaking from the holes they had been hiding in." He would add,

> *Bare-headed women, their arms filled with every descripton of goods, plundered from warehouses and shops, their hair hanging about their ears, were rushing one way to deposit their plunder and return for more, while a current of the empty-handed surged in a contrary direction towards the scene.*
>
> *The roaring and crackling of the burning houses, the trampling and snorting of our horses over the paved streets as we swept along, wild sounds of every description, while the rising sun came dimly through the cloud of smoke that hung like a pall around him, made up a scene that beggars description, and which I hope never to see again—the saddest of many of the sad sights of war—a city undergoing pillage at the hands of its own mob, while the standards of an empire were being taken from its capitol, and the tramp of a victorious enemy could be heard at its gates.*
>
> *Richmond had collected within its walls the refuse of the war—thieves and deserters, male and female, the vilest of the vile were there, but strict military discipline had kept it down. Now, in one moment, it was all removed—all restraint was taken off—and you may imagine the consequences. There were said to be 5,000 deserters in the city, and you could see the grey jackets here and there sprinkled in the mob that was roaring down the street.*
>
> *When we reached somewhere between Twentieth and*

*Twenty-fifth streets—I will not be certain—the flames swept
across Main Street so we could not pass. The column turned to
the right, and so got into the street above it. On this [Franklin
Street] are many private residences; at the windows we could see
the sad and tearful faces of the kind Virginia women, who had
never failed the soldier in four long years of war and trouble,
ready to the last to give him devoted attendance in his wounds
and sickness, and to share with his necessities the last morsel.*

He paused to watch "a low white man—he seemed a
foreigner—about to strike a woman over a barrel of flour,
under my horse's nose." At that juncture "a stout negro" came
to her aid, threatening to throw the man in the canal. "All this
occurred at one of those momentary halts to which the rear of a
marching column is subjected; in another moment we moved
on, the crowd closed in, and we saw no more."

Boykin was racing for the bridge to Manchester when he
saw what he identified as "about forty of Kautz's cavalry"
galloping "easily up Main Street." This was, if Boykin were
correct, the First Division of Major General August Kautz,
which thus would have become the first in the capital. The
Federal troops "fired a long shot" at other retreating Confederates still on the bridge and then continued on up the street.

Captain Sulivane was witness to the same spectacle, "a
line of blue-coated horsemen galloping in furious haste up
Main Street. . . . they fired a few random shots at us."

Nellie Grey, still watching in awe from her window as the
day grew brighter,

*saw a Confederate soldier on horseback pause almost under
my window. He wheeled and fired behind him; rode a short
distance, wheeled and fired again; and so on, wheeling and firing
as he went until he was out of sight. Coming up the street from
that end toward which his fire had been directed and from which
he had come, rode a body of men in blue uniforms. It was not a
very large body, they rode slowly, and passed just beneath my
window.*

Sulivane, Boykin, Haskell and others all now accelerated
their commands over the burning Mayo's Bridge. Boykin, as
Ewell had before him, halted momentarily on the slopes of
Manchester to survey the city behind him:

By this time the fire appeared to be general. Some magazine or depot for the manufacture of ordnance stores was on fire about the centre of the city; it was marked by the peculiar blackness of smoke; from the middle of it would come the roar of bursting shells and boxes of fixed ammunition, with flashes that gave it the appearance of a thunder cloud of huge proportions with lightning playing through it. On our right was the navy yard, at which were several steamers and gunboats on fire, and burning in the river, from which the cannon were thundering as the fire reached them.

The old war-scarred city seemed to prefer annihilation to conquest—a useless sacrifice, however much it may have added to the grandeur of the closing scene; but such is war.

Colonel Duke, who, like so many, thought he was the last Confederate out of Richmond, paused "on the slope beyond the bridge" to observe the sun "peep over the eastern hills":

I turned and looked back; the city of Richmond was in flames. From all the windows of the Gallego Mills tongues of flame were bursting out; dense clouds of smoke, sparks and flames were reaching skyward. The sight was awfully grand . . . sublime spectacle. . . . I felt the end was near.

But others were still departing, either overlooked by the advanced riders of the Union cavalry, or not regarded as especially important. Secretary Breckinridge himself, handsome and apparently as fearless as ever, took a swig out of his saddle bottle and became perhaps the very last to cross Mayo's. Wise enough to recognize Jefferson Davis's chauvinism, the Confederate general was uncertain whether to follow the helter-skelter cabinet to Danville or keep on for Mexico—and the West Indies, perhaps Cuba?

De Leon credited Breckinridge with the conceivably dubious distinction of being the last to flee the capital: "Over its [the bridge's] burning embers rode General Breckinridge and his staff—the last group of Confederates was gone: Richmond was evacuated!"

However, Admiral Semmes, "still opposite the city of Richmond," would write:

Amid flames and smoke and tumult and disorder, the enemy's hosts were pouring into the streets of the proud old capital. Long lines of cavalry and artillery and infantry could be seen, moving like a huge serpent through the streets, and winding their way to State-House Square. As a crowning insult, a regiment of negro cavalry, wild with savage delight at the thought of triumphing over their late masters, formed a prominent feature in the grand procession. Alongside of the black savage marched the white savage.

The die-hard rebel's luck did not desert him. He found another engine, fired it, and his trainload of very mixed shipmates was soon "thundering" along "at five or six miles an hour," heading only for the next woodpile to keep the boilers hot.

Kautz's cavalry had made far better time than other Federal units or, indeed, the surrender party itself. While the horsemen in blue were reportedly pounding up Main Street and their opposites trying to get across the burning bridge, a drama in sotto voce was quietly unfolding at the junction of the Osborne Turnpike and the Newmarket Road, two miles from the Capitol and about a mile east of the port Rocketts. There Major Atherton Stevens, a provost marshal, Major E. E. Graves, aide-de-camp of the Fourth Massachusetts Cavalry, and Lieutenant Royal Prescott, of the Thirteenth New Hampshire Infantry, were the first to spot "a shabby carriage" or "barouche" flying a white flag.

The officers, part of a detachment of forty, had been halted at Gillie's Creek, running past the intersection. En route they had traversed varied terrain: woods; hard, open ground "much trampled by the Confederate troops"; and abandoned fortifications, some with unspiked guns, "the ammunition piled ready for use," and surrounded by "bits of bright-colored cloth attached to little sticks, rising a few inches above the ground" warning of torpedoes.

Now the eerie stillness beside Gille's Creek, in contrast to the early morning explosions from the "vicinity of Richmond," was interrupted by the creaking wheels of a weary conveyance. When the carriage rolled into sight, "a few rods south of the little stream," it was, as near as Prescott could determine, "between six and a half and seven o'clock."

Major Stevens asked, "Who is in command of this flag-of-truce?"

"It is Mr. Mayo, the mayor of the city of Richmond," Judge Meredith replied.

The jurist thereupon introduced the mayor and all of his associates to the Federal cavalry officers.

"The Mayor," Meredith would recall, "handed the letter to him [Major Stevens]." It purportedly stated: "It is proposed to formally surrender to the Federal authorities the city of Richmond, hitherto the capital of the Confederate States of America, and the defenses protecting it up to this time."

The proceedings, however, would be witnessed from differing and not always reconcilable perspectives. For example, another version of the same letter would be published in the Richmond press:

> *General:*
> *The Army of the Confederate Government having aban-*
> *doned the City of Richmond, I respectfully request that you will*
> *take possession of it with an organized force, to preserve order and*
> *protect women and children and property. . . .*
> *Respectfully,*
> *Joseph Mayo, Mayor.*

Judge Meredith would record that "in reading it, he [Major Stevens] remarked that they had learned that morning of the evacuation of the city, and that stringent orders had been issued to protect persons and property, and that we need not feel any apprehension on that subject."

On the other hand, Lieutenant Prescott would report,

> *The Mayor . . . then tendered to me the surrender of the city*
> *of Richmond, and offered to place in my hands a package, in the*
> *act of so doing, containing, I presume, papers and the keys of the*
> *public buildings. I was about to take the package, but just then I*
> *saw Gen. Godfrey Weitzel, with his staff, coming down the hill,*
> *riding along the turnpike, and I at once referred the Mayor to*
> *him, as the proper officer with whom to treat.*

Meredith was not aware of Weitzel's presence, as he continued, "after some conversation about the best mode of preserving order in the city he [Stevens] proposed to the Mayor to accompany him, and they moved rapidly on to the city. The rest of us followed in carriages."

Prescott, however, continued, "The Mayor then proceeded southward down the turnpike to meet Gen. Weitzel." Then, the lieutenant reported that "in a few minutes" the general came up to him "and ordered me to follow him into the city, which I proceeded at once to do. . . . We soon, however, lost sight of Gen. Weitzel in the dense smoke of the burning city."

Weitzel, in his report, noted his arrival at the Osborne–New Market junction, but made no mention of seeing the mayor. Finding that "only one man was killed in passing through the rebel torpedo lines," he wrote that Devens's division took the pike for Richmond "by virtue of seniority in rank," while others "struck out straight across the fields."

It became a race to be among the first into Richmond, according to Major Graves, now done with his meeting of the surrender party.

> As we approached the inner line of defenses we saw in the distance divisions of our troops, many of them upon the double-quick, aiming to be the first in the city; a white and colored division were having a regular race, the white troops on the turnpike and the colored in the fields.

It was much the same story with the First Connecticut Light Battery, which had been filing through abandoned rifle pits, abattis and all sorts of earthworks which, the soldiers agreed, could not have been stormed without a "fearful" loss.

> As soon as the order was given to march to Richmond, [wrote Pvt. Herbert Beecher] there was a wild rush. The Battery did not attempt to march along the road; the infantry blocked that. The Battery boys set to work with their shovels and filled in the ditches with dirt, and then broke a passageway through the front of the fort to get their pieces through. Then they went across lots—any way to get ahead.
>
> There were no stragglers that day, for every soldier was making a rush pell-mell for Richmond and all were anxious to get there first. Never did schoolboys show more enthusiasm; never did the wildest of fanatics make a more vigorous rush for the goal. All were singing, shouting, and "On to Richmond!" burst from thousands of voices in that crowd of patriots who had waited four years for that grand climax.

Weitzel himself was making good time. When he arrived just below Rocketts, he encountered a bewildered Confederate sentry "in a bright and gorgeous militia uniform" who informed the general he had not been relieved and wondered why not. Weitzel, who decided the man was an Alsatian, found he "spoke poor French and worse German." With bemused compassion, he took the man's rifle and told him to hurry home to his family.

> When we entered Richmond we found ourselves in a perfect pandemonium. Fires and explosions in all directions; whites and blacks, either drunk or in the highest state of excitement, running to and fro on the streets, apparently engaged in pillage or in saving some of the scanty effects from the fires; it was a yelling, howling mob. . . .
>
> To add to the horrors of the scene, the convicts broke out of the penitentiary and began an indiscriminate pillage and cut the hose of some of the fire engines.
>
> When the mob saw my staff and me, they rushed around us, hugged and kissed our legs and horses, shouting hallelujah and glory. This continued until we arrived at Capitol Square. I escaped considerable of this disagreeable infliction by an amusing circumstance. Major William V. Hutchings, of Roxbury, Mass., rode by my side. He was dressed in full uniform except epauletts and had the regulation equipments, &c., on his horse. He had quite a venerable and very handsome appearance. I was in undress uniform.
>
> The mob naturally supposed Hutchings to be the General, and he received the bulk of the caresses and attentions. A sad sight met us on reaching Capitol Square. It was covered with women and children who had fled here to escape the fire. Some of them had saved a few articles of furniture, but most had only a few articles of bedding, such as a quilt, blanket, or pillow, and were lying upon them. Their poor faces were perfect pictures of utter despair.

With his modest-sized band of pickets, Lieutenant Prescott tried valiantly to keep up with General Weitzel, but the crowds in the city pressed in on their ranks, offering to carry their packs and "urging liquors" upon them:

"I smashed several vessels of liquor with my sword," Prescott recalled, "to prevent its effect upon the men. The heat at the corner of Fourteenth and Main Streets was so intense that we were forced to turn aside . . . towards Franklin Street.

We had to double-quick as fast as possible, and our whiskers, hair and clothing were singed by it."

Hardened campaigners, the First Brigade pickets nonetheless were moved by "the condition of the poor people . . . pitiable in the extreme." They shared their rations of "hard bread and meat."

Prescott watched "one brawny man" put aside his rifle to "thrust a ten dollar greenback—all the money he had—" into the hand of a shoeless woman with four pale, emaciated children.

The lieutenant thought it was about "7:20 o'clock" when the troops finally reached the Capitol grounds. Weitzel was informed by his busy assistants, Graves and Stevens, that they had already hoisted two bright cavalry guidons atop the Capitol, reportedly to the cheers and applause of many below. However, these apparently were not the first flags attesting to the presence of the Union to be flown this morning, nor would they long remain.

Earlier yet, some time after dawn, Elizabeth Van Lew sent a servant to the roof of her home at Church Hill and unfurled the big flag she had been secreting. In fact, very soon the cry rang through this same eminence, overlooking Richmond, Rocketts and the river, that "the Yankees were a-coming!"

This alarmed Amelia Gorgas sufficiently to grab up her son and run from her partially denuded apartment in the Armory "through bursting shells" to the home of her sister, Mrs. Bayne, who was sheltering her younger children.

Dallas Tucker, returning home with a piece of mutton "as big as my two fists," heard the cry, "The Yankees are coming!" Along with several friends who had accompanied him, Dallas turned,

> and, sure enough, there came the advance guard of the Federal army up Main Street. Now, we were, or at least we thought we were, a lot of very brave fellows, but I must say the alarm and sight of the Federal troops so demoralized the whole crowd that we took to our heels, leaving almost all of our booty in the alley.

Lieutenant de Peyster, of the Thirteenth New York Artillery, who from a signal tower had been among the first to spot the fires in Richmond, was early into the city carrying a flag entrusted to him by Brigadier General George F. Shepley,

Army of the James and Devens's chief of staff. The flag formerly belonged to the Twelfth Maine Volunteers and had also flown over occupied New Orleans, part of the time atop the St. Charles Hotel. There General Butler had made his headquarters.

"Arriving at the Capitol," de Peyster wrote to his mother that Monday,

> I sprang from my horse, first unbuckling the Stars and Stripes, a large flag I had on the front of my saddle. With Captain [Loomis L.] Langdon, Chief of Artillery, I rushed up to the roof.
> Together we hoisted the first large flag over Richmond and on the peak of the roof drank to its success . . .
> I found two small guidons, took them down, and returned them to the Fourth Massachusetts Cavalry where they belong.

And below the Capitol roof, ". . . men, women and boys, colored and white all shouting welcome. The excitement was intense; old men gray and scarred by many battles, acted the part of boys, shouting and yelling at the top of their voices. . . ."

The shouts were "deafening," according to Beecher, of the Connecticut Light Battery, impressed as well by the "fiery flakes from the adjacent conflagration" sweeping just above the newly raised American flag.

"The colors of the enemy fluttered in the early morning light over the Capitol of the Confederacy," Editor Pollard wrote simply. His colleague, Lawley of the London *Times,* wrote that "the Stars and Stripes floated in triumph from its rebellious roof." (Since he was on the train towards Fredericksburg, the correspondent filed on the basis of secondhand information.)

"I did not move, I could not," confessed Mary Fontaine,

> but watched the blue horseman ride to the City Hall, enter with his sword knocking the ground at every step, and throw the great doors open, and take possession of our beautiful city; watched two blue figures on the Capitol, white men. I saw them unfurl a tiny flag, and then I sank on my knees, and the bitter, bitter tears came in a torrent.

The "horrible Stars and Stripes over our beloved Capitol!" was the equally emotional reaction of Emmie Sublet. "O the *horrible wretches!* I can't think of a name dreadful enough to call

them. It makes us fifty times more Southern in our feel-
ings . . .''

"God help us!" exclaimed Anita Dwyer Withers, a Texas
girl with a little baby, "The United States flag is flying over our
Capitol!" She added that the entry of the Union Army seemed
to possess "the solemnity of a processional entering church."

Nellie Grey thought it was "exactly at eight o'clock" when

> the Confederate flag that fluttered above the Capitol came
> down and the Stars and Stripes were run up. We knew what that
> meant! The song "On to Richmond!" was ended—Richmond
> was in the hands of the Federals. We covered our faces and cried
> aloud. All through the house was the sound of sobbing. It was as
> the house of mourning, the house of death.

Dallas Tucker watched the flag-raising from "the largest
tree I could find" on the square. When he thought of his "dead
soldier brother," his heart "was filled with bitter hate, and my
lips, which had never before uttered an oath, poured maledic-
tions on our triumphant foes. Then I went home. . . .''

As the "folds of . . . the ensign of our subjugation," wrote
Sallie Brock,

> were given to the breeze, while still we heard the roaring,
> hissing, crackling flames, the explosions of the shells and the
> shouting of the multitude, the strains of an old, familiar tune
> floated upon the air—a tune that, in days gone by, was wont to
> awaken a thrill of patriotism. But now only the most bitter and
> crushing recollections awoke within us, as upon our quickened
> hearing fell the strains of "The Star Spangled Banner." For us it
> was a requiem for buried hopes.

What, Judith McGuire asked herself, was the matter?

> I seemed to be answered by a hundred voices, "The Yankees
> have come!" . . . I turned to come home, but what was my
> horror, when I reached Ninth Street, to see a regiment of Yankee
> cavalry come dashing up, yelling, shouting, hallooing, scream-
> ing! All Bedlam let loose could not have vied with them in
> diabolical roarings. I stood riveted to the spot; I could not move
> nor speak.

Then I saw the iron gates of our time-honoured and beautiful Capitol Square, on the walks and greensward of which no hoof had been allowed to tread, thrown open and the cavalry dash in. I could see no more; I must go on with a mighty effort, or faint where I stood. I came home amid what I thought was the firing of cannon. I thought that they were thundering forth a salute that they had reached the goal of their ardent desires.

At 8:15, Weitzel arrived at City Hall where he formally, with no ceremony and as few words, accepted the surrender of Richmond from Mayor Mayo. He then dictated a dispatch to General Grant: "We took Richmond at a quarter past eight this morning. . . ."

At once, he issued a series of orders for the occupation and governing of the city, as well as for extinguishing the flames. Devens—already setting up headquarters in the senate chamber of the Capitol—would have the latter responsibility. Brigadier General George F. Shepley would become military governor since "he had occupied a similar position in New Orleans after its capture in 1862 and was eminently fit for it by education and experience."

Weitzel's first published order read:

Headquarters Detachment Army of the James,
Richmond, Va., April 3, 1865.
Major General Godfrey Weitzel, commanding detachment of the Army of the James, announces the occupation of the city of Richmond by the Armies of the United States, under command of Lieutenant General Grant. The people of Richmond are assured that we come to restore to them the blessings of peace, prosperity, and freedom, under the flag of the Union.

The citizens of Richmond are requested to remain, for the present, quietly within their houses, and to avoid all public assemblages or meetings in the public streets. An efficient provost guard will immediately re-establish order and tranquility within the city.

Martial law is, for the present, proclaimed.

Brigadier General George F. Shepley, United States Volunteers, is hereby appointed military governor of Richmond.

Lieutenant Colonel Fred L. Manning, provost marshal general, Army of the James, will act as provost marshal of Richmond.

Commanders of Detachments doing guard duty in the city will report to him for instructions.

By command of
Major General Weitzel.

D. D. Wheeler, Assistant Adjutant General

Into Richmond, close behind General Devens, came the First Brigade of the Twenty-fourth Corps, led by Brigadier General Edward H. Ripley (recently colonel of the Ninth Vermont and addressed interchangeably in the ranks). Lieutenant Royal Prescott and his pickets, already in the city, watched with pride as their regiment, the Thirteenth New Hampshire, led the First Brigade up Franklin Street, "their colors flying and their drum corps playing 'Yankee Doodle.' "

Major N. D. Stoodley noted that only "some few cavalry and a part of our picket line were in before us . . . but ours was the first Flag." As they marched along, the drum corps changed its tune to the "Battle Cry of Freedom."

"The sides of the streets were crowded with people, mostly negroes," Stoodley continued. . . . "They shouted, they danced, cried, prayed, sang, and cut up all manner of wild capers."

The fires at this time, between 8 and 9 A.M., were, according to another soldier,

> *raging with unabated fury, and the shells are continually exploding in the neighborhood of the arsenal. . . . As we march into Capitol Square, we find it strewn . . . with furniture and household implements . . . numbers of women and children, black and white . . . hungry, destitute, helpless.*

General Ripley, reporting immediately to Weitzel, was ordered to garrison the city with his First Brigade. "The central figure," Ripley would recall "of this brilliant historical scene, was standing at the east front of the Confederate Capitol . . . looking down into a gigantic crater of fire, suffocated and blinded with the vast volumes of smoke and cinders, which rolled up over and enveloped us." Weitzel, according to Ripley, added, "I have no orders further to communicate; except to say that I wish this conflagration stopped, and this city saved if it is in the bounds of human possibility, and you have carte blanche to do it in your own way."

The Capitol of the Confederate States, originally the Virginia State Capitol, was an imposing marble structure fashioned after Thomas Jefferson's favorite Maison Carré at Nimes, France. In Capitol Square, Jefferson Davis was inaugurated President of the Confederacy on Washington's birthday, 1862. Little more than three years later, Major General Godfrey Weitzel, commanding the occupying force of Union troops, stood on its porch "looking down into a gigantic crater of fire, suffocated and blinded with the vast volumes of smoke and cinders. . . ." *Library of Congress*.

To Ripley it seemed an "apparently hopeless task. . . ."

Major Stevens, set up in the city hall, was himself issuing orders, talking rapidly with the mayor and Judge Meredith, while interrupting himself to snap out "very stringent" commands to his aides "for the protection of the citizens of the town and their property." Meredith reported:

> *He advised us to repair to the fire, and set an example to the people of the city to arrest, if possible, the progress of the fire. All of us, except the Mayor, at once repaired to the fire. We found the engine at work on Thirteenth Street between Main and Cary Streets near the corner of Main. We went to work, and continued at work about fifteen minutes, when the fire, which was then*

*advancing from Cary to Main Street, forced us to move the engine
to another point.*

*I then left for breakfast, having been up all night and with-
out anything to eat.*

The troops continued to roll in, past the abandoned Confederate works. Arthur Henry, the *New York Tribune* correspondent who claimed to be the first in the city, found

> *seven distinct lines of fortifications—very formidable, but no
> more so than those encountered at Petersburg. Nearly all were
> overgrown with last summer's vegetation while some were badly
> washed by late rains.*
>
> *The enemy removed none of the heavy guns—their black
> forms dot the parapets and you look into their black throats as you
> approach the city.*
>
> *An inspection of the rebel works disclosed the fact of their
> having left in great haste. Many of their quarters were left
> without a thing being taken out of them. Pistols, revolvers,
> carbines, and arms of every description . . . in abundance and in
> some of the officers' quarters were found their private correspon-
> dence, diaries, etc. . . . .*
>
> *Our army was greeted with enthusiastic cheers by the popu-
> lace. . . . The colored population were excessively jubilant and
> danced for very joy at the sight of their sable brethren in arms.
> . . . That part of the city along the river front known as the main
> business part was one vast sheet of flame.*
>
> *What with the roaring and dashing and clashing, burning
> and tumbling buildings, the shouts of our soldiers moving up the
> main streets to the Capitol, the music of Union bands playing the
> Star Spangled Banner, the shouts of welcome and excitement of
> the people was a scene of grandeur and magnificence never to be
> effaced from our memory. . . . .*

A Negro band playing the "Year of Jubilee" inspired
perhaps the greatest applause. Old men, "battle-scarred and
resting on crutches, acted like schoolboys," wrote Beecher of
the Connecticut First Light Battery, "shouting, singing, throwing their hats in the air and yelling at the top of their voices."
Eddie Watehall watched as "some women and boys stood on
the corner and waved little Union flags."

The spectacle of the incoming troops and the emotions
they evoked depended on the particular observer and where he

Experts at rapidly stretching pontoon or even trestle bridges, U.S. Army engineers had spanned the James River even as embers of the original destroyed structures glowed. *Library of Congress.*

or she happened to be, physically, during the morning. "Long lines of negro cavalry swept by the Exchange Hotel," wrote Sallie Brock,

> *brandishing their swords and uttering savage cheers, replied to by the shouts of those of their own color, who were trudging along under loads of plunder, laughing and exulting over the prizes they had secured from the wreck of the stores, rather than rejoicing at the more precious prize of freedom which had been won for them. On passed the colored troops, singing, "John Brown's body is mouldering in the grave," etc.*

Mary Fontaine, virtually paralyzed with fascination over the endless columns of the incoming army, wrote to her friend of the "fat horses" as they came

> *trotting up that heavy hill [Broad Street] dragging the cannon as tho. they were light carriages, the trappings were gay, and I commenced to realize the fearful odds against which our gallant little army had contended.*
>
> *Then the Cavalry thundered at a furious gallop. We haven't been used to that, you know, and it startled us; indeed I imagined that there never was such riding before, unless at Bull Run. Then*

the infantry came playing "The Girl I Left Behind Me," that dear old air that we heard our brave men so often play; then the negro troops playing "Dixie," and they certainly were the blackest creatures I ever saw. I am almost inclined to the belief that they are a direct importation from Africa.

Then our Richmond servants were completely crazed, they danced and shouted, men hugged each other, and women kissed and such a scene of confusion you have never seen. Imagine the streets crowded with these wild people, and troops by the thousands, some loaded with plunder from the burning stores, whole rolls of cloth, bags of corn, etc. chairs, one old woman was rolling a great sofa; dozens of bands trying to drown each other it seemed; gorgeously dressed officers galloping furiously about; men shouting and swearing as I never heard men do before. . . .

Pollard recorded similar observations:

Here were the garish Yankee troops sweeping up towards the Capitol Square, with music and wild cheers; everywhere, almost, the pandemonium of fire and pillage; and in the midst of all the wild agony, the fugitive distress of women and children rushing towards the open square for a breath of pure air, all that was now left them in heaven's great hollowness. And even that was not to be obtained there.

The air, even in the square of the Capitol, was almost choking; and one traversed it blinded by cinders and struggling for breath. Beneath the trees, on the sward, were piles of furniture, dragged from the ruins of burning homes; and on carpets, stretched on the slopes of the hill, were family groups, making all sorts of uncouth arrangements to protect their little ones, and to patch up, with broken tables and bureaus, some sort of home in the open air.

De Leon, who had watched columns of "blue-coats" as they first materialized over the crests east of Chimborazo Heights, soon heard "the clatter of cavalry, sabers drawn and at a trot; still cautiously feeling their way into the long-coveted stronghold." To him, the entry was

a solemn and gloomy march; little resembling the people's idea of triumphal entry into a captured city. The troops were quiet, showing little elation; their officers anxious and watchful ever; and dead silence reigned around them, broken only by the roar and hiss of flames, or the sharp explosion as they reached some magazine. Not a cheer broke the stillness; and even the wrangling, half-drunken bummers round the fires slunk sullenly away; while but few negroes showed their faces, and those ashen-black from indefinite fear; their great mouths gaping and white eyes rolling in curious dread that took away their faculty for noise.

As Nellie Grey saw the unfolding scene, there was little demonstration except by the "negroes," who "falling on their knees before the invaders hail them as their deliverers, embracing the knees of the horses, and almost preventing the troops from moving forward."

The Federal cavalrymen were "well mounted, well accoutered, well fed," by the marveling assessment of Phoebe Pember. "Company after company, regiment after regiment, battalion after battalion, and brigade after brigade, they poured into the doomed city—an endless stream."

For at least one cavalryman, the moment was epochal. Charles Francis Adams, Jr., was a descendant of two U.S. presidents, both staunch opponents of the slave system. As a colonel with the Fifth Massachusetts Cavalry, Adams led his black troopers into "burning Richmond at the moment of its capture—the one event which I should most have desired as the culmination of my life in the Army."

Some of the soldiers already had stacked arms in Capitol Square, according to John Leyburn, but many more still were pounding into the city, as Matron Pember had herself witnessed. Leyburn added:

Here and there a man waved his hat and huzzaed. The most marked demonstrations were the shaking of hands by those nearest with the passing troops. . . . Some of the women courtesied and bowed at a great rate. . . . No sooner had the [black] cavalry fairly comprehended by whom they were surrounded then they returned the greeting with a will, rising in their stirrups, waving their flashing sabres, their white eyes and teeth gleaming from rows of dark visages, and rending the air with wild huzzas.

Those with the Thirteenth New Hampshire attested to the same welcome, punctuated by shouts: "The Yankees! the Yankees! God bless de Yankees! We's free . . . we's free! Bless de Lord. . . !"

The sight of even one cavalryman could inspire acute emotions, often contrasting.

"I can never forget the man's appearance," wrote Emmie Crump,

> and the thrill of horror that went through me; his blue jacket with the yellow stripes down the back is vivid in my mind's eye today. . . . We went into the house, locked all the doors, shut the front shutters and felt as if we were in a state of siege.

The Federals "swarmed in every highway and byway," according to Phoebe Pember, "rose out of gullies, appeared on the top of hills, emerged from narrow lanes, and skirted around low fences." There was scarcely "a spot" in the whole city "not occupied by a blue coat," she concluded.

On and on they marched and rode in. Even by midmorning, according to Jones, the war clerk, the streets "filled with *negro* troops, cavalry and infantry . . . and were cheered by hundreds of negroes at the corners."

Their heavy boots and well-shod horses' hooves alike crunched over the broken glass—"pulverized," as Jones seconded others' description—and assorted flotsam, the random cerements of a dying city, nearly defunct government and a way of life on its way to extinction. Among the litter was the morning's edition of the *Richmond Whig*, a number of issues of which had somehow come off the presses before Sunday's rioting. From its torn and soiled pages, kicked and trampled on the streets and into the gutters, plaintively philosophized the editorial:

> One has only to read the records of battle and campaigns in which the Bible abounds to see how frequently, how generally indeed the weaker party in numbers and materiel of war came out victorious.

With no time to peruse editorials, or any other part of Monday's very final edition, the president of the city council, David Saunders, hurried past the incoming soldiers to City Hall. Taking out his minutes book, he meticulously noted: "The City was on this day occupied by the United States forces, and the Council did not, therefore, meet." Federal officers watched impassively his devotion to routine.

THE FIELD OF OPERATIONS IN VIRGINIA.

Judge Meredith, for one, had no thought of council, or other, meetings:

> As soon as I had breakfasted I returned to the fire, and found the engine on Ninth Street between Main and Cary. I remained there but a short time as we were forced to move by the advance of the fire and the explosion of shells which had been stored by the Confederate authorities in a building nearby. This was between 10 and 11 o'clock I think.
>
> I then repaired to the Capitol Square, the lower side of which was covered with furniture removed for safety from the adjoining

buildings. I soon saw that the State Court was in danger, the fire having progressed to the corner of Twelfth and Franklin Streets. The portico of the State court house soon caught on fire and I then united with the clerk and such other persons as I could induce to aid us in removing many of the papers, and depositing them in the auditor's office.

He encountered "Mr. H. Exall" in the southern portico of the Capitol "and learned from him that one of the windows" in that structure was ablaze. "Near the same time the railing around the steeple of St. Paul's Church caught on fire."

Dr. Davidson went "up to the upper part of my house and looked out" to witness

a column of smoke rising perpendicularly. For some time it seemed to stand perfectly still and straight, without moving, except upwards.

In a little while it commenced to bend towards Main Street. Very soon I could feel the wind blowing—the morning had been very still before—and the smoke was drawn toward my house and over the city by the wind.

He then witnessed the collapse of the roof of the Gallego Mill which sent showers of "fire, that is coal and shingles, chunks of burning brands, to Main Street and beyond onto the tops of houses. . . ."

Combating this searing storm were Ripley's regiments,

distributed . . . in various sections . . . into this sea of fire with no less courage and self-devotion as though fighting for their own fireside and families, stripped and plunged the brave men of the First Brigade.

None of the usual fire-fighting machinery was at hand. The retreating army of Ewell had cut the hose; the Richmond firemen were unequal to the task, so the First Brigade had to depend upon blowing up and pulling down buildings in the pathway of the flames to check them. Happily the wind blew down the river and carried the flames and cinders in a straight line through the business and away from the residence section. . . .

The Confederacy, like a wounded wolf, died gnawing at its own body in insensate passion and fury.

11:00 A.M.

Ripley's men kept rounding up "thousands of Confederate stragglers and pillagers and clapped them in Libby and Castle Thunder, giving them a taste of their own prisons." But there wasn't much fight left in these "wolves."

In hospitals and in private houses, according to Lieutenant Prescott, "we find about 5,000 sick and wounded," abandoned by the enemy "in his haste."

Jones, by 11 A.M., having bought a bushel of potatoes for seventy-five dollars and watched, like a man in a dream, as "a battery (United States) passed my house on Clay Street," asked

> one of the command if guards would be placed in this part of the city to prevent disturbance, etc. He paused, with his suite, and answered that such was the intention, and that every precaution would be used to preserve order. He said the only disturbances were caused by our people. I asked if there was any disturbance. He pointed to the black columns of smoke rising from the eastern part of the city, and referred to the incessant bursting of shell.
>
> I remarked that the storehouses had doubtless been ignited hours previously. To this he assented, and assuring me that they did not intend to disturb us, rode on. But immediately meeting two negro women laden with plunder, they wheeled them to the right about, and marched them off, to the manifest chagrin of the newly emancipated citizens.

Shortly after eleven o'clock Petersburg had a visitor— President Lincoln. At the invitation of Grant, he had left City Point about 8 A.M. by special train with his two most distinguished admirals, David G. "Davy" Farragut and David D. Porter, also Lincoln's son Tad. At Meade Station, en route, soldiers caught sight of a familiar bearded face and stovepipe hat at the car window. They cheered "most heartily," according to the *Boston Journal* correspondent Charles Carleton Coffin, who added:

> He acknowledged the enthusiasm and devotion of the soldiers by bowing and thanking them for the glorious achievement

of their arms. On Friday he looked careworn, but the great victory had smoothed the deep wrinkles on his brow.

Coffin, however, was going the other way—towards City Point to catch a boat for Richmond.

About a mile east of Petersburg, at Patrick Station, the President left his train and continued in an ambulance, the most comfortable conveyance available. He was welcomed at the now empty residence of Thomas Wallace on Market Street by General Grant and also General Meade. Grant, Coffin had observed before his own departure, was "cool, calm, and evidently well pleased with the aspect of affairs."

The commanding general, nevertheless, was not certain that his troops were actually in Richmond, since the telegraph lines stopped three miles short of the city and cavalry couriers had to carry dispatches the intervening distances. Not having received Weitzel's dispatch, Grant hurried off two messages: "I do not doubt that you will march into Richmond unopposed. Take possession of the city and establish guards, and preserve order until I get there. . . ." This was followed by "How are you progressing? Will the enemy try to hold Richmond? . . . I am waiting to hear from you. . . ."

What Lincoln saw in Petersburg was in likelihood much the same as observed by the correspondent for the *Cincinnati Gazette*, Whitelaw Reid, who signed himself "Agate." He would send to his paper:

> *In my peregrinations I went by some of the markets. They were empty markets for nothing was there for sale—no meat, no vegetables, nor anything else. . . . Food was so scarce that the poor went out to our camp to pick up the rations of beef and lard lying about there and many carried off the blankets they found lying in the log huts. There was a total lack of business to be seen in the city, and the writer only wondered that the people managed to live. All wore a sallow look of half want.*

Yet another correspondent paused "along the Boydtown road" on the outskirts of Petersburg to notice a dead Confederate:

> *The dark, swarthy countenance almost led one to believe, until he touched his cold and pulseless hand, that life still lingered in his emaciated, half-clad body. He lay in a ditch or*

gully along the highway, with the water from a pure, perennial spring trickling musically beneath him; his blanket was neatly rolled and slung across his shoulder; his head was resting upon his arm as if in repose, but the death-glaze upon his eyes told that he slept the sleep that knows no waking.

In Petersburg the reporter saw closed doors and shuttered windows, while

> *the eastern portion of the town exhibits on every side marks of the solid shot and shell thrown by our guns during last summer. The buildings in Bolingbroke street, which run nearly east and west, are literally perforated in every part. Chimneys have been razed on every building, windows knocked and splintered to pieces, brick walls crumbled and torn, porches carried away—ruin and desolation reign supreme. Almost every house is deserted in this street, but in the center and other portions of the city but little damage seems to have been done by our fire.*

Cadwallader, the *Herald* correspondent, had accomplished the seemingly impossible—a round trip of two hours by horseback to City Point in order to send his dispatches on "the 10 o'clock mailboat for Fortress [Fort] Monroe." He was back before eleven "in the public square of Petersburg," where he found Lincoln, Grant, the admirals and General Meade sitting on the Court House steps. The Court building was a ten-minute walk east of the Wallace house on Market Street.

Cadwallader, however, was attached to Grant's headquarters, and he was now only marking time to be off with the general again.

Sara Pryor, meanwhile, was experiencing difficulties with a Union soldier, trying to feed him in her "basement kitchen." When he "set his bayonet" and appeared to be coming after her, she bolted him inside and raced into the street where she enlisted the aid of a young cavalry officer. Dismounting, he followed her to the kitchen, unbolted the door, then Sara ". . . had the satisfaction of seeing him lay about with the flat of his sword to good purpose." The officer "placed a guard around the house."

Shortly, General Pryor returned, after having been paroled—for the second time—"until exchanged" by the President himself. The proud Confederate officer had declined Lincoln's invitation for a "conference," explaining that Lee was

"We sat all day in the front room, watching the splendidly equipped host as it marched by . . . on its way to capture Lee." So wrote Sara Pryor. This dramatic Brady photograph shows Grant's seemingly endless supply train crunching through the mud and ruts of Petersburg, the "Cockade City," continuing on to Amelia Court House. Evidence of the heavy downpour which impeded the Union advance on Five Forks lies in the fields and on the road. Cavalry are at top of hill. *Library of Congress.*

"still in the field," and, as a "paroled prisoner," he had no authority to deal with "the head of the opposing army." As a matter of fact, Sara and the general were old friends of Admiral Porter.

So, for the moment, the Pryors "sat . . . in the front room, watching the splendidly equipped host" as they "passed continually," and "our hearts sank within us."

Noon

Headquarters Military Governor of Richmond
Richmond, Va., April 3, 1865.
I. The armies of the rebellion having abandoned their effort to enslave the people of Virginia, have endeavored to destroy by fire the capital which they could not longer occupy by their arms. Lieutenant-Colonel Manning, provost marshal general of the Army of the James and provost-marshal of Richmond, will immediately send a sufficient detachment of the provost-guard to arrest, if possible, the progress of the flames. The fire department of

the city of Richmond, and all the citizens interested in the preservation of their beautiful city, will immediately report to him for duty, and render every possible assistance in staying the progress of the conflagration. The first duty of the Armies of the Union will be to save the city doomed to destruction by the armies of the rebellion.

II. No person will leave the city of Richmond, without a pass from the office of the provost-marshal.

III. Any citizen, soldier, or any person whatever, who shall hereafter plunder, destroy, or remove any public or private property of any description whatever, will be arrested and summarily punished.

IV. The soldiers of the command will abstain from any offensive or insulting words or gestures towards the citizens.

V. No treasonable or offensive expressions, insulting to the flag, the cause, or the Armies of the Union, will hereafter be allowed.

VI. For an exposition of their rights, duties, and privileges, the citizens of Richmond are respectfully referred to the proclamations of the President of the United States in relation to the existing rebellion.

VII. All persons having in their possession, or under their control, any property whatever of the so-called Confederate States, or of any officer thereof, or the records or archives of any public officer whatever, will immediately report the same to Colonel Manning, provost marshal.

In conclusion, the citizens of Richmond are assured that, with the restoration of the flag of the Union, they may expect the restoration of that peace, prosperity, and happiness which they enjoyed under the Union, of which that flag is the glorious symbol.

G. F. Shepley, Brigadier General U.S.V., [Volunteers] and Military Governor of Richmond

The fires still burned, individually and collectively. To expedite their control and reduce duplication of effort, Weitzel sent all Union troops out of the city except the First Brigade, which totalled 300 officers and 4,200 men. Far too many soldiers in blue to be effectively managed were wandering like sightseers around the half-ruined city. Unit by unit, the mostly aimless extra soldiers began marching out to the old inner line of defenses.

Unchecked, the flames had flowed with the imponderable quality of lava out from the business district and were threatening private homes, including that of General Lee on Franklin Street. There his wife persisted in failing health.

To Dr. Davidson, it appeared that all of the mills were on fire. When the roof of one fell in,

> some of the coals were driven through the open dormer windows of my house, and my house caught on fire. I think it was about the first house that caught fire on that square.
>
> We put the fire out, and then I got on top of my house and fought the fire—that is to say, put out the coals and shingles with buckets of water as they fell on top of my house. A great many persons were engaged in this way on the houses on that street. As the fire increased the shower of coals also increased.
>
> After awhile I could not longer stand upon my house and had to give it up. Other houses on the street caught from the top about the same time . . . the wind was then blowing very strong. My house was consumed.
>
> Was or [was] not the wind strong enough from the first time you saw the fire after breakfast to carry the fire over the city by its own force?
>
> Certainly it was, for it actually did carry the fire over the city. The wind grew stronger until . . . a large portion of the city had burned. A great many persons carried their furniture to Capitol Square, where they had to protect it from the falling coals blown by the wind. A good deal of this furniture which was not properly protected was burnt up. . . . [There were] a good many persons on the square whose clothes were on fire, caused by coals dropping on their backs.

Jones found "the grass of Capitol Square . . . covered with parcels of goods snatched from the raging conflagration, and each parcel guarded by a Federal soldier.

> A general officer rode up and asked me what building that was—pointing to the old stone United States Custom House— late Treasury and State Departments, also the President's office. He said, "Then it is fire-proof, and the fire will be arrested in this direction." He said he was sorry to behold such destruction; and regretted that there was not an adequate supply of engines and other apparatus.

Shells are still bursting in the ashes of the armory, etc.

*All the stores are closed; most of the largest (in Main Street)
have been burned.*

Rumors abounded. A lawyer friend from the Eastern
Shore, "Mr. T. Cropper," told Jones that St. Paul's was on fire,
and that he himself had just been "burnt out." Jones, usually
the last to learn important or even verified news, quickly discovered that St. Paul's was intact although the Second Presbyterian was "in ruins," and by early afternoon "the leaping
and lapping flames were roaring in Main Street up to Ninth;
and Goddin's Building (late General Post Office) was on fire, as
well as all the houses in Governor Street up to Franklin."
Would it never stop? wondered Emmie Crump:

*All day long the fire raged, till finally the old Court House in
the Square caught and we watched it burn with increasing anxiety.*

*Our house caught fire several times on the roof, but with the
aid of an old gentleman neighbor and the servants, was controlled
and did little damage. It added, however, to the strain of anxiety
and excitement we endured that memorable day. We tied all the
clothes and valuables we could in blankets and sheets, ready to
move if necessary. The authorities did all they could to extinguish
the fire, but not only much property, but many valuable papers
were destroyed.*

*One company of soldiers stopped just at our gate and had all
sorts of things they had rescued from the fire on their way
through it. . . . [She saw] a barrel of sugar, hams, dry goods,
shoes, etc. Many of the negroes would beg from them and generally received something.*

*Uncle Simon, our butler, was on very good terms with them
and would steal up and pull a ham or a pair of shoes through the
railings while they were not looking. We young people, in spite of
our grief, were amused at many things which occurred. . . .*

The fire kept "creeping steadily nearer" to Mary Fontaine's
house as those next door "caught, and we prepared to leave."
Neighbors likened this Monday to "judgment day," while "the
heavens were black as with a thunder cloud, great pieces of
shells flying about. . . . Oh, it was too awful to remember!"
Fannie Walker, her belongings tied up in preparation for a

sudden departure, helped bucket parties on the roof by drenching blankets with water. This expedient saved her residence, as it had others.

The only thing that spared Arlington House, where Nellie Grey was staying with her mother, "was an open space between us and the nearest house which had been on fire. Even so, wet blankets were spread over the roof and hung at the windows. At one time, however," remembered Nellie, "cinders and smoke had blown into my room till the air was stifling and the danger great."

"By one o'clock," wrote Sallie Brock,

> confusion reached its height. . . . The wind had risen from the south, and seemed likely to carry the surging flames all over the northwestern portion of the city.
>
> The Capitol Square now presented a novel appearance. On the south, east, and west of its lower half, it was bounded by burning buildings. The flames bursting from the windows, and rising from the roofs, were proclaiming in one wild roar their work of destruction. Myriads of sparks, borne upward by the current of hot air, were brightening and breaking in the dense smoke above.
>
> On the sward of the Square, fresh with the emerald green of early spring, thousands of wretched creatures, who had been driven from their dwellings by the devouring flames, were congregated. Fathers and mothers, and weeping, frightened children sought this open space for a breath of fresh air. But here, even, it was almost as hot as a furnace. Intermingled with these miserable beings were the Federal troops in their garish uniform, representing almost every nation on the continent of Europe, and thousands of the Corps d'Afrique.
>
> All along on the north side of the Square were tethered the horses of the Federal cavalry, while, dotted about, were seen the white tents of the sutlers, in which there were temptingly displayed canned fruits and meats, crackers, cheese, etc.
>
> The roaring, crackling and hissing of the flames, the bursting of shells at the Confederate Arsenal, the sounds of instruments of martial music, the neighing of the horses, the shoutings of the multitude, in which could be distinctly distinguished the coarse, wild voices of the negroes, gave an idea of all the horrors of Pandemonium. Above all this scene of terror, hung a black

shroud of smoke through which the sun shone with a lurid angry glare like an immense ball of blood that emitted sullen rays of light, as if loth to shine over a scene so appalling.

Remembering the unhappy fate of the citizens of Columbia and other cities of the South, and momentarily expecting pillage, and other evils incidental to the sacking of a city, great numbers of ladies sought the proper military authorities and were furnished with safeguards for the protection of themselves and their homes. These were willingly and generously furnished.

At the same time, Sallie expressed "grateful thanks to General Weitzel," to be seconded by De Leon, among others, who believed that "old, dry and crammed . . . cotton" was largely fueling the warehouse flames. Describing the "dense pall of smoke" hanging over the chimney pots of the city, as noted by other inhabitants, De Leon wrote:

Through it shone huge eddies of flames and sparks, carrying great blazing planks and rafters whirling over the shriveling buildings. Little by little these drew closer together; one vast, livid flame roared and screamed before the wind, from Tenth Street to Rocketts; licking its red tongue around all in its reach and drawing the hope—the very life of thousands into its relentless maw!

Should the wind shift, that rapidly-gaining fire would sweep uptown and devour the whole city; but, while the few men left looked on in dismayed apathy, deliverance came from the enemy. The regiments in Capitol Square stacked arms; were formed into fire-squads; and sped at once to points of danger. Down the deserted streets these marched; now hidden by eddying smoke—again showing like silhouettes, against the vivid glare behind them. Once at their points for work, the men went at it with a will; and—so strong was force of discipline—with no single attempt at plunder reported!

Military training never had better vindication than on that fearful day; for its bonds must have been strong indeed, to hold that army, suddenly in possession of a city so coveted—so defiant—so deadly, for four long years.

DeLeon watched the soldiers work "with good will," even to the extent of moving furniture out of houses in the path of flames which "could not be stayed," then placing a guard over the belongings.

> Richmond's best and tenderest-nurtured women moved among their household goods, hastily piled in the streets, selecting this or that sacred object, to carry it in their hands—where?
>
> Poor families, utterly beggared, sat wringing their hands amid the wreck of what was left, homeless and hopeless; while, here and there, the shattered remnant of a soldier was borne, on a stretcher in kindly, if hostile, hands, through clouds of smoke and mourning relatives to some safer point.
>
> Ever blacker and more dense floated the smoke-pall over the deserted city; ever louder and more near roared the hungry flames. And constantly, through all that dreadful day, the whoo! of shells from magazines, followed by the thud of explosion, cut the dull roar of the fire. For —whether through negligence or want of time—charged shells of all sizes had been left in the many ordnance stores when the torch was applied.
>
> These narrow brick chambers—now white hot and with a furnace-blast through them—swept the heaviest shells like cinders over the burning district. Rising high in air, with hissing fuses, they burst at many points, adding new terrors to the infernal scene; and some of them, borne far beyond the fire's limit, burst over the houses, tearing and igniting their dry roofs.
>
> Slowly the day, filled with its hideous sights and sounds, wore on. . . .

John Leyburn, in quest of some personal "valuable" papers, located on the fourth floor of a commercial building, entered a street-level store to find

> a colored man . . . filling a bag with shoes from the shelves, all the while talking to himself, and swearing he would have them. And have them he did for there was no longer any one there to dispute his right.
>
> Ascending to the tailor's shop, I found it deserted, and the rolls of cloth for which hundreds of dollars a yard had been asked [were] lying there waiting to be burned up.
>
> While getting together my papers the flames burst through the windows opposite, and came lashing halfway across the

street. There was no time to lose; and as I emerged from the front door, the heated atmosphere was already most stifling.

I cast a farewell look up Main Street. The Dispatch *and* Enquirer *newspaper offices were all in a blaze, the banks and the American Hotel were just catching, and from the doors and windows of some of the fashionable stores volumes of flame were bursting.*

Leyburn then evoked considerable amusement from "one of the Federals" when he volunteered that "unless they went to work to arrest the conflagration the entire city would be swept away." Then in the next block he was heartened by the sight of "crowds of blacks" organized by the troops as a "fire corps" to create fire blocks and assist with those steam engines that were functioning.

But, even so, Leyburn noted,

Well on in the afternoon flame and smoke and burning brands and showers of blazing sparks filled the air, spreading still further the destruction, until it had swept before it every bank, every auction store, every insurance office, nearly every commission house, and most of the fashionable stores, together with one of the fashionable churches . . . immense mills, manufacturies, foundries, etc. . . .

John Leyburn, however, was not the only citizen of Richmond on the prowl. Curiously, perhaps, many women kept themselves in almost uninterrupted motion throughout the fire-spawned confusion. Van Lew, for one, now a much-sought-after female, was very difficult to find "as she flew from place to place." Weitzel, who had been instructed from higher authority to place a guard around her mansion first off, would subsequently be joking that this turned out to be a "mobile guard."

Judith McGuire made two visits to City Hall to secure guards for her property. The first time she was advised, "Our troops are perfectly disciplined and dare not enter your premises." To this Judith snapped back: "I am sorry to be obliged to undeceive you, sir, but when I left home seven of your soldiers were in the yard of the residence opposite to us, and one has already been in the kitchen."

She won her case and returned with a guard. Shortly the latter became drunk "and threatened to shoot the servants in the yard." She started back to City Hall, wending through the flames and noting the destruction:

> The fire was progressing rapidly, and the crashing sound of falling timbers was distinctly heard. Dr. Read's church was blazing. Yankees, citizens, and negroes were attempting to arrest the flames. The War Department was falling in; burning papers were being wafted about the streets. The Commissary Department, with our desks and papers, was consumed already. Warwick & Barksdale's mill was sending its flames to the sky. Cary and Main Streets seemed doomed throughout; Bank Street was beginning to burn, and now it had reached Franklin. At any other moment it would have distracted me, but I had ceased to feel anything.

Judith returned with another guard, who first carried off his predecessor "by the collar."

The indomitable Mrs. Sampson from Arlington House also took to the rubble-strewn streets to find General Weitzel, or some officer. Three Union men "fully armed" had entered the boarding house "to search . . . for rebels." Nellie Grey thought one "was very drunk. Anxious to get rid of him quickly I helped him in his search." She threw over her mattress and opened up closets and bureau drawers, while he kept protesting, "I'm good Secesh as you."

But downstairs, the other two men "tumbled their things about outrageously" until Mrs. Sampson clapped on her chicken-feather hat and declared she was going to report them to General Weitzel.

The Arlington was one-half of a double house with a veranda serving both halves. When a "regiment of Yankees . . . quartered themselves next door," the families in the boarding house had no further trouble with stragglers. The children were overjoyed to see the "Yankees" move in, certain they had plenty to eat and to share. Indeed, the blue-uniformed neighbors gave the half-starved youngsters all kinds of goodies, making them quite ill.

At about this time of the afternoon, Connie Cary and her cousin Edith also took their "courage in both hands" when their "Aunt M's condition became so much worse" due to all the excitement. They made their way to Capitol Square in search of a guard for the house. The girls were appalled at the scene before them:

> Looking down from the upper end of the square, we saw a huge wall of fire blocking out the horizon. . . . The War Department was sending up jets of flame. Along the middle of the streets smouldered a long pile, like street-sweepings, of papers torn from the different departments' archives . . . from which soldiers in blue were picking out letters and documents that caught their fancy.

Connie and Edith believed that only the Customs House remained of the buildings "environing the square." The green lawn sweeping down from the Capitol enclosure was "scorched out or trampled down by the hoofs of cavalry horses picketed at intervals about it."

The homes of many friends around the same square were burned. "Luckily the Lee house and that side of Franklin stand uninjured. General Lee's house has a guard camped in the front yard."

The girls were treated with "perfect courtesy and consideration" at the headquarters of "the Yankee General in charge of Richmond." A young lieutenant escorted them home through the confusion, and a guard was immediately placed there.

Connie retreated at once to her garret room, with no wish to venture forth again into the town which she thought already "wore the aspect of one in the Middle Ages smitten by pestilence. The streets, filled with smoke and flying fire, were empty of the respectable class of inhabitants, the doors and shutters of every house tight closed."

Connie spent the afternoon sewing her mother's securities into the trimming of a skirt. They had been entrusted to her the day before by the president of the family's bank which had disappeared "in the track of the awful Main Street fire."

So "here I am," Connie wrote her mother, "with the family fortune stitched into my frock, which I have determined to wear every day with a change of white bodices, till I see you or can get to some place where it is safe to take it off. . . ."

The manuscript of Connie's first—and only—book had, however, "gone up in flames and smoke" along with Messrs.

West and Johnson, publishers. She consoled herself that it was probably no great loss to posterity.

During this time, Emma Mordecai and Rosina's daughter, Augusta ("little A."), started for Richmond "in a covered cart drawn by a mule and driven by George (a negro boy)." The purpose was to place Augusta in the home of "some friends," to deposit a trunk containing "valuable clothing," mostly Augusta's and her mother's, with other acquaintances, to secure "a box of very valuable plate at the bank," and to pick up a barrel of flour "at Mr. Gordon's store."

If all went as planned, Emma would return with the plate later in the evening.

> . . . as we proceeded along the military road we met soldiers, generally in couples, hurrying away, loaded with whatever they possessed. Some spoke to us, asked if we were going to Richmond, and said, 'You are going to a bad place!'
>
> I asked of all we met whether the enemy had yet entered—they were expected. When we got to Camp Lee [the old Fair Grounds] the white tents lately occupied by our returned prisoners were silent and forsaken.
>
> Two youths, bending under the weight of some tobacco they had found there, were the only living creatures we saw. We stopped at a house a little further on to make inquiry of some women we saw talking to a returned soldier, whose home it was.

Only then did Emma learn that Richmond had been occupied since early morning, "that they had come in 'very quietly.'" Now she understood the meaning of the "smoke and even flames" she had been noticing all the way in, as well as the "incessant reports of cannon or bursting shells."

"I knew tobacco, etc., had to be burned, and all the works destroyed, so this did not astonish or unnerve me." But on the other hand "A. felt terrified, and was crazy to get back home.

> These persons told us that they had been in the city that morning, that they did not think that George would be troubled if he went on with the cart; that he could load the cart with flour and meat that was thrown open to the people, and as there was a possibility of his getting Mr. W. to get the silver, I decided to leave the baggage with these people, who seemed very kind, and

*promised to take good care of it, to let George proceed, as he was
very anxious to do, and Augusta and I would walk back home.*

*So these kind people, whose name was Turk, and who knew
this family . . . carried the things into the house, and we all
separated, A. and I walking rapidly homeward—fire and smoke
behind us, while the incessant roar of one explosion after another,
or of many together, were multiplied by the repeated reverbera-
tions from hill to hill in terrible grandeur. I don't think we saw a
living creature about the road except now and then a crow
lighting to feed, and the little birds that find in this troubled
world of ours an untroubled world of their own. We had met a
young negro woman shortly after we left Turk's, hurrying into
the town. She said, without slacking her pace, "Missis, you going
away from dem nasty Yankees?"*

"We are going home," I said. "Where are you going?"

She indicated she was off in search of her "young Mistie,"
who Emma assumed was her daughter. . . . "I'll risk my life to
get her."

Emma at last reached home, and Augusta "rejoiced to get
back to her mother, whom she had left most reluctantly. . . .
The day seemed never-ending. . . ."

"All day long . . . the brave men of the Northern army
battled with desperate courage and splendid self-sacrifice to
save the apparently doomed capital . . .," reported Colonel
Ripley. But he had additional challenges: the restless women.

"My office," he continued,

*was besieged and taken possession of by crowds of terror-
stricken ladies whose minds had been filled with the wicked and
outrageous calumnies heaped upon the Northern troops by the
Richmond papers and who expected that the regime initiated by
their own people was but the prelude to the reign of terror which
the "Yankee monsters" would inaugurate when settled in the
possession of the city.*

*Old ladies came and threw themselves on my neck in
paroxysms of terror and implored me to save them; others clung
to my arms until they had extracted a personal pledge from me;
others threw themselves on the floor and grasped my knees until I
would promise them a soldier safeguard in their own house. One
lady, deeply veiled, came in great excitement, and leaning on my*

shoulder whispered in my ear, "I am the daughter of General Keim of Pennsylvania and I appeal to you as a Northern woman for protection."

Ripley replied that a woman from the North did not "need to make such an appeal," but provided her with a guard anyhow. Another, claiming to be recently widowed by the fighting before Petersburg, asserted she was left with many small children, they had nothing but bean soup for subsistence, and that they had been compelled to burn up the staircase banisters for fuel.

The colonel turned her over to the Sanitary Commission and, in addition, supplied her with rations from his own officers' mess. And so on. If he did not in each case provide a personal sentry, he worked out a system where one was centrally posted to guard several houses where women were alone, and whose safety was not wholly assured.

This sort of solicitude caused the French Consul, Alfred Paul, to observe that by afternoon

> *the inhabitants were fraternizing with them [the Federals] without fear, without exaggeration of any kind, but very sincerely, especially when it was understood that there was nothing to fear.*
>
> *Moreover, there was a strong bitterness against the Confederate authorities who, in spite of all promises, persisted in destroying the properties and the principal city of a people who had bent every effort in their behalf.*

He, too, was furnished guards for his consulate, and also for what tobacco, earmarked for the Regie Imperiale, had managed to survive the immolation of the warehouses.

Ladies who did not care to fraternize or did not solicit special protection stayed home or scurried in partial mufti behind "veiled faces," according to Phoebe Pember. Her own Chimborazo was "attended to," although rations or fresh medical supplies were slow in arriving. For the moment, anyhow, the large hospital complex would remain open.

Phoebe proved equal to a sudden, emboldened assault of "hospital rats," malingerers she never had "been able to get rid of." When they tried to rush the matron to make off with Chimborazo's whiskey stores, she produced her "friend," a large revolver, and informed the "rats" that "even a woman" at close range could not likely "miss six times."

Clerk Jones, in midafternoon, was informed by a Federal officer "that a white brigade will picket the city tonight; and he assured the ladies standing near that there would not be a particle of danger of molestation." He added that

> we had done ourselves great injury by the fire, the lower part of the city being in ashes, and declared that the United States troops had no hand in it. I acquitted them of the deed, and told him that the fire had spread from the tobacco warehouses and military depots, fired by our troops as a military necessity.

Whitelaw Reid, from the *Cincinnati Gazette*, arrived in the city at about that time, traveling from Petersburg by ambulance. Signing in at the Spotswood as "Agate," he wrote:

> Somewhat to my astonishment, I confess, the rebel landlord stood in the office. "I want a private parlor and bedroom attached."
> "Certainly, will be delighted to accommodate you."
> I had the pleasure of registering my name below a swarm of rebel officers—the first arrival direct from Washington or the North. A negro waiter seized the baggage and seemed to me a trifle more attentive than eyes of mine ever beheld negro before.
> The rooms were as good as the Continental or Fifth Avenue would have given—except that the furniture, carpets and curtains were all at least four years old. . . . On the whole the Spotswood seemed to be a very fair house.

Other Northern reporters came, breathless, into Richmond within minutes of one another. Coffin, of the *Boston Journal*, had opted to continue from City Point by horse instead of by boat—or ambulance. He nearly broke his neck en route when the animal stumbled:

> I tried to pass through Main Street but on both sides the fire was roaring and walls were tumbling. I turned into a side street, rode up to the Capitol, and then to the Spotswood Hotel. Dr. Reed's church in front was in flames. On the three sides of the hotel the fire had been raging, but was now subdued, and there was a fair prospect that it would be saved.

"Can you accommodate me with a room?"

"I reckon we can, sir, but like enough you will be burnt out before morning. You can have any room you choose. Nobody here."

Charles Coffin was dirty, bone weary. He was not pampered by any "city room on wheels," used for their war correspondents by the *New York Times* and the *New York Herald*. These were wagons equipped with many comforts for living in the field including cots, soap, some food and wardrobes. The Spotswood, with real beds and linen, was to Coffin an unfamiliar and unexpected oasis of luxury. But with no time yet to enjoy his suite's niceties, Coffin threw up the window sash and "looked out upon the scene." He saw

> *. . . swaying chimneys, tottering walls, streets impassable from piles of brick, stones and rubbish. Capitol Square was filled with furniture, beds, clothing, crockery, chairs, tables, looking glasses.*
>
> *"Women were weeping, children crying. Men stood speechless, haggard, woebegone, gazing at the desolation.*

He would recall that in Charleston

> *the streets echoed only to the sound of my own footsteps or the snarling of hungry curs. There I walked through weeds, and trod upon flowers in the grassy streets; but in Richmond I waded through Confederate promises to pay, public documents and broken furniture and crockery. Granite columns, iron pillars, marble facades, broken into thousands of pieces, blocked the streets. . . .*

(Coffin's fertile imagination had sprouted weeds, grass, and flowers in the streets of a city—Charleston—which had fallen only in mid-February!)

The *New York Tribune* correspondent, freshly arrived, reported much the same about Richmond:

> *Private and public papers and documents are scattered over the street, subject to the winds and the rapacity of the piccaninnies who in innumerable swarms—in danger of falling walls— were diving with their little black hands into every place that suggested a reward for their plunder.*

A panoramic view of the Richmond waterfront with the Capitol in the background showing the vast extent of the ruins left from the fire set by the retreating Confederates and extinguished finally by Union troops. Many church spires were left standing, including that of St. Paul's. *Library of Congress.*

But even in the midst of smouldering embers and the debris-strewn streets there were already whispers that the arteries of a stricken city would be pumping life again: for example, the railroads. Not all the trains had chugged off to Danville, Petersburg or even to Fredericksburg.

"A large force," wrote the correspondent for the *Cincinnati Commercial*, "including 400–500 negroes have been to work on the railroad to Petersburg which will be running in a short time. Abundance of cars and engines were found here, unharmed, and we shall make good use of them as soon as possible."

Federal transportation officers, stumbling about the litter of the yards, counted as many as twenty-eight available locomotives, if in various states of disrepair, forty-four passenger/baggage cars and more than one hundred freight cars.

In Petersburg they were also at work on the tracks, refurbishing "the old line . . . from Petersburg to City Point," augmenting the military tracks along much of the same right-of-way. According to Surgeon Liddell, by afternoon the trains were about ready to roll, also towards Richmond.

At City Point, Lincoln, back aboard the comfortable *U.S.S.
Malvern*, Admiral Porter's flagship, dictated a telegram to Secretary Stanton, who had been concerned for the President's
safety:

> *Thanks for your caution; but I have already been to
> Petersburg, staid there with Gen. Grant an hour and a half, and
> returned here. It is certain now that Richmond is in our hands,
> and I think I will go there tomorrow. I will take care of myself.*

In Petersburg, as the shadows of late afternoon grew long
over its quiet shuttered homes and stores, the crack of saluting
rifles suddenly echoed from the yard of Grace Episcopal
Church. The drama in low key within a far greater one had
commenced a few hours earlier when Mary Morrison, who
had "said goodbye at midnight" to the last Confederates, discovered a Southern soldier propped "stiff and stark," against
the wall of the Second Presbyterian Church, blanket rolled
across his chest—forgotten in death by his swiftly retreating
comrades.

Mary Morrison, with the aid of the Reverend Churchill
Gibson, minister of Grace Church and recently a neighbor of
Sara Pryor, several elderly parishioners and a few faithful servants, dug a shallow grave. The pastor was just starting to read
from the Book of Common Prayer when interrupted by the
tramp-tramp of a company of Federal infantry, swinging past.

There snapped the bristling command, "Company, halt!"
The captain, who had become aware of what was happening,
ordered an honor guard into the church grounds, while the
bulk of his unit stood at parade rest. In moments, muskets
firing skyward spoke their singular requiem for a fallen foe: full
military honors.

As the captain led his company away at double time—
following military tradition after a burial—he was heard to say,
according to Mary Morrison, but to none in particular:

"My God! This brings war home to a man!"

6:00 P.M.

The fires, not out, were under control, even if the whole city
reeked of embers and masonry. A wind shift followed by
abatement had to share honors with the incessant efforts of the

Federal troops, using to great advantage the expedient of tearing down structures to create fire blocks or "dead zones."

Now General Weitzel, understandably, was "desirous to obtain lodging and food." He would write:

> Upon inquiry I found that Major Graves, in the course of his reconnaissance, had found the Davis mansion, and that the housekeeper, under instructions from Mr. Jefferson Davis, had surrendered it for the occupancy of the commanding officer of the Federal troops which might occupy the city.
>
> In addition to the housekeeper a few servants remained. The supplies in the larder were very scant, but everything else in the house was in good order and furnished elegant quarters for my staff and me.

None was in agreement exactly when the fires were extinguished. Weitzel would attest only that they were "subdued" by "2 P.M." Campbell, vaguer yet, noted that "the conflagration continued till the afternoon." Ripley would report officially that the fires burned "into the night."

De Leon, in flowery generalities, observed that "the fire was, at last, kept within its own bounds" sometime after the day "wore on," as he continued that it was then "gradually forced backward, to leave a charred, steaming belt between it and the unharmed town." But at the same time, "within this, the flames still leaped and writhed and wrangled in their devilish glee; but Richmond was now comparatively safe, and her wretched inhabitants might think of food and rest."

Though food was still very scarce and rest a need rather than a realized state, it was possible this evening to make an accounting of the damage. Pollard, who would soon be under temporary arrest as a leading secessionist editor, was an obvious one to take inventory. He wrote,

> It [the fire] had consumed the very heart of the city. A surveyor could scarcely have designated more exactly the business portion of the city, than did the boundaries of the fire. Commencing at the Shockoe warehouse, the fire radiated front and rear, and on two wings, burning down to, but not destroying, the store No. 77 Main-street, south side, half way between Fourteenth and Fifteenth Streets, and back to the river, through Cary and all the intermediate streets. Westward, on Main, the fire was stayed at Ninth-street, sweeping back to the river. On the north side of

*Main the flames were stayed at Mitchell and Tyler's Jewelry Store
between Thirteenth and Fourteenth streets. From this point the
flames raged on the north side of Main up to Eighth-street, and
back to Bank-street.*

*Among some of the most prominent buildings destroyed
were the Bank of Richmond, Traders' Bank, Farmers' Bank, all
the banking houses, the American Hotel, the Columbian Hotel,
the Enquirer building on Twelfth-street, the Dispatch office and
job rooms, corner of Thirteenth and Main-streets; all that block of
buildings known as Belvin's Block; the Examiner office, engine,
and machinery rooms; the Confederate Post-office Department
building; the State Courthouse, a fine old building situated on
Capitol Square at its Franklin-street entrance; the Mechanics'
Institute, vacated by the Confederate War Department, and all
the buildings on that square up to Eighth-street and back to
Main-street; the Confederate arsenal and laboratory, Seventh-
street.*

*The streets were crowded with furniture, and every descrip-
tion of wares, dashed down to be trampled in the mud or burned
up where it lay. All the government storehouses were thrown
open, and what could not be gotten off by the Government was
left to the people.*

*Next to the river the destruction of property was fearfully
complete. The Danville and Petersburg Railroad depots, and the
buildings and shedding attached, for the distance of half a mile
from the north side of Main-street to the river, and between
Eighth and Fifteenth streets, embracing upwards of twenty
blocks, presented one waste of smoking ruins, blackened walls,
and solitary chimneys.*

Gallego, Shockoe, many of the mills, warehouses and
other business structures which were levelled had not long
been in existence. Their predecessors had been destroyed by a
major fire in 1848.

The *Whig*, reborn under strict Northern sponsorship,
added this to Pollard's account:

*The familiar aspect of and face of Main Street is changed so
completely that those best acquainted with the buildings cannot
point them out with certainty. The busy street of a few days ago is
a ghost of its former self, an amphitheater of crumbling walls and
tottering chimneys.*

The Customs House, late Confederate Treasury, passed

Ruins of the Arsenal yard with the skeleton of the Franklin Paper Mill looming in the background near the remains of a Richmond and Petersburg Railroad aqueduct. *Library of Congress.*

through the ordeal of fire unscathed, from the fact that the edifice is of granite and fireproof. The Bank of the Commonwealth presents a granite front, but is a mere shell as also is the Bank of Virginia. At one time during Monday morning the Spotswood Hotel was in great danger, the flames leaping towards its location with great rapidity; but a merciful Providence caused a lull in the breeze, and blew the flames out of their track.

A dozen drug stores went up in hot cinders. There was a consolation since most of their shelves were bare anyway and, as Sallie Brock wrote of one which had been "an extortionate vender of drugs":

This incident points a moral which all can apply. Riches take to themselves wings, and in a moment least expected elude our grasp. Many who shirked the conscription, who made unworthy use of exemption bills, for the purpose of heaping up and watching their ill-gotten treasures, saw them in a single hour reduced to ashes and made the sport of the winds of heaven. Truly man knoweth not what a day may bring forth.

The *Whig* account continued:

> *Old boundaries and landmarks are so entirely obliterated*
> *that it is with the greatest difficulty that the sites of particular*
> *stores can be pointed out, the debris of brick and granite and iron*
> *destroying any trace of the cross streets; they can be distinguished*
> *only by the openings in the ruins.*

Publishing was all but obliterated. In addition to West and Johnson, where Connie's manuscript perished in the ashes, were these other houses and presses: *The Southern Literary Messenger*, of Edgar Allen Poe fame and to which Connie Cary was a contributor; the *Illustrated News*, a slavish copy of its London namesake; the *Evening Courier*, the *Central Presbyterian*, *Southern Churchman*, and *Religious Herald*. Others were at least scorched.

As 9 P.M. curfew neared, ladies still hurried to the provost for "protection papers," since, as De Leon thought,

> *the deserted women of Richmond dreaded not only the pres-*
> *ence of the victorious enemy, but also that of the drunken and*
> *brutalized "bummers" and deserters who stayed behind. . . .*
> *By nightfall, the proud Capital of the Southern Confederacy*
> *was only a Federal barrack!*

Even with a guard, Fannie Walker shared turns with the household "watching . . . while others slept," and "we gradually adapted ourselves to the forlorn situation."

Few were wholly relaxed.

"When night came," wrote Emmie Crump,

> *it was cool and we had a wood fire in the large grate in our*
> *beautiful dining room, [and] had to burn candles as the fire had*
> *practically destroyed the gas works.*
> *At every sound we would start and listen and when the bell*
> *rang mother would open the door with a lighted candle in her*
> *hand and all of us watching behind her, trembling with fear. . . .*

Fannie and Emmie were among the fortunate who still had a roof over their heads, even a warm fireside.

"As night came on," noted Nellie Grey,

> *"many people were wandering about without shelter, amid*
> *blackened ruins. In the Square numbers huddled for the night*
> *under improvised shelter or without any protection at all. But*

profound quiet reigned—the quiet of desolation as well as of order. . . .

Outside the city, Emma Mordecai remained "in a state of indefinite terror . . . intolerably increased by every usual or unusual sight or sound. I told Cyrus if we got scared I should ring the bell, and he promised to come as soon as he heard it."

There was also some protection quite out of the ordinary. Mrs. Robert E. Lee, suffering from "a very serious disposition," peeked through the shutters of her Franklin Street home that evening to notice that the cavalry sentry posted in front of her picket fence was a black man! She reacted as though stricken.

When she recovered her composure, she sent a servant running to the provost, with the indignant message that the black presence was "perhaps an insult!"

Federal officers, as a matter of fact, had always been solic-itous of Mrs. Lee. During the Peninsular campaign McClellan's headquarters were for a time at the "White House," the old Custis estate on the Pamunkey River where Mrs. Lee had gone after leaving Arlington. Since she herself was in residence, McClellan pitched his own tent on the grounds rather than commandeer the mansion.

However, General Lee accepted the Union commander's offer to send his wife to Richmond. Mrs. Lee was seated in a carriage drawn by a mule ridden by a black boy. Federal cavalry escorted her to the Confederate lines, under a flag of truce.

Again, while harboring no sympathy for her bias, the Union forces acquiesced to Mrs. Lee's wishes. Believing there was "not much hope of her recovery," Ripley's provost removed the black guard and substituted a white man.

In the darkened city, meanwhile, reporters kept arriving. Lawley, for example, quit his northbound train before reaching Fredericksburg that afternoon, belatedly realizing that he may have "forfeited the chance to witness one of the most momentous events in history—the surrender of the Confederate forces."

At a way station, Lawley flagged down what was possibly the first Federal supply train swaying along the line from Fredericksburg to Richmond. Suspecting this pompous, high-domed individual with the odd accent to be a spy, an army guard squinted at his papers and shortly concluded that he was just another of those crazy war correspondents—the more odd yet as a foreigner.

His reception by American counterparts was no warmer. After all, had he not aided and abetted the Confederates all the war long? This was the Francis Lawley who had cheered the South on at Gettysburg, with almost sycophantic praise for Lee and Longstreet, conveying the alleged quote from a "Union prisoner" who supposedly remarked it was "no wonder we are thrashed upon every field" with such as Longstreet as adversaries.

The Northern press corps members turned their backs on the London *Times* representative in the Spotswood Hotel as he hastened arrangements for renting a horse, then was off "towards Lee's headquarters near Amelia Court House." In his pocket was a slip of paper, the best the U.S. garrison could do for him: a pass to the Confederate lines.

George Alfred Townsend arrived at about the same time, having cruised by "great hulks of vessels" in the James, the remnants of Semmes' scuttled fleet. The *New York World* correspondent, who usually signed himself "Gath," wrote:

> There is a stillness, in the midst of which Richmond, with her ruins, her spectral roof, afar, and her unchanging spires, rests beneath a ghastly, fitful glare—the night stain which a great conflagration leaves behind it for weeks. Struggling silently with colossal shadows along the foreground, two hideous walls alone arise in front, shutting these gleams. They are the Libby Prison and Castle Thunder. Right and left, and far in the moonlighted perspective beyond, there is a soft glitter upon cornices and domes.
>
> A haggard glow of candles faintly defines the thoroughfares that have not suffered ruin; while massive, and upon a height overlooking all, stands the Capitol, flying its black shadow from the sinking moon across a hundred crumbling walls, until its edges touch the windows of the Libby.
>
> We are under the shadow of ruins. From the pavements where we walk far off into the gradual curtain of the night, stretches a vista of desolation. The hundreds of fabrics, the millions of wealth, that crumbled less than a week ago beneath one fiery kiss, here topple and moulder into rest. A white smoke-wreath rising occasionally, enwraps a shattered wall as in a shroud. A gleam of flame shoots a grotesque picture of broken arches and ragged chimneys into the brain. Huge piles of debris begin to encumber the sidewalks, and even the pavements, as we

The churches, except for one, survived Richmond's firestorm, "her unchanging spires" still pointing skyward. *Library of Congress.*

The Capitol dominates this scene as viewed by the newly arrived Federal troops—"flying its black shadow from the sinking moon across a hundred crumbling walls . . ." as Townsend wrote. *Library of Congress.*

go on. The streets in some places are quite choked up from walking. We are among the ruins of half a city.

The wreck, the loneliness, seem interminable. The memory of lights in houses above, beheld while upon the steamer, alone keeps despondency from a victory over hope; and although the continued existence of the Spotswood Hotel is vouched for by authority, my lodge in such a wilderness seems next to impossible. Away to the right, above the waste of blackened walls, around the phantom-looking flag upon the capitol—the only sign betwixt heaven and earth, or upon the earth, that Richmond is not wholly deserted—beyond and out of the ruins, we walk past one or two open doorways where the moon serves as a candle to a group of negroes.

. . . there is no sound of life, but the stillness of a catacomb, only as our footsteps fall dull on the deserted sidewalk, and a funeral troop of echoes bump their elfin heads against the dead walls and closed shutters in reply, and this is Richmond. Says a melancholy voice: "And this is Richmond!"

But nonetheless a shot here and there, according to Captain Clinton of the Connecticut Light Battery: a die-hard Confederate, drunk, levelling his musket at a sentry from a darkened window; a momentary outcry as a curfew violator was ordered off the streets; or commotion briefly within a house whose owner had not extinguished at 10, P.M. such illumination as he possessed. Otherwise, Richmond this night was much the city of the dead as Townsend painted it. "Not a human being" did Ripley encounter on a late inspection through the darkened streets.

On every alternate corner stood the motionless form of a sentry; not a ray of light from a house gave hint of life within, except at a corner grocery, where light was detected through a crack in the shutters.

The sharp rap of an aide's sabre hilt on the door brought out a panic-stricken German grocer, who had been too frightened to go to bed, and who was sitting up with the few worldly goods he had left.

And again Ripley and his staff "passed up and down the streets, which echoed with the clatter of our horses' hoofs and the jingle of our sabres. . . ."

As midnight neared, Judith McGuire would pen, "Almost every house is guarded; and the streets are now perfectly quiet. The moon is shining brightly on our captivity.

"God guide and watch over us!"

Another woman of the city, Anna Deane, invoked the Deity with different emotions. She would write her sister, "I can't believe that God has deserted us, and given us over to our enemys. [sic] . . ."

So great had become the contrasting silence that Nellie Grey would postscript, "Our next door neighbors were so quiet with only a wall between we sometimes forgot their presence."

To John Leyburn, it was "as if that day would never end." And to Emma Mordecai, "the day seemed neverending," until at last "the noise from the city ceased . . . and the night was quiet.

"Thus ended Monday."

La Salle Pickett pronounced her own amen: "The Queen City of the South had fallen."

April 3, 1865, was about to be tolled into history, the day that Richmond—as the capital of the Confederate States of America—died.

Epilogue

Late Tuesday morning, President Lincoln arrived in Richmond, via Rocketts. He had gone as far as Admiral Porter's *Malvern* could steam into the shallows, then was rowed in a captain's gig the remaining distance. The visit was a profound embarrassment to General Weitzel, whose honor guard and ambulance-carriage arrived too late to escort the presidential party. Twelve sailors substituted for the soldiers.

No stranger to walking considerable distances, the tall man from Illinois made his way on foot to Capitol Square, "closely followed," according to Weitzel, "by a rabble mostly composed of negroes." There was bitter humor at one point when certain segments of the "rabble," obviously with impaired vision, thought Jefferson Davis was returning and cried, "Hang him!" Union sentries quickly hustled them off.

From Admiral Porter, her friend of prewar Washington days, Sara Pryor would recap some of the morning:

> The day was warm, and the streets dusty, "owing to the immense gathering of the crowd, kicking up the dirt." Mr. Lincoln took off his hat and fanned his face, from which the perspiration was pouring, and looked as if he would give his Presidency for a glass of water.

From Sara's pen pal, Agnes, another impression: "I had a good look at Mr. Lincoln. He seemed tired and old—and, I

President Lincoln arrived in Richmond on Tuesday, April 4, 1865, the day after Federal troops marched in. He was followed by curious crowds, "a rabble mostly composed of negroes," in the opinion of the commanding general. Many, according to Sallie Brock, pushed close "to press or kiss his hand." While the average resident, white or black, was awed by the significance of the occasion, one girl, Emmie Sublet, dismissed the whole affair as "a monkey show." The sketch of the President's visit to the former residence of Jefferson Davis was by an artist from *Leslie's Illustrated Newspaper*, a weekly. *U.S. Naval Historical Center.*

must say, with due respect to the President of the United States, I thought him the ugliest man I had ever seen. . . ."

According to Sallie Brock,

> *Hundreds of the colored population thronged about him, to get a look at him, to shake his hand, to hear the tones of his voice, or otherwise to testify their admiration or secure his notice. He made his way to the Capitol. On the Square a superb carriage was in readiness for him, in which he was conveyed through the principal streets of the city. In the carriage were seated his son, Admiral Porter, and Captain Bell, while in attendance was an escort of negro cavalry.*

All along his triumphal passage, sable multitudes of both sexes and every age gathered and pressed around the vehicle to press or kiss his hand, or to get a word or look from him. As the carriage rolled up the streets they ran after it in furious excitement, and made the welkin ring with the loud and continuous cheering peculiar to their race. Mr. Lincoln visited the late residence of Mr. Davis, and the principal places of interest in Richmond.

Far less impressed, or respectful, Emmie Sublet stamped the visit a "monkey show." She "peeped" at the presidential party through her parlor shutters, not wishing to reveal her curiosity.

Bolder, Nellie Grey's friend, Mrs. Sampson, still resplendent in her chicken-feather hat, paused to gape from the sidewalks, holding as far from her nose as possible—a codfish. The determined housekeeper had sallied forth to the commissary, expounding, "I'll take anything I can get out of the Yankees!" The dried but redolent cod was that "anything."

Lincoln evinced especial fascination with the Confederate White House, now headquarters for Weitzel, his tardy host, and "quite a small affair compared with the White House," according to Sara Pryor, alluding of course to the executive mansion in Washington. For once, the phrasemaker appeared at a loss for colorful speech as sitting before Jefferson Davis's desk, he observed blandly:

"This must have been President Davis's chair."

General Weitzel, who did not know the mansion much better than his Commander in Chief, nonetheless took his distinguished visitor on a tour, room by room. When they had finished, Judge Campbell was waiting in the parlor to see Lincoln.

"His manner," wrote Campbell,

indicated that he expected some special, and perhaps authorized, communication to him from the Confederate Government. I disabused his mind of this by saying I had no commission to see him. I told him that in parting with General Breckinridge, the Secretary of War of the Confederate States, I had informed him I should not leave Richmond, and that I should take the earliest opportunity to see Mr. Lincoln on the subject of peace, and should be glad to have a commission to do so, but I had no

The Virginia State Capitol at Richmond as it looks today. No trace or memory of the agonies it witnessed can be found in its peaceful parklike surroundings. Only the square bell tower—Jones's "tocsin"—still standing at the edge of the Capitol grounds—is a reminder of less happy times. *Virginia Conservation Commission.*

reply, and received no commission. I then told the President that the war was over, and all that remained to be done was to compose the country.

Recapping the "pith" of the talk, General Weitzel would report:

Mr. Lincoln insisted that he could not treat with any rebels until they had laid down their arms and surrendered; and that if this were first done, he would go as far as he possibly could to prevent the shedding of another drop of blood; and that he and the good people of the North were surfeited with this thing and wanted it to end as soon as possible. Mr. Campbell and the other gentlemen assured Mr. Lincoln that if he would allow the Virginia Legislature to meet, it would at once repeal the ordinance of secession and that then General Robert E. Lee and every other Virginian would submit; that this would amount to the virtual destruction of the Army of Northern Virginia and eventually to the surrender of all the other rebel armies, and would ensure perfect peace in the shortest possible time.

While Lincoln was tramping about the fallen capital, a unique observance was taking place throughout the nation. At all military posts, arsenals and naval establishments, at noon—"the meridian," as the official order read—a one-hundred-gun artillery salute was fired.

The noisy honor to Grant's army did not long anticipate the end of the Army of Northern Virginia. Five days after Lincoln's visit to Richmond, on April 9, Lee accepted Grant's generous surrender terms at Appomattox Court House. Among the more literate observers of the historic occasion was Colonel William Blackford, who had so recently accompanied the refugees out of Richmond.

After Lee had left the McLean house, where he had surrendered only the Army of Northern Virginia, his principal field command, Blackford spoke of "a general rush from each side of the road to greet him as he passed, and two solid walls were formed along the whole distance."

> *Their officers followed and behind the lines of men were groups of them, mounted and dismounted, awaiting his coming. I saw something unusual was about to happen, so I sprang upon "Magic" and followed, keeping a short distance behind, but near enough to hear what was said as General Lee passed. As soon as he entered his avenue of these old soldiers, the flower of his army, the men who had stood to their duty through thick and thin in so many battles, wild heartfelt cheers arose which so touched General Lee that tears filled his eyes and trickled down his cheeks as he rode his splendid charger, hat in hand, bowing his acknowledgments.*
>
> *This exhibition of feeling on his part found quick response from the men, whose cheers changed to choking sobs as with streaming eyes and many cries of affection they waved their hats as he passed. Each group began in the same way with cheers and ended in the same way with sobs, all the way to his quarters. Grim bearded men threw themselves on the ground, covered their faces with their hands and wept like children. Officers of all ranks made no attempt to conceal their feelings, but sat on their horses and cried aloud. . . .*

The sands of an incredible four years were running out faster than Lincoln, or anyone else, could have foreseen. The war president was assassinated in Ford's Theater on April 14 by John Wilkes Booth.

Four days later, on April 18, the Confederacy's last effective army, Joe Johnston's, surrendered to Sherman, who offered terms at least as magnanimous as those tendered Lee by Grant—so magnanimous that Secretary Stanton's wrath was provoked. But not until May 10, in dense pine woods near Irwinville, Georgia, was the fast-moving diehard, Jefferson Davis, captured—more or less through chance by troopers of the Fourth Michigan Cavalry.

At long last, the final curtain of the last act of the Civil War—or, the War of the Rebellion—had been rung down. And for many actors, lesser in stature than Abraham Lincoln, their moments in history had also passed, if less violently.

Davis, a prisoner for two years under somewhat less than the most healthful conditions, would live into his eighty-second year without ever fully understanding why the Federal government had been so angry with him. Lee vanished within the shaded campus of Washington College (later Washington and Lee), to die of heart disease only five years after Appomattox. His wife, Mary Custis, always in fragile health, nonetheless survived her husband by three years. Indeed, she outlived her third and favorite daughter Agnes by a month.

Alexander H. Stephens, upon his capture, was found to be "slim as a skeleton . . . nothing but skin, bone and cartilage, and is so feeble as to be hardly able to move about." However, the former vice-president of the Confederacy rallied to serve nine years as a U.S. Representative from Georgia, commencing in 1873. He died in office in 1883, at the age of 71, as governor of Georgia.

Secretary Trenholm, back in Charleston, staggered under claims for damages and wartime duties owed the U.S. Treasury. Nonetheless, he was back in the export business at the time of his death in 1876.

James Chesnut returned to the slow-paced role of country lawyer in his home town, Camden, South Carolina. His extremely articulate wife, Mary Boykin, kept up a correspondence with Varina Howell Davis and other wives of Richmond until her death in 1886, one year after that of her husband.

John Beauchamp Jones, the faithful war clerk–diarist, who could never wholly forgive the War Department for withholding so much from him, passed on short months after the fall of Richmond.

Cooper De Leon returned to much the same literary limbo whence he had sprung. It was true as well of Sallie Brock who merged with history's mists as Mrs. Richard Putnam, and even the busy authoress La Salle Pickett, who never answered, or perhaps was unable to answer, the question posed by the title of her memoir, "What Happened to Me?"

Immortality for most soldiers and statesmen was molded, chiselled and hammered into the shapes of statuary in their own village greens. "Fighting Joe" Hooker, astride his horse, fiercely guards the State House in Boston. In Washington, another "almost" commander, George Brinton McClellan, still guides his bronze mount in the general direction of Richmond. The name "Devens" lives as a familiar army post in Massachusetts.

But not all the old soldiers would simply fade away. Some could yet contemplate the apex of their careers. Grant would become a two-term president; Sherman a respected chief of staff before retiring to indulge mellow-years fancy for the theater, in New York; the names of Sheridan and Custer would carry the ring of "Indian fighter," one tragically so.

General Weitzel, electing to remain in the Army, served as an able engineer for two decades. On the other side, Longstreet, Lee's old "war horse," proved that bygones were bygones by being appointed United States minister to Turkey. Old "Fitz" Lee, of fish-fry fame at Five Forks, commanded the U.S. Seventh Army Corps during the Spanish-American War.

Judah Benjamin, with a keenly honed sense of self-preservation, fled to England. As "Queen's counsel," he pursued a lucrative law practice for nearly two decades. He died in Paris, still the home of his expatriate wife, in 1884.

Breckinridge followed his cabinet officer confrère to Great Britain, via Cuba. He returned to Lexington, Kentucky, under a full pardon from President Grant, who held no grievance against the Confederate officer corps. The handsome one-time vice-president of the United States became a successful railroad attorney, his career cut short by his death in 1875. He was only fifty-four.

The legal profession seemed to dominate the careers of the participants in rebellion. Secretary Mallory resumed a career as admiralty lawyer in Florida. He died in Pensacola in 1873. Like others of the cabinet with neither the agility nor funds to flee the country, Mallory had spent time in prison before cool heads in Washington had prevailed over the sometimes vindictive President Andrew Johnson, and the Congress.

Even Roger Pryor, Sara's husband, turned to the law, in New York, working as a twenty-five-dollar-a-week reporter for the *Daily News* while studying for his law degree. Ultimately, he became a justice of the Supreme Court of New York. Sara, who wrote a number of books and essays, succumbed in 1912 at the age of eighty-two.

The robes of the bench were also in Louise Wigfall's future. She married Daniel Giraud Wright of Baltimore, that "shaky" Union town, where Wright distinguished himself as a lawyer and jurist. Louise herself was a firm-jawed rallying figure for the United Daughters of the Confederacy.

Horace Porter, Grant's literate chronicler, served as ambassador to France under McKinley. He later thumped for preparedness prior to the United States' entry into the "Great War," then spent his short remaining years declaring that the League of Nations wouldn't work—until his death in 1921, when Harding was President.

Connie Cary, to the surprise of none of her friends, married Burton Harrison, who, as an aide to President Davis, had been jailed upon apprehension. He had the dubious distinction of being confined in the old Washington Penitentiary, on the Arsenal grounds, at the time of the hanging of Mary Surratt and the other Lincoln conspirators.

Connie, as a prolific novelist, continued to wear out pen points. Traveling extensively with her husband on various governmental missions, she met such diverse personages as Sir Arthur Conan Doyle, Richard Harding Davis, Rudyard Kipling, Thomas Hardy, Cyrus Field, Samuel J. Tilden, Charles Dana Gibson (who married a Richmond beauty) and Emma Lazarus, whose poem would lend voice to the Statue of Liberty, "Give me your tired, your poor. . . ."

Two of her sons would attain high positions: Francis, governor general of the Philippines, and Fairfax, president of the Southern Railroad. She survived until 1920, with much of the beauty that had distinguished her in wartime Richmond still evident in her eighties. She is buried in Ivy Hill Cemetery in her native Alexandria, Virginia, where a simple stone cannot hope to recall the vivacious spirit that was Connie. Who now is to pause by her grave, much less weep?

War's battles, with all their death and horror, nonetheless

acted as a magnet to some. George Alfred Townsend, the correspondent, returned to South Mountain (scene of the fighting preliminary to Antietam) to build a handsome estate, "Gathland." On this lofty property, between Frederick and Harper's Ferry, "Gath" Townsend created something unique: a tall stone arch bearing names of many of the correspondents and artists who had made this history's first thoroughly reported and depicted war. Some from "the other side" were as well memorialized—with at least one notable exception, Francis Lawley, the gentleman from *The Times* of London.

Gath, a portly man with a tightly waxed black moustache, became a familiar postwar figure on the lecture circuit. Then, as competition grew, especially accenting the personages and the avoirdupois of admirals and generals, the verbal spate swelled into a Niagara of personal reminiscences. All at once, no one—North or South—wanted to hear any more about the war. Townsend settled down to the life of a gentleman farmer and author. Before his death in 1914, Gath had published some two dozen works: fiction, nonfiction, essays and even a few poems.

Sylvanus Cadwallader headed up the New York *Herald*'s Washington Bureau immediately after the war. He moved to Milwaukee in 1868, becoming assistant secretary of state for Wisconsin. He lived thereafter in several states including Missouri and California, although it was not until 1896, when he was in his seventies, that Cadwallader wrote his memoir—and took his place beside the immortals of James Gordon Bennett's *Herald*, such as Henry Villard, John Russell Young and Henry M. Stanley.

But there were yet others whose life currents were not significantly altered by the war: Richmond's well-known preachers, for example. The Reverend Moses Hoge returned from Danville, where he had roomed with Judah Benjamin and undoubtedly urged the secretary of state to make tracks for England, to set some sort of an ecclesiastical record: he served as the Second Presbyterian Church's rector for fifty-three years. Only death had sufficient clout to terminate his pastorate, which it did in 1898—even as Dr. Hoge was turning his thoughts to another war, that with Spain.

Dr. Minnigerode, who predeceased Hoge by four years, approximated but could not equal Hoge's tenure.

The youngsters of Richmond's war years grew up, went away, and faded from the pages of recorded history. Dallas

Correspondents' Arch, South Mountain, near Frederick, Maryland, and the name of George Alfred Townsend on it. A correspondent for the *New York World* and *New York Herald*, Townsend had "covered" the battle of South Mountain in September 1862. He was so impressed with the locale that he returned after Appomattox and built an estate on the mountaintop, as well as the arch to memorialize the correspondents and artists who had made the American Civil War history's first thoroughly reported and depicted war. *From the Authors' collection.*

Tucker entered the ministry, Emmie Crump became Mrs. William Lightfoot; but what happened to the widowed Hetty Cary, to Emmie Sublet, to the elusive Nellie Grey, to John Leyburn, Eddie Watehall, Mann S. Quarles, the law student George Cary Eggleston, or the sleepy drummer John Woods?

Elizabeth Van Lew was rewarded for her spy work by President Grant with Richmond's postmastership. But her neighbors continued to regard "Crazy Bet" with mingled suspicion and disdain, some even crossing to the other side of the street when they saw her approaching.

Unlike many, perhaps the majority, of her contemporaries, Elizabeth lived until the turn of the century—but barely. She passed away on September 21, 1900. Thereafter, her mansion on Church Hill was demolished to make way for the Bellevue Elementary School. Whatever secrets remained in the great structure were further entombed by the wreckers' claws and hammers. Soon the cries of children would ring stridently where in an improbable yesterday the stealthy footfalls of servants and others bore clandestine testament to an opposition to secession.

Today, tourists walk past this wholly unmarked spot—in a deteriorating neighborhood—en route to the adjacent St. John's "Patrick Henry" Church. In Richmond, Lizzie Van Lew remains, more than one hundred years later, "unrehabilitated."

Matron Pember left Chimborazo not, so far as is known, to return to nursing. She was believed to have travelled extensively in the United States and abroad before her death in Pittsburgh, in 1913. She rests in her native Savannah, beside her husband who died in the second year of the Civil War.

Phoebe herself would be a stranger to the site of her famous old hospital. Chimborazo is a park, overlooking factories (with tobacco still king), the river, a wholly rebuilt Richmond, and modern highways. A small museum operated by the National Park Service conveys through pictures and relics much of the flavor of far more frenetic times.

But there is not much at all in or about Richmond to whisper that Phoebe or Connie Cary or clerk Jones were ever here—no frame structures; no gas lamps; no rutted, frequently muddy streets; certainly no bandaged soldiers hobbling on crutches. The bell tower still stands on Capitol Square. Nearby is St. Paul's. A stack and some walls of the Tredegar Works mock time and "progress." The White House of the Confederacy hints at another era; here and there a very old brick structure seems to be trying to suggest that it defied good soldier Ewell's fiery night.

Yet there is no abundance of physical tattletales to affirm that Richmond as capital of the Confederacy ever existed at all, except perhaps as the fabrication of overtaxed historians.

Looking back, De Leon mused, "The trials, the strain, the suffering of those years remain with us but a memory."

And, now, there is not even memory.

Not much is left of the Tredegar Works which pumped out so much iron plate, rails, guns and munitions for the Confederacy. A short walk from the Capitol, beside the James River, it endures in broken abandonment. *From the Authors' collection.*

Bibliography

Libraries, Universities

. . . the fire creeping steadily nearer us, until houses next to us caught, and we prepared to leave; and above all, inconceivably terrible, the 700,000 shells exploding at the laboratory. I say imagine, but you cannot; no one who was not here will ever fully appreciate the horrors of that day.

Confederate Museum—among the treasures here in the old Jefferson Davis mansion (complete with modern annex), Richmond, is this letter, excerpted above, from Mrs. Mary A. Fontaine to her friend Mrs. Marie Burrows Sayre, describing a fallen capital's death throes. Other documents at the museum: a letter from thirteen-year-old Emmie Crump (Lightfoot) to a friend, written a few days after the occupation (somewhat expanded by her in a 1933 article entitled "The Evacuation of Richmond" in the *Virginia Magazine of History and Biography*, with the notation that it was for the benefit of her children and grandchildren—it is not clear when the then Mrs. Lightfoot wrote this article although there is an oblique notation in the same issue of the magazine that she had attended a patriotic ceremony in Capitol Square in 1927); a letter from Miss Emma Mordecai to a Confederate officer, from Rosewood Plantation, Henrico County, Virginia, dated April 5, 1865; a letter from Quartermaster Frank Potts to his brother, written at Clarksville and dated April 25, 1865 (also describing the surrender at Appomattox and published in the *Museum Newsletter* of July 1969); excerpts from the diary of Mrs. William A. Simmons, of Atlanta, Georgia, wife of a Confederate officer; a letter from Emmie Sublet (aged thirteen, to Emily Anderson, a friend, written from her home in Richmond, Waverly Place, April 29, 1865; and the Richmond Soup Association report, which tells graphically, if in terse official language, of the suffering of the people.

Duke University—the William R. Perkins Library. The ever-growing collection of Civil War manuscripts and the like at Duke include the unpublished memoir of Colonel John Cheeves Haskell, CSA, who lost a pair of $1,250 boots in the confusion of retreat; and the papers of the Fleming family. Contained therein is a letter from Anna Deane, in Richmond, to her sister Mary Eliza Fleming, and another, dated April 12, 1865, to a friend, "Sallie." Both describe the last hours of the Confederate capital and the entrance of Federal troops. Here, too, is the short but descriptive memoir of Mann S. Quarles, the Treasury's youngest teller.

University of Florida—While, as previously noted, the Yonge Library on the Gainesville campus does not hold Patrick papers relative to the fall of Richmond, its open shelves filled in gaps encountered elsewhere by the authors: notably the Kean and Nellie Grey accounts.

Library of Congress—Many if not most of the books cited in the acknowledgments (as well as newspapers) are in this nation's "national library," The Library of Congress. Regimental histories, while not fully assembled for review, are well represented. One of the richest sources for this account's needs is the history of the Thirteenth New Hampshire, more than 700 pages proud, with the accounts of some half dozen officers quoted.

Maine State Library—This fine collection in a modern building on the Capitol grounds in Augusta formerly had to share space in cramped quarters with stuffed moose heads, owls, chipmunks, and the like. What other libraries may lack in New England Civil War regimental histories is compensated for here, and quite appropriately. In contrast to Sherman's army, made up primarily of rawboned westerners, Grant employed Yankees and easterners to produce the winning Sunday punch. For example, waiting on the shelves to charge again is the First Light Battery of Connecticut Volunteers. Its youthful members raced across fields to be among the first into Richmond. Here too reposes a leather-bound memorial to Brigadier General Charles Devens, promoted late in the campaign from Third Division commander to commander of the Twenty-fourth Army Corps, and who "led the advance into Richmond." The tribute by George F. Hoar, published in Worcester, Massachusetts in 1891, when the general died, recalls that he had been so crippled with rheumatism during the fierce fighting at Cold Harbor that he could neither mount a horse nor stand—he had to be carried along the lines on a stretcher.

New York Public Library—The guns had barely cooled when book publishers joined representatives of libraries as well as historical and learned societies in the North (especially New England) and headed south. They knew a treasure in the printed word awaited them; and when they returned, their wicker suitcases were full. New York's Astor, Lenox and Tilden libraries (later to merge into the New York Public Library) were in the forefront, with the result that their successor would house a formidable Civil War collection. Principally used for the purposes of this book are the Elizabeth Van Lew papers. While chronologically they are full of gaps, these documents represent the best library holdings of "Crazy Bet" that can be found.

University of North Carolina (Southern Historical Collection)— Consulted principally in this collection: James W. Albright, *Diary;* Berry Greenwood Benson, *Reminiscences;* John A. Campbell-George R. Colston, papers; Leeland Hathaway, *Recollections;* Edward Hitchcock McDonald, *Reminiscences;* Emma Mordecai, mistress of Rosewood Plantation, diary; Isaac C. Richardson, letters; James R. Sheldon, *Last March of the Army of Lee;* Anna Holmes Trenholm, diary; Anita Dwyer Withers, diary. Similar original source material proved to be the "heart" of this book.

Virginia Historical Society—"No thought of evacuation before 1 o'clock on this day and by midnight the evacuation was completed." So noted John Coles Rutherford, member of the Virginia Legislature on April 2, 1865. His papers are to be found at the Virginia Historical Society, Richmond. Of particular value are indexes to old publications, not available elsewhere—for example, an excellent index to the Southern Historical Society Papers. Newspaper articles and books treating in some way Richmond, 1861–65, are also carefully referenced here.

University of Virginia—In the manuscript section of the Alderman Library is the diary of Miss Mary Taylor, who worried about obtaining warm things for the boys in the trenches before Fredericksburg. It is part of the larger collection of the Charles Elisha Taylor papers. The library's complete set of the *Confederate Veteran* is not easily duplicated. Alderman's shelves are heavy with Civil War literature.

College of William and Mary—Of interest to historians who may wish to concentrate on the siege of Petersburg is the large Charles Campbell collection in the Swem Library. Campbell, who kept a diary like most literate people in that age, took part in a local defense company and made his basement available as a shelter during shellings.

A number of public libraries figured in this research including the District of Columbia, Montgomery County (Maryland) and Fairfax County (Virginia). *McClure's Magazine* of December 1900, for example, was located at the Martin Luther King central library, in the District of Columbia. It contains excerpts from the Stephen R. Mallory papers, published under the title, *The Last Days of the Confederate Government.*

Magazines

The excitement was so great that the (Federal)
cavalry paid no attention to us. I got separated
from my squad, who were nearly all Virginians.
I still had my guns, and went to Capitol Square
to one of the gates, and while standing there
with an old Texas soldier I saw our flag pulled
down from the Capitol and the Stars and Stripes
hoisted in its place.

So wrote S. A. Gerald, of Matador, Texas, in an article entitled, "Last
Soldiers to Leave Richmond," published in the *Confederate Veteran*,
1910. Much of the wealth of reminiscences in the various issues of the
Veteran go beyond the time frame of this book, such as John Southall's
"Recollections of the Evacuation of Richmond," vol. 37, as he
watched Lee return after Appomattox:

> *General Lee crossed the river and turned into Cary Street on his
> way to his home. He was riding Traveller, and looked neither to the right
> nor to the left, but straight ahead. The streets were filled with debris . . .
> and it was difficult to make your way through even in the middle of the
> roadway.*

Other sources from the *Confederate Veteran* include Amelia Gorgas, "The Evacuation of Richmond," 1917; E. T. Watehall, "Fall of
Richmond," 1909; Fannie Walker Miller, "The Fall of Richmond,"
1905; and Private John L. G. Woods, "Last Scenes of War—How I Got
Home," 1919.

Edward M. Alfriend's article, "Social Life in Richmond During
the War," appeared in *Cosmopolitan*, December 1891.

John Leyburn penned his vivid "The Fall of Richmond" in
Harper's New Monthly Magazine, vol. 33, 1866.

As previously noted, Stephen R. Mallory, secretary of the Confederate Navy, wrote "Last Days of the Confederate Government,"
published in *McClure's*, December 1900, long after his death.

In the Summer 1969 issue of *Virginia Cavalcade* William J. Kimball
wrote "Richmond, 1865: the Final Three Months."

In addition to the Emmie Crump Lightfoot letter published in
1933 in the *Virginia Magazine of History and Biography*, noted previously, there are at least two other items of interest from that
magazine. The letter of French Consul Alfred Paul to Drouyn de Llys,
Ministre des Affaires Etrangères, dated 11 April, 1865, was published
as part of an article by Warren F. Spencer entitled "A French View of
the Fall of Richmond," in the April 1965 issue. In the same issue a
short article edited by William Rachal quotes Colonel Christopher

Tompkins encountering "Extra Billy" Smith in Goochland County after the evacuation. The governor, who fled on horseback, had trouble crossing the canals in the dark. After steed and rider stumbled several times, according to Tompkins:

> . . . *together they extricated themselves, both injured, the Gov. with a black eye and the horse with a gash under his forearm which seemed to pain him.*

The colonel, who believed "Extra Billy" was a teetotaller, offered him "a dram" and "for once . . . he acquiesced."

Both articles are excerpted by permission of Editor William Rachal.

There is much in the *Southern Historical Society Papers* including:

Lieutenant Colonel R. T. W. Duke, "Burning of Richmond," vol. 25.

Lieutenant General Richard S. Ewell, "Evacuation of Richmond," vol. 13.

G. Powell Hill, "First Burial of General Hill's Remains," vol. 19.

Captain McHenry Howard, "Closing Scenes of the War About Richmond," vol. 31.

Colonel Loomis L. Langdon, "The First Federal to Enter Richmond," vol. 30 (concerning Major A. H. Stevens, from the *Richmond Dispatch*, 10 February 1893).

Dallas Tucker, "The Fall of Richmond," vol. 29 (from *Richmond Dispatch*, 3 February 1902).

Colonel Charles S. Venable, "Letter from a Courier,—further Details on the death of General A. P. Hill," vol. 12.

W. S. White, "Stray Leaves from a Soldier's Journal," vol. 11.

The Southern Historical Society was founded in 1869 in New Orleans, and was afforded initial impetus by such dignitaries as Generals Beauregard, Jubal Early and Pickett, Governor Letcher and Admiral Semmes. Although the final issue of its "Papers" came off the press in 1943 (vol. 49) with a new cast, including the scholarly Douglas Southall Freeman, fires cooled and memories dimmed after the turn of the century. Volumes became spasmodic. By 1900 or so most Confederate general officers who still survived were in their eighties or close thereto. Besides, there was not much more to recall about the War of Secession. It all seemed to have been said. The society dwindled to two members, then one. Finally it was absorbed into the Virginia Historical Society which, in effect, pronounced obsequies over the brainchild of old Jubal Early.

Newspapers

On April 3, 1935—the seventieth anniversary of the end of the capital of the Confederacy—the *Richmond News-Leader* published a reminiscence of Miss Lelian M. Cook, who as a young lady was living at the home of the Reverend Moses D. Hoge. She was in 1935 a resident of Blackstone, Virginia. One could then speculate if she were the last survivor of wartime Richmond.

Other papers consulted from the period of 1861–1865:

Baltimore Clipper
Baltimore Sun
Boston Daily Advertiser
Boston Journal
Charleston Daily Courier
Chicago Tribune
Cincinnati Daily Gazette
New York Herald
New York Times
New York Tribune
New York World
Petersburg Express
Grant's Petersburg Progress
Philadelphia Inquirer
Philadelphia Ledger
Philadelphia Press
Richmond Enquirer
Richmond Examiner
Richmond Times
Richmond Evening Whig
Washington Chronicle
The Evening Star (Washington)
National Intelligencer (Washington)
National Republican (Washington)

Books

This listing represents but a portion of those books consulted and which proved useful. (See commentary at end.)

Adams, Charles Francis. *A Cycle of Letters.* Edited by W. C. Ford. New York/Boston: Houghton Mifflin Co., 1920.

———. *Charles Francis Adams, 1835–1915-an Autobiography.* New York: Houghton Mifflin Co., 1916.

Andrews, Matthew Page. *The Women of the South in War Times.* Baltimore: Norman, Remington Co., 1920.

Avary, Myrta Lockett. *A Virginia Girl in the Civil War.* New York: Appleton & Co., 1903.

———. *Dixie After the War.* Boston: Houghton Mifflin Co., 1937.

Battles and Leaders of the Civil War. Four volumes (comprised principally of personal memoirs originally published as articles in *The Century Magazine*). Introduction by Roy F. Nichols. New York: Thomas Yoseloff, 1956. Among those quoted (although other sources for most are also referenced) are Brig. Gen. Joseph R. Anderson; Judah P. Benjamin; Edward M. Boykin; Constance

Cary; Capt. James B. Fry; Thomas Thatcher Craves; Brig. Gen. Horace Porter; and Capt. Clement Sulivane.

Beals, Carleton. *War Within a War*. Philadelphia: Chilton Books, 1965.

Beecher, Herbert W. *History of the First Light Battery Connecticut Volunteers 1861–1865*. New York: A. T. De La Mare Printing and Publishing Co., 1901.

Bill, Alfred Hoyt. *Beleagured City*. New York: Alfred A. Knopf, 1946.

Blackford, Susan Leigh, compiler. *Letters from Lee's Army*. New York: Charles Scribner's Sons, 1947.

Blackford, Lt. Col. William W. *War Years with Jeb Stuart*. New York: Charles Scribner's Sons, 1945.

Boykin, E. M. *The Falling Flag*. New York: E. J. Hale & Son, 1874.

Cadwallader, Sylvanus. *Three Years with Grant*. Edited by Benjamin P. Thomas. New York: Alfred A. Knopf, Inc., 1955.

Campbell, John A. *Recollections of the Evacuation of Richmond*. Baltimore: John Murphy & Co., 1880.

Cary, Constance [Mrs. Burton Harrison]. *Recollections Grave and Gay*. New York: Charles Scribner's Sons, 1911.

Catton, Bruce. *Grant Takes Command*. Boston: Little Brown, 1969.

Chamberlain, Joshua L. *The Passing of the Armies*. New York: G. P. Putnam's Sons, 1915.

Chesnut, Mary Boykin. *A Diary from Dixie*. Edited by Myrta Avary. New York: D. Appleton & Co., 1905.

Christian, W. Asbury. *Richmond Past and Present*. Richmond: L. H. Jenkins Co., 1912.

Claiborne, Dr. John H. *Seventy-five Years in Old Virginia*. New York: Neale Publishing Co., 1904.

Coffin, Charles Carleton. *Four Years of Fighting*. Boston: Ticknor and Fields, 1866.

Commager, Henry Steele, ed. *The Blue and the Gray*. New York: The Bobbs-Merrill Co., Inc., 1950.

Cunningham, H. H. *Doctors in Gray, the Confederate Medical Service*. Baton Rouge: Louisiana State University Press, 1958.

Dabney, Virginius. *Richmond, the Story of a City*. New York: Doubleday & Co., 1976.

Daniel, F. S., ed. *The Richmond Examiner During the War, or the Writings of John M. Daniel*. New York: privately printed, 1868.

Davis, Burke. *To Appomattox—Nine April Days 1865*. New York: Rinehart, 1959.

Davis, Jefferson. *The Rise and Fall of the Confederate Government*. New York: Thomas Yoseloff, 1958.

Davis, Varina Howell. *Jefferson Davis*. New York: Belford Co., 1890.

De Leon, Thomas C. *Four Years in Rebel Capitals*. Mobile: The Gossip Printing Co., 1892.

De Peyster, Livingston. *The Colors of the United States First Raised over the Capitol of the Confederate States*. Morrisania, New York: privately printed, 1866.

Douglas, Major Henry Kyd. *I Rode With Stonewall*. Chapel Hill, North Carolina: University of North Carolina Press, 1940.

Dowdey, Clifford. *Experiment in Rebellion*. Freeport, New York: Books for Libraries, 1970.

Durkin, Joseph T. S. J. *Stephen R. Mallory, Confederate Navy Chief*. Chapel Hill, North Carolina: University of North Carolina Press, 1954.

Eggleston, George Cary. *A Rebel's Recollections*. New York: G. P. Putnam's Sons, 1905.

Fowler, Philemon H. *Memorials of William Fowler*. New York: A. D. F. Randall & Co., 1875.

Freeman, Douglas Southall. *Robert E. Lee, a Biography*. 4 vols. New York: Charles Scribner's Sons, 1934–37.

Grant, Ulysses S. *Personal Memoirs*. 2 vols. New York: Charles L. Webster & Co., 1886.

Hatcher, Edmund N. *The Last Four Weeks of the War* (compilation). Columbus, Ohio: privately published, 1891.

Hoge, Peyton Harrison. *Moses Drury Hoge, Life and Letters*. Richmond: Presbyterian Committee of Publication, 1899.

Hoole, W. Stanley. *Lawley Covers the Confederacy*. Tuscaloosa, Alabama: Confederate Publishing Co. Inc., 1964.

Horn, Stanley F. *The Robert E. Lee Reader*. New York: Bobbs-Merrill Co., Inc., 1949

Jones, John B. *A Rebel War Clerk's Diary*. 2 vols. Philadelphia: John B. Lippincott Co., 1866.

Jones, Katherine M. *Ladies of Richmond; Confederate Capital*. New York: Bobbs-Merrill Co., Inc., 1962.

Jones, Virgil Carrington. *Eight Hours Before Richmond*. New York: Henry Holt & Co., 1957.

Kimball, William Joseph. *Richmond in Time of War*. Boston: Houghton Mifflin Co., 1960.

Kimmel, Stanley. *Mr. Davis's Richmond*. New York: Coward-McCann, 1958.

Lewis, Lloyd. *Sherman, Fighting Prophet*. New York: Harcourt Brace, 1932.

Liddell, Surgeon John A. His reports and comments published in Official Records, *War of the Rebellion*. Both consulted and excerpted through permission of Louis H. Manarin.

Long, E. B. *The Civil War Day by Day—an Almanac 1861–1865*. New York: Doubleday and Co., Inc., 1971.

Manarin, Louis H., ed. *Richmond at War, The Minutes of the City Council 1861–65*. Chapel Hill, North Carolina: University of North Carolina Press, 1966.

McCabe, James D. Jr. *Life and Campaigns of General Robert E. Lee*. New York: Blelock & Co., 1867.

McElroy, Robert. *Jefferson Davis, The Unreal and the Real*. New York: Harper & Brothers, 1937.

McGuire, Judith White Brockenbrough. *Diary of a Southern Refugee During the War*. New York: E. J. Hale & Son, 1868.

Meade, Robert Douthat. *Judah P. Benjamin, Confederate Statesman*. New York: Oxford University Press, 1943.

Miers, Earl Schenck. *Lincoln Day by Day, a Chronology*. Washington: Lincoln Sesquicentennial Commission, 1960.

Miller, Francis Trevelyan. *The Photographic History of the Civil War*. 10 vols. New York: Thomas Yoseloff, 1957. Of especial pertinence to the research of this book were the biographies, accounts of the Richmond and Petersburg campaigns, and treatments of such specialized subjects as hospitals, prisons, the military telegraph and the railroads.

Nepveux, Ethel Trenholm Seabrook. *George Alfred Trenholm, The Company that Went to War*. Charleston: privately printed, 1973.

Nevins, Allan. *The War for the Union*. The Organized War to Victory, vol. 4. New York: Charles Scribner's Sons, 1959–71.

Parker, William H. *Recollections of a Naval Officer*. New York: Charles Scribner's Sons, 1883.

Patrick, Rembert. *The Fall of Richmond*. Baton Rouge: Louisiana State University Press, 1960. Permission to use as background kindly granted.

Peck, George B., Jr. *A Recruit Before Petersburg*. Providence, Rhode Island: N. Bangs Williams & Co., 1880.

Pember, Phoebe Yates. *A Southern Woman's Story*. Edited by Bell Irvin Wiley. Jackson, Tennessee: McCowat-Mercer Press, 1959. [Original printings, which appeared shortly after the war, are virtually unobtainable.]

Pickett, LaSalle Corbett. *What Happened to Me*. New York: Bretano's, 1917.

Pollard, Edward A. *Southern History of the War*. New York: Charles B. Richardson, 1866.

Prussian Officer. *The Defence of Richmond*. New York: George F. Nesbitt & Co., 1863.

Pryor, Sara. *My Day, Reminiscences of a Long Life*. New York: MacMillan, 1909.

———. *Reminiscences of Peace and War*. New York: MacMillan, 1904.

Putnam, Sallie A. Brock. *Richmond During the War*. New York: Carleton & Co., 1867.

Reagan, John H. *Memoirs*. Edited by Walter F. McCaleb. Washington: Neale Publishing Co., 1906.

Richmond Civil War Centennial Committee. *Confederate Military Hospitals in Richmond*. Official Publication no. 22. Richmond, Virginia, 1964.

Ripley, Edward H. *The Capture and Occupation of Richmond, April 3, 1865*. New York: G. P. Putnam's & Sons, 1907.

Rowland, Dunbar. *Jefferson Davis Constitutionalist, His Letters, Papers and Speeches*. Jackson, Mississippi: Mississippi Department of Archives and History, 1923.

Semmes, Admiral Raphael. *Service Afloat*. New York: P. J. Kenedy, 1903. [His many editions commenced with London imprints immediately following the war.]

Sheridan, General Philip. *Personal Memoirs of P. H. Sheridan*, vol. 2. New York: Charles L. Webster & Co., 1883.

Sherman, William T. *Memoirs of William T. Sherman.* 2 vols. New York: D. Appleton & Co., 1875.

Simkins, Frances Butler, and Patton, James W. *The Women of the Confederacy.* Richmond: Garrett & Massie Inc., 1936.

Taylor, Walter H. *General Lee, His Campaigns in Virginia.* Norfolk: Nusbaum Book and News Co., 1906.

Thompson, S. Millett (Lieutenant, Thirteenth Regiment New Hampshire Volunteers). *Thirteenth Regiment of New Hampshire Volunteer Infantry in the War of the Rebellion 1861–1865.* Boston: Houghton Mifflin Co., 1888. Marching through the pages of this fat volume are such old friends as Brigadier General Charles Devens, onetime Third Division commander in the Twenty-fourth Army Corps, briefly corps commander; Lieutenant Colonel Bamberger; Major E. E. Graves; Lieutenant Royal B. Prescott; Colonel Edward H. Ripley; Major Atherton Stevens; Major Nathan Stoodley and Major General Godfrey Weitzel.

The Times Reports the American Civil War. London: Times Books, 1975.

Townsend, George Alfred. *Campaigns of a Non-Combatant.* New York: Blelock and Co., 1866.

Vandiver, Frank E., ed. *The Civil War Diary of General Josiah Gorgas.* Alabama: University of Alabama Press, 1947.

Official Records of the Union and Confederate Armies. *War of the Rebellion.* Series I, vol. 46 (Parts 1, 2 and 3), "The Richmond Campaign." Washington: U.S. Government Printing House, 1894–95.

Weitzel, Major Godfrey. *Richmond Occupied, Entry of the United States Forces into Richmond, Virginia, April 3, 1865.* Edited by Louis Manarin. Richmond: Richmond Civil War Centennial Committee, 1965.

Wiley, Bell Irvin. *Confederate Women.* Westport, Connecticut: Greenwood Press, 1975.

Wright, Mrs. D. Giraud [Louise Wigfall]. *A Southern Girl in '61, The Wartime Memories of a Confederate Senator's Daughter.* New York: Doubleday, Page & Co., 1905.

Younger, Edward, ed. *Inside the Confederate Government, The Diary of Robert G. H. Kean, Head of the Bureau of War.* New York: Oxford University Press, 1957.

Some random notes on these many books . . .

While often said, it is nonetheless true that books become old friends. Certainly, the great majority of the people who have wandered through the pages of these volumes are very real to the authors. Some we have already met in unpublished diaries, letters, memoirs, articles and the like. It was with a sense of great loss that we closed the covers and said goodbye. But a few words in adieu:

Where is the letter of Charles Francis Adams, supposedly describing in depth his entry into Richmond? It is alluded to in various publications by or about the distinguished soldier-author, but no trace of it has been exhumed.

Concerning Myrta Lockett Avary, who gave us the sympathetic characters of Nellie Grey and Mrs. Sampson (the latter with her chicken-feather hat)—history will never know if Nellie was one or a composite of two or three people, or in greater part the creation of Myrta's fertile brain. Yet, "A Virginia Girl in the Civil War" presents Nellie as flesh and blood. And we rather prefer to think of her that way.

Connie Cary comes through as one of the warmer personages of wartime Richmond. Afterward, she wrote much, but nothing quite equalled the simple, straightforward story she recounted of 1861–1865. Although she probably never understood it, her career as an author had already peaked when she was a young belle in the Confederacy's capital.

Mary Chesnut penned voluminously. Over the years there have been several versions of her memoir, all mirroring her sharp tongue, personal conflicts, strong opinions and penchant for name-dropping. Ben Ames Williams, the late novelist who was asked to edit one of the longer Chesnut "diaries," used her in part as a model for Cinda Dewain in *House Divided*. The attractive matron of Richmond and points south may indeed have lived again in the persons of other fictional heroines of that time period, possibly even as a hint in the tempestuous Scarlett O'Hara.

The original Chesnut papers are in the South Caroliniana Library, University of South Carolina, Columbia, where Mary Boykin remains a Lorelei for historians. A scholar from Connecticut has been at work on yet another compilation of her diaries. James Chesnut himself left a considerable collection of papers, state and otherwise, divided among at least four university libraries including Chapel Hill.

Jefferson Davis, in tracing "The Rise and Fall of the Confederate Government," nonetheless did not remove the mask from the man who presided over that downfall. He wrote with angry pen and often in detail, but he omitted—perhaps intentionally—all shadings, depth and color. What were his emotions the night he fled the capital, when he took the oath of office, or when he watched and listened to the ambulance trains crunching in from the battlefields? He does not succeed in making even one day of those many come alive.

John B. Jones, war clerk, was a recorder of generally disparate vignettes: the price of a chicken, the amount of snowfall, or the death of a pet cat. Although a novelist and editor, he shared Jefferson Davis' inability to breathe life into his people or draw up curtains to illuminate otherwise darkened scenes.

Phoebe Pember, the matron of Chimborazo, leaves much unsaid about herself and her associates as well as about the big hospital. Nor can her able editor and respected Civil War author, Bell Irvin Wiley, be expected to fill in the many gaps. The longtime professor of history at Emory University kindly granted permission to excerpt from the musings of Phoebe.

Sara Pryor, vivid chronicler of Petersburg's changing panorama, bequeathed history at least one teasing mystery: *who* was Agnes, her penpal in Richmond? Not the daughter of Lee by the same name, this Agnes may well have been a pseudonym. Also, what is the location of any of the several residences of Sara in Petersburg? Determined local historians have yet to pinpoint a single one.

Sallie Brock's colorful, girlish writing was influenced by others. In fact, the agile Sallie was not averse to lifting entire passages from Editor Pollard.

The account of Sylvanus Cadwallader lay, curiously enough, in the Illinois State Historical Library for more than half a century before being discovered and edited into book form. Excerpting here is through the kind permission of the Alfred A. Knopf publishers.

Francis Lawley, who cut such a figure in social Richmond, never bothered to write his own memoir. *The Times* of London printed many of his dispatches recently in a slim volume with just one omission. Their distinguished war correspondent was never identified. Lawley attempted a biography of Judah Benjamin, which he never completed. Before his demise in 1901 he had written short articles and essays on a variety of subjects, from badminton to horse racing.

However, *finis* must inevitably be pronounced, even though this chronicle continued in many respects long after April 3, 1865.

Index